Managing Mailing Lists

Managing Mailing Lists

Alan Schwartz

O'REILLY™

Cambridge · Köln · Paris · Sebastopol · Tokyo

Managing Mailing Lists
by Alan Schwartz

Published by O'Reilly & Associates, Inc., 101 Morris Street, Sebastopol, CA 95472.

Editor: Paula Ferguson

Production Editor: Mary Anne Weeks Mayo

Printing History:

    March 1998:   First Edition.

ISBN: 1-56592-259-X

Table of Contents

Preface

This book is about helping groups of people communicate with one another using email—in short, about designing and running mailing lists. Email is the universal Internet application, which makes mailing lists an ideal vehicle for creating electronic communities. All you need to run a mailing list is access to a system that is connected to the Internet, a mailing list management software package, and a bit of know-how. In this book, I'm going to give you the information you need to run effective mailing lists.

Mailing lists are extremely flexible; you can create many different styles of electronic forums, depending on what you are trying to accomplish. For example, you can create a moderated mailing list, so that you can control the content on the list, or you can let anyone post whatever they want, for a more free-form discussion group. If you want to limit membership based on certain criteria, you can also exercise control over who can subscribe to a list. You can give your subscribers the option to receive individual messages or message digests, and you can archive list postings and make them available to your readership.

There are two primary tasks involved in running a mailing list: managing the mailing list itself and administering the software, often called a *list server*, that controls the mailing list. This book details what is involved for both of these tasks. If you are going to be handling both tasks yourself, you'll find everything covered herein. If you are only interested in managing a mailing list or administering a list server, this book tells you what you need to know and explains what you need to communicate to the people handling the other aspect of the system.

The Software

This book covers four free mailing list management (MLM) packages:

- *Listproc* 6.0c, by Anastasios C. Kotsikonas

- *Majordomo* 1.94.4, initially written by Brent Chapman, later developed by John Rouillard, and currently maintained by Chan Wilson

- *SmartList* 3.10, by Stephen van der Berg

- *LISTSERV Lite* 1.8d, L-Soft International, Inc.'s free version of LISTSERV

In addition, the book examines what you can do using only *sendmail*, the most common Unix mail transport agent, and some other general tools.

Why Unix?

Mailing list management software is available for nearly every computer platform. There are three reasons why this book focuses on Unix mailing list software:

- The Unix operating system and its mail system is mature. Unix tends to have greater compliance with Internet standards than other platforms. Unix is stable and powerful and it remains the operating system of choice for major Internet mail hubs.

- Unix mailing list management software is mature. The software discussed in this book has been widely tested; even new versions that are developed are based on a proven core.

- The Unix mailing list servers covered in this book are not only stable, flexible, and powerful, but *free*. All but LISTSERV Lite even include complete source code (LISTSERV Lite includes partial source code). Supporting good free software is important to me.

Unix isn't the only choice; it may not even remain the best choice for long. Windows NT 5.0 promises to include a mailing list server component. While LISTSERV Lite is already available for Windows NT (among other platforms), I feel that it is premature to discuss NT-based list servers until NT 5.0 sets some standards. Perhaps a future edition of this book will reexamine Windows NT as a platform for mailing lists.

The Contents of the Book

The first two chapters of this book explain email, mailing lists, and mailing list software in general; everyone should read these chapters. Chapters 3 through 8 are for list maintainers; they provide examples of mailing list design, management, and troubleshooting under specific Unix mailing list management software.

Chapters 9 through 12 are for server administrators; they detail the installation and configuration of each MLM package. The appendixes provide a reference to each package for users, list owners, and server administrators.

Chapter 1, *Introduction*, reviews the basics of email messages and email software. It introduces mailing lists and mailing list management software, and gives an example of interaction with a list server.

Chapter 2, *Designing a Mailing List*, outlines the principles for designing a mailing list. It covers the choices a list manager must make about subscriptions, moderation, digests, archives, peer lists, and newsgroup gateways. It also includes a guide to choosing a list server and a comparison of this book's list server software.

Chapter 3, *Maintaining Lists with Listproc*, explains how to create, configure, and manage a list using Listproc.

Chapter 4, *Maintaining Lists with Majordomo*, explains how to create, configure, and manage a list using Majordomo.

Chapter 5, *Maintaining Lists with SmartList*, explains how to create, configure, and manage a list using SmartList.

Chapter 6, *Maintaining Lists with LISTSERV Lite*, explains how to create, configure, and manage a list using LISTSERV Lite.

Chapter 7, *Maintaining Lists with sendmail*, discusses ways to use *sendmail* and other Unix tools to build your own mailing lists, list servers, and file servers.

Chapter 8, *Troubleshooting Your Lists*, details some of the common problems faced by list managers and server administrators and offers ways to track down and solve them.

Chapter 9, *Administering Listproc*, is a guide for the Listproc server administrator. It covers installation, configuration, and maintenance of the Listproc server.

Chapter 10, *Administering Majordomo*, is a guide for the Majordomo server administrator. It covers installation, configuration, and maintenance of the Majordomo server.

Chapter 11, *Administering SmartList*, is a guide for the SmartList server administrator. It covers installation, configuration, and maintenance of the SmartList server.

Chapter 12, *Administering LISTSERV Lite*, is a guide for the LISTSERV Lite server administrator. It covers installation, configuration, and maintenance of the LISTSERV Lite server.

Appendix A, *Listproc Reference*, is a reference for Listproc commands, files, and configuration options.

Appendix B, *Majordomo Reference*, is a reference for Majordomo commands, files, and configuration options.

Appendix C, *SmartList Reference*, is a reference for SmartList commands, files, and configuration options.

Appendix D, *LISTSERV Lite Reference*, is a reference for LISTSERV Lite commands, files, and configuration options.

Additional Resources

In addition to this book, the documentation that comes with each list server, and the help files available from the servers themselves, there are two other resources for list managers and server administrators: Usenet news and, of course, mailing lists.

Usenet Newsgroups

The Usenet newsgroup hierarchy *comp.mail.** is devoted to groups related to email. *comp.mail.sendmail* is of particular note to people who are running list servers and file servers using only *sendmail.*

The *comp.mail.list-admin.** hierarchy is devoted to topics of interest to mailing list server administrators. It includes *comp.mail.list-admin.policy*, a discussion of mailing list policies, and *comp.mail.list-admin.software*, a discussion of mailing list server software. Frequently Asked Questions (FAQ) postings about mailing list management software appear in the latter group.

Mailing Lists

Naturally, there are mailing lists about mailing lists! One of the best (and busiest: be prepared for multiple large digests daily) is *list-managers-digest@greatcircle.com*. To subscribe, send email to *majordomo@greatcircle.com* with **subscribe list-managers-digest** in the body of the message.

Each of the software packages discussed in this book has one or more associated mailing lists for users to discuss problems and ideas with one another:

- Listproc users can join *unix-listproc@avs.com* by sending email to *listproc@avs.com* with **subscribe unix-listproc** *your-name* in the body. This list may move from *avs.com* to *emailsol.com* in the future.

- Majordomo users can join *majordomo-users@greatcircle.com* for discussion about installing, configuring, and using Majordomo, and *majordomo-announce@greatcircle.com* to receive announcements about new versions and patches. Follow the instructions for joining *list-managers-digest.*

- SmartList users can join *smartlist@informatik.rwth-aachen.de* by sending email to *smartlist-request@informatik.rwth-aachen.de* with `subscribe` as the Subject of the message.

- LISTSERV Lite users can join *listserv-lite@peach.ease.lsoft.com* by sending email to *listserv@peach.ease.lsoft.com* with `subscribe listserv-lite your-name` in the body of the message.

Conventions Used in This Book

Italic is used for:

- Pathnames, filenames, and program names
- New terms where they are defined
- Mailing list names and Internet addresses, such as domain names, URLs, and email addresses
- Comments to the reader in sample command lines and code examples

`Constant Width` is used for:

- Requests that can be sent to mailing list servers
- Parameter names and values that are set in configuration files
- Environment variables
- Command-line options

`Constant Italic` is used for:

- Placeholders that indicate that an item is replaced by some actual value in your own configuration file
- Placeholders in command-line options

`Constant Bold` is used for:

- Command lines and options that should be typed verbatim on the screen. Note that the % character represents the regular prompt in command lines and the # character represents the root user's shell prompt.

Getting the Scripts

Throughout the book, I provide scripts that may be useful in running your mailing lists. There are also a few such scripts that I mention but do not show. All of the scripts are available at *ftp://ftp.oreilly.com/pub/examples/nutshell/mailing_lists*.

Request for Comments

Please help us to improve future editions of this book by reporting any errors, inaccuracies, bugs, misleading or confusing statements, and plain old typos that you find anywhere in this book. Email your bug reports and comments to us at *bookquestions@ora.com*. We take your comments seriously and will try to incorporate reasonable suggestions into future editions.

Acknowledgments

No book is a solo effort. Along the way, I've had help from many of good folks.

Tim O'Reilly agreed to do the book, and I'd like to thank him for the vote of confidence. Paula Ferguson at O'Reilly was a terrific editor: insightful, thoughtful, and helpful. Adrian Nye and Frank Willison served as editors for this book during its earlier stages before Paula took over.

O'Reilly's production group put the finishing touches on this book. Mary Anne Weeks Mayo was the project manager and copy/production editor. Claire Cloutier LeBlanc was the proofreader, and quality was assured by Nancy Wolfe Kotary, Nicole Gipson Arigo, and Sheryl Avruch. Joel S. Berson created the index, with help from Seth Maislin. Len Muellner tweaked the troff tools to finesse the interior design. Robert Romano prepared the crisp illustrations. The book's interior was designed by Nancy Priest. Edie Freedman designed the front cover, and Kathleen Wilson designed the back cover.

Jerry Peek, who once planned to write a book like this, kindly donated many megabytes of archived notes, mailing list messages, and ideas. I am also indebted to Dave Barr, Nathan Brindle, Anastasios C. Kotsikonas, Lydia Leong, Ellen Siever, and Chan Wilson, who provided technical reviews of a draft of the book. Naturally, any remaining mistakes are my own.

The many subscribers to the many mailing lists I've run over the years certainly deserve mention. Not only were those lists my practical training for this book, but they provided many interesting conversations and informative discussions, as mailing lists should.

My wife M.G. writes children's books. She understands evenings and weekends spent at the computer. I'd surely have taxed her patience beyond endurance had she been anything other than her wonderful self. Luckily for me, she wasn't. :)

1

Introduction

This chapter provides an introduction to how email works, why mailing lists are useful, and what mailing list management software does. If you're already knowledgeable about email and mailing list software, you can safely skim or skip ahead. If not, this chapter will provide the basic information.

Email Basics

Before we look at mailing lists, let's review how email works from the user's standpoint. In many ways, email is a lot like regular postal mail. When you write a postcard to a friend, you put her address on the card so the post office knows where to deliver it. You include a return address, so the post office can return your postcard to you if it has a delivery problem, and so your friend can write back even if she doesn't already have your address. You drop your postcard into a mailbox, and it's received by your local post office, which stamps it with a postmark and sends it to the central post office. From there, the postcard travels to your friend's post office, and finally, to her address.

Similarly, an email message you receive from your friend includes not only the message itself, but also your email address, her return email address, and "postmarks" from all the computers through which your message passed.

Mail Messages

Simple email messages have two parts: a *header* and a *body*. The header contains all the "postal" information: the sender, the recipient, and the computers that transferred the mail. It also includes the date the message was sent and the subject of the message. The body is the actual text of the message. A blank line separates the header and the body.

Here's an example of an email message:

```
From uhuru@starbase.starfleet.gov  Thu Feb 13 12:40:32 1997
Received: from mailhost.starfleet.gov (mailhost.starfleet.gov
    [1.4.4.4]) by enterprise.starfleet.gov (8.8.5/8.8.5) with ESMTP id
    MAA00395 for <kirk@enterprise.starfleet.gov>; Thu, 13 Feb 1997
    12:40:32 -0700
Received: from starbase.starfleet.gov (starbase.starfleet.gov
    [1.4.4.2] by mailhost.starfleet.gov (8.6.10/1.40)  id MAA21172;
    Thu, 13 Feb 1997 12:40:30 -0700
Message-Id: <v02110101abea9b0dcf86@[1.4.4.2]>
Date: Thu, 13 Feb 1997 12:41:35 -0800
To: Captain Kirk <kirk@enterprise.starfleet.gov>
From: uhuru@starbase.starfleet.gov (Lt. Uhuru)
Subject: Testing Base-to-Ship Communications

Captain, this is a test of the starbase-to-starship communications.

    - Uhuru
```

The majority of this message is the header; the body begins with the note to the Captain.

Standard mail headers

Let's take a look at the headers in our example message. There are two headers that begin with "From." Here's the first one:

```
From uhuru@starbase.starfleet.gov  Thu Feb 13 12:40:32 1997
```

This one, which has no colon after the word From, is the envelope From or SMTP From. This header is inserted by the computer that sends the message. (Actually, by the sending mail transport agent (MTA), as discussed below.) It identifies the user and computer from which the mail was sent. This header is used by most mail readers as well to determine where one message in a mailbox ends and the next begins.*

Here's the other From header:

```
From: uhuru@starbase.starfleet.gov (Lt. Uhuru)
```

This From is followed by a colon. It is set by the user who sends the mail; usually, it indicates the best email address at which to respond to the sender.

---

* If a mail message contains the word "From" at the beginning of one of its lines, the mail reader can become confused and think that it is the beginning of a new message. That's why message lines beginning with "From" are commonly escaped by adding a ">" to the beginning of the line, resulting in a line like ">From the beginning, electronic mail was exciting." The ">" is usually inserted by the final recipient's computer. This can sometimes cause problems; for example, when I sent a copy of this chapter to the book's editor without encoding it, many ">" signs crept into the text by mistake!

The two From headers can be different. This commonly occurs when an organization has a central mail-receiving computer that distributes mail to the individual computers belonging to users. In that situation, the headers often look like this:

```
From puma@whiskers.cats.com  Thu Feb 13 12:40:32 1997
From: The Pink Puma <puma@cats.com>
```

The distinction between these two forms of the From header becomes important in later chapters, when we look at how mailing list software verifies subscriber addresses.*

You may have noticed that there are a few different ways to write valid email addresses. According to RFC 822, the document that defines the standards for the format of Internet mail messages, any of the following formats are okay:

```
gatsby@host.net
gatsby@host.net (The Great Gatsby)
The Great Gatsby <gatsby@host.net>
"The Great Gatsby" <gatsby@host.net>
```

Internet RFCs

As more networks were connected to the Internet, and email began to pass between these networks, standards for how to format, transport, and read email came into being. Internet standards are defined by documents called *Requests for Comment*, or more colloquially, *RFCs*. The Internet RFCs are numbered; RFC 1206, for example, is a list of frequently asked questions by new Internet users.

You can get the RFCs that are mentioned in this book (or any other RFC) by FTP from *ftp.internic.net* in the *rfc* directory or on the World Wide Web at *http://www.internic.net/ds/dspg0intdoc.html* or *http://www.cis.ohio-state.edu/hypertext/information/rfc.html*.

Just as post offices stamp the letters they process with postmarks, computers add headers to email messages they accept for delivery. The Received headers show the path our message traveled:

```
Received: from mailhost.starfleet.gov (mailhost.starfleet.gov
   [1.4.4.4]) by enterprise.starfleet.gov (8.8.5/8.8.5) with ESMTP id
   MAA00395 for <kirk@enterprise.starfleet.gov>; Thu, 13 Feb 1997
   12:40:32 -0700
Received: from starbase.starfleet.gov (starbase.starfleet.gov
```

---

* A further complication, or simplification, depending on your perspective, is that some MTAs use the Return-Path: header rather than the envelope From header to record the SMTP From information.

```
[1.4.4.2] by mailhost.starfleet.gov (8.6.10/1.40) id MAA21172;
Thu, 13 Feb 1997 12:40:30 -0700
```

The lower Received header shows that Uhuru's message was sent from *starbase.starfleet.gov* and received by an intermediate computer, *mailhost.starfleet.gov*. The upper header shows the message was passed from *mailhost.starfleet.gov* to *enterprise.starfleet.gov*. These headers also give the date and time the email was received and information about the mail software being used by each receiving machine.

The Message-Id header shows the unique identifier assigned to the message by the sender's mail software.* It can be useful if you are a mail administrator trying to debug your mail software or trace a particular message:

```
Message-Id: <v02110101abea9b0dcf86@[1.4.4.2]>
```

A message ID is usually composed of a unique string of characters, an at sign (@), and the hostname (or Internet Protocol (IP) address in brackets) from which the message was originally sent, all enclosed in angle brackets (<>).

When you reply to a message, many systems insert an In-Reply-To or References header that gives the message ID of the message you're replying to.

The remaining headers are self-explanatory:

```
Date: Thu, 13 Feb 1997 12:41:35 -0800
To: Captain Kirk <kirk@enterprise.starfleet.gov>
Subject: Testing Base-to-Ship Communications
```

Other headers

You may see other headers on a message. Here's a list of some possible headers:

Cc and Bcc

Lists email addresses of people that were sent copies of the message. Bcc stands for "blind carbon copy"; recipients in the To or Cc headers won't see the Bcc header.

Reply-To

May be added by the sender to indicate where replies to the message should be sent. This is commonly used when people send email from one computer, but wish to receive replies on another computer.

Errors-To

This header is *not* part of RFC 822, but is used by older mail systems to indicate the address to which delivery errors should be sent.

---

* It's supposed to be unique, but some broken Windows mail software has been known to use the same message ID for every message, which wreaks havoc with mailing lists.

Sender

According to RFC 822, this header should list the email address of the single person or computer who actually sent the message. It appears only when the From: header has been rewritten to show the name of the person who wanted the message sent, instead of the actual sender. This practice is common when messages are sent out by mailing list software; the From address shows the person who sent the message to the list, while the Sender address is the address of the manager of the mailing list. (Some mailing list programs misuse the Sender header, setting it to the address of the list, rather than the list owner.)

Resent-

Headers that begin with "Resent-" indicate that the message has been forwarded. In other words, an intermediate account received the mail and resent it to its final destination. These headers include Resent-From, Resent-Reply-To, and Resent-To; they provide information about the intermediate recipient who resent the message.

Precedence

Can be used to instruct the sending computer that a message does not need immediate delivery. Mailing list messages are often sent with `Precedence: bulk` or `Precedence: junk`, which helps the sending computer manage the large number of messages typical of mailing lists. In addition, programs like *vacation*, which automatically respond to email, often ignore low-precedence messages; if they didn't, mailing lists would be deluged with automatic "I'm on vacation" responses.

X- Headers that begin with "X-" are user-defined headers. Because no standard header begins with "X-", any header that does can be safely added to a message without fear that it will be misinterpreted. Examples include X-Mailer, followed by the name of the email program that sent the message, X-Face, followed by an encoded picture of the sender's face; and X-Comment, followed by almost anything.

MIME

Email messages aren't limited to just text. Internet RFCs 2045–2049 define the standard for Multipurpose Internet Mail Extensions, or MIME. MIME messages can contain any kind of data: text, sound, pictures, and even video. Binary data sent by email is encoded into an all-text format when it is sent; it is later decoded by the recipient (or more accurately, her email program).

A MIME message is identified by some extra headers that describe the contents of the message:

```
MIME-Version: 1.0
Content-Type: image/gif
Content-Transfer-Encoding: base64
```

These headers identify the message as a MIME message that contains an image in Graphics Interchange Format (GIF), translated by the `base64` encoding into text that can be sent reliably by email.

A MIME message can contain more than one type of data. `Content-Type: multipart/mixed` indicates that a message contains multiple sections. Each section includes its own Content-Type header that describes the type of data it contains. This mechanism allows users to attach files to text messages. Mail readers that support MIME can then decode the attachments and save them as individual files on the recipient's computer.

Mail User Agents

When you want to send email, you use your *mail user agent* (MUA) to compose the message. Some common Unix MUAs include *Mail, mailx, mh, elm, pine,* and *Z-Mail.* MUAs for other platforms include *Eudora, Netscape Communicator, Microsoft Outlook Express,* and *Pegasus.* MUAs usually provide:

- A place to compose and edit the message you plan to send. Most MUAs allow you to compose your message in your favorite text editor.

- A way to read mail that you've received and reply to it, forward it to other people, or store it in a file.

- An address book that contains *aliases* for people and groups whom you email frequently. For example, you might use the alias *pres* to refer to the email address *president@whitehouse.gov.* This feature saves you from having to remember complex email addresses. Because an alias can refer to a group of email addresses, instead of a single email address, aliases can be used as mailing lists. For example, John, Paul, George, and Ringo might each establish an alias for the group. In Paul's MUA, the alias might be *beatles*; in George's, it might be *fab4.* If the group gets larger, however, making sure that everyone's aliases are complete and correct can become a serious problem.

Mail Transport Agents

When you finish composing your email message, your MUA hands the message over to the *mail transport agent* (MTA) on your computer system. The MTA is responsible for delivering the message. On most Unix systems, the MTA is a version of the *sendmail* program; throughout this book, that's the MTA I'll assume you're using. Other MTAs include *smail, Zmailer, qmail,* and *MMDF.*

If you send your message to someone else on the same computer, the MTA just passes the message to the *local delivery agent*, a program that puts the message in the recipient's mailbox.

If the message is for a user on another computer, it is the MTA's responsibility to interpret the recipient's email address, connect to the MTA at the computer that receives email for the recipient, and pass the message along. Most Internet MTAs speak to each other using SMTP, the Simple Mail Transfer Protocol. Here's an example of how a *sendmail* program at *almond.nuts.com* might deliver a message from *banzai@almond.nuts.com* to *johnb@yoyodyne.com*:

```
Banzai's mailer contacts yoyodyne.com by SMTP,
and yoyodyne's sendmail announces that it's ready:
220 yoyodyne.COM Sendmail 5.65/DEC-Ultrix/4.3 ready at Tue, 11 Feb 1997
13:03:24 -0700
>>> HELO almond.nuts.com                    Banzai's mailer identifies itself
250 yoyodyne.COM Hello almond.nuts.com, pleased to meet you
>>> MAIL From:<banzai@almond.nuts.com>      Banzai's mailer identifies the sender
250 <banzai@almond.nuts.com>... Sender ok
>>> RCPT To:<johnb@yoyodyne.com>            Banzai's mailer identifies the recipient
250 <johnb@yoyodyne.com>... Recipient ok
>>> DATA                                    Banzai's mailer wants to send the message
354 Enter mail, end with "." on a line by itself
>>> .                                       Done with the message
250 Ok
>>> QUIT                                    Done with the connection
221 yoyodyne.COM closing connection
```

Figure 1-1 illustrates the flow of the message. The figure shows that *banzai* writes a message in his MUA, which passes it to his MTA. *banzai*'s MTA transports the mail to *yoyodyne.com*'s MTA, which places it in *johnb*'s mail spool.

If *johnb@yoyodyne.com* had set up his account to forward his email to another computer, *yoyodyne.com* would add a Received: header and begin an SMTP transaction with the new computer to pass the message on.

Knowing how to speak SMTP can be useful in troubleshooting mail problems, as discussed in detail in Chapter 8, *Troubleshooting Your Lists*.

As the message travels, it may pass through a number of MTAs. Each system the message visits "postmarks" it (by adding another Received: message header) and passes it on.

What Is a Mailing List?

Email is a marvelous tool for person-to-person communication. But often, you'd like to send the same message to many people and conduct a group conversation. As mentioned above, address book aliases can simplify the process of sending a

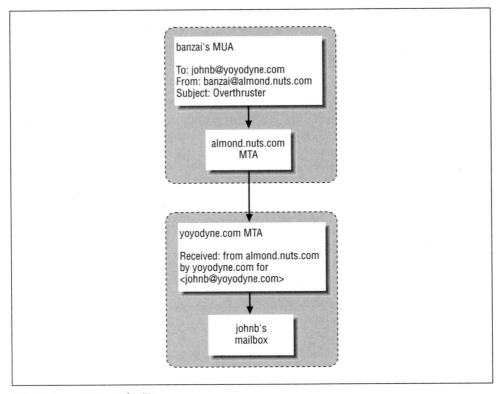

Figure 1-1: MUAs and MTAs

message to a group, but everyone in the group must update their address books when the group gains or loses members.

A *mailing list* is a group of email addresses that can all be reached by sending a single message to one address: the *list address*. Messages sent to the list are distributed to each of the list's *subscribers*. By sending messages to the list, subscribers can have ongoing discussions with each other and need only keep track of one address. Figure 1-2 graphically illustrates a mailing list. The figure shows that the sender writes a message, addressed to the mailing list, in her MUA, which passes it to her MTA. The MTA transports the mail to the host MTA for the mailing list, which distributes it to the MTAs of all the list subscribers.

Mailing lists are good for many things, including:

Distributing information

O'Reilly announces new products on its *ora-news* mailing list.

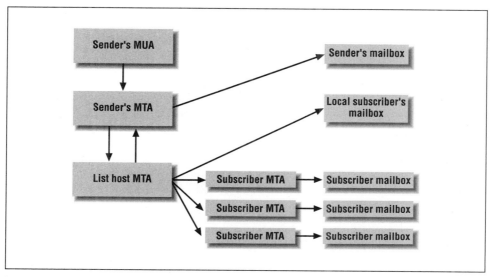

Figure 1-2: How mailing lists work

Discussing a project among several participants
> For example, a group of authors could collaborate on a book by distributing chapters on a mailing list.

Exchanging questions and answers with other users of a product or service
> Users of the Listproc mailing list software discuss questions and problems on the *unix-listproc* mailing list.

The list of subscribers can be maintained by hand using a *mail reflector*, or with an automated *mailing list manager* (MLM) system like Listproc, LISTSERV Lite, Majordomo, or SmartList.

Mail Reflectors

Small mailing lists are often set up using the built-in facilities found in most MTAs (such as *sendmail*). The list of subscribers is stored as a *mail alias*, a single email address that the MTA expands into the complete list when a user sends email to it. (Don't confuse MTA aliases, which are email addresses that are expanded by the MTA, with the personal MUA aliases discussed earlier. Your personal aliases are like a private address book: only you can use them. MTA aliases are like listings in a public telephone directory: anyone can send mail to an MTA alias and the message is forwarded to the recipients).

Usually, a human being is responsible for maintaining the list of subscribers. People who want to subscribe to the list or cancel their subscription send email to the maintainer, who edits the subscription list.

Mail aliases have uses other than mailing lists, however. For example, the mail alias *postmaster* should be defined at every site that receives email; it should direct mail to the person responsible for the system's mail software. Mailing list aliases are often called *mail reflectors* or *mail exploders* to distinguish them from these simpler aliases.

Mail aliases can also do more than simply forward mail. For example, they can be set up to save messages to a file or to pass them on to a program or shell script. All of the mailing list software described in this book uses MTA aliases to pass incoming mail to the list software.

Mailing List Management Software

As mailing lists get larger, maintaining the subscriber list by hand becomes unwieldy. Mailing list management software automates the process of managing subscriptions. In addition to the list address, an MLM has a special email address for user requests to subscribe and unsubscribe. Popular MLMs like Listproc, LISTSERV Lite, Majordomo, and SmartList provide many features. They can:

- Automatically process subscription requests or forward them to the list maintainer for approval. In many cases, they can also redirect requests mistakenly sent to the list itself and prevent them from being distributed to subscribers.

- Support *moderated lists.* When a message is sent to a moderated list, the MLM forwards it to the list moderator for approval before sending it to the subscribers.

- Distribute messages as *digests.* A digest is a single mail message that contains several complete messages from the list, often with a summary or description of the contents. Some users prefer receiving a single digest on a regular basis to receiving each list message individually.

- Archive list messages, digests, or other files, making them available to subscribers who request them.

- Provide some help in handling bounced messages. MLMs can often be configured to remove subscribers to whom they can no longer deliver mail.

- Prevent *mail loops*, which can occur when a subscriber is using software to automatically respond to his mail. When the automatic response is sent back to the mailing list, distributed again, responded to again, and so on, a mail loop is created. MLMs take precautions to prevent this.

Many of these features were pioneered by LISTSERV, the granddaddy of MLMs. LISTSERV managed mailing lists on the now defunct BITNET network of IBM mainframes. It now runs under VM, VMS, Unix, Windows 95, and Windows NT. A free (for noncommercial use) version, LISTSERV Lite, is covered in this book. Although the complete commercial version is not covered here, it remains a standard to which other MLMs are compared.

Most of the rest of this book is devoted to setting up and using mailing list management software to maintain mailing lists. We'll look at four popular free Unix MLMs: Listproc, Majordomo, SmartList, and LISTSERV Lite. In addition, we'll see how to use *sendmail*'s features to create mailing lists and other mail services.

Though the examples in this book focus on Unix-based MLMs, MLM software is available for VMS, IBM VM, Macintosh, MS-DOS, and Windows platforms as well. A good source of information about MLMs (and advice about how to choose one) is Norm Aleks's mailing list management software FAQ. The FAQ is regularly posted to the *comp.mail.list-admin.software, comp.answers,* and *news.answers* newsgroups. You can also get a copy by FTP from *rtfm.mit.edu* in *pub/usenet/comp.answers/mail/list-admin/software-faq.*

Usenet News

Usenet newsgroups provide another way for groups to hold ongoing discussions. Like a mailing list, postings to a newsgroup can be read by the group's subscribers. A newsgroup can also have a moderator to approve postings. Unlike a mailing list, however, there's no central control over subscribers; it's impossible to know who is reading the newsgroup or to limit it to specific individuals. On the other hand, once created, newsgroups usually require less maintenance.

In general, a mailing list is better than a newsgroup when the topic is:

- Narrowly focused, or only interesting to a small group of people

- Private, so security or control of readership is important

- Urgent, as most people read their email more often than news

- Highly interactive, as Usenet news is generally propagated more slowly than email

- Of interest to readers who can receive email but can't read Usenet news (and there are a lot of these people!)

Want the best of both worlds? Some MLMs can be configured to exchange messages with a newsgroup. Messages sent to the list are posted to the newsgroup, and messages posted to the newsgroup are sent to the list subscribers. This enables users to choose how they prefer to read their messages, and it can make a newsgroup accessible to those who have access only to email.

Using Mailing List Software

From a user's point of view, mailing lists maintained by MLMs are not difficult to use. Let's take a look at a series of messages from Andrea Thompson to the Majordomo MLM at Illuminati Online (*io.com*) and the responses she gets back. (Try these examples yourself, if you'd like to.) Andrea knows that *io.com* has a mailing list for people who love to peruse used bookstores, and she's heard that the email address for the MLM is *majordomo@lists.io.com*.

Asking for Help

Andrea first sends a message containing two requests: `help` and `lists`. (Although different MLMs use different commands, those two are fairly standard.) The first request asks for general help; the second asks for a description of the available mailing lists. Here's her message:

```
From andrea@mac23.mogo.edu  Sat Feb 15 10:51:03 1997::digests
Date: Sat, 15 Feb 1997 11:51:03 -0600 (MDT)
From: Andrea Thompson <andrea@mogo.edu>
To: majordomo@lists.io.com
Subject: information

help
lists
```

Some MLMs, like Listproc, Majordomo, and LISTSERV Lite, expect requests to appear in the body of the message, so they can process multiple requests in one message. Others, like SmartList, expect requests to be in the Subject header and can process only one request at a time.

The MLM reads her message and sends a message in return. (Some MLMs send multiple messages in response to multiple requests; Majordomo sends one message in reply to all of the requests.) Here are parts of that message:

```
From Majordomo-Owner@lists.io.com  Sat Dec  6 13:19:46 1997
Date: Sat, 6 Dec 1997 11:09:55 -0800 (PST)
To: andrea@mac23.mogo.edu
From: Majordomo@lists.io.com
Subject: Majordomo results: information
Reply-To: Majordomo@lists.io.com

--

>>>> help

This help message is being sent to you from the Majordomo mailing list
management system at Majordomo@lists.io.com.

This is version 1.94.4 of Majordomo.
```

```
If you're familiar with mail servers, an advanced user's summary of
Majordomo's commands appears at the end of this message.
```

   . . .
   And near the end of the message:
   . . .

```
>>>> lists
Majordomo@lists.io.com serves the following lists:
  GrandCouncil
  aah-digest
  aah-l
  aamen
  aamen-digest
  . . .
  bsj-digest             Book Store Junkies Digest
  bsj-l                  Book Store Junkies
  . . .
```

```
Use the 'info <list>' command to get more information
about a specific list.
```

The output tells her about a command named `info` that gives more information about a list and mentions the *bsj-l* list.

Now Andrea sends another message to *majordomo@lists.io.com* with the commands `help subscribe` and `info bsj-l`. Back comes detailed information about the `subscribe` command and a few paragraphs of information about the *bsj-l* list.

Subscribing to a List

Andrea decides to subscribe to the *bsj-l* list, so she sends a third message to *majordomo@lists.io.com* with this line in the body:*

```
subscribe bsj-l
```

If *bsj-l* is a list that's open to the public (and it is), Andrea's email address is added to the mailing list. The MLM then sends her the following confirmation:

```
From owner-bsj-l@lists.io.com  Sat Dec  6 13:47:57 1997
Date: Sat, 6 Dec 1997 13:47:09 -0600
To: andrea@mac23.mogo.edu
From: Majordomo@lists.io.com
Subject: Welcome to bsj-l
Reply-To: Majordomo@lists.io.com

--
```

---

* Different MLMs have different syntax for subscription commands. For instance, Listproc requires Andrea to put her full name after the name of the list. The `help` message tells Andrea how to use Majordomo's `subscribe` command.

```
Welcome to the bsj-l mailing list!

Please save this message for future reference.   Thank you.
```

         ... A welcome message ...

The next time someone sends an announcement to the *bsj-l* list, Andrea automatically gets a copy:

```
From owner-bsj-l@lists.io.com  Sat Dec  6 15:47:57 1997
Date: Sat, 6 Dec 1997 15:47:09 -0600
To: bsj-l@lists.io.com
From: larry@almond.nuts.com (Larry Legume)
Subject: Chicago-area bookstores
```

         ... Message from Larry here ...

She keeps getting copies of list messages until she sends an **unsubscribe** request to *majordomo@lists.io.com*.

Addresses and More Addresses

Each mailing list managed by an MLM usually has a number of addresses. Here's an explanation of the common ones:

- Messages sent to the *list address* are distributed to all subscribers. In the example above, the list address was *bsj-l@lists.io.com*.

- Requests to subscribe, cancel a subscription, or perform other functions (sometimes called administrivia) are sent to the *request address*. This address is either the name of the MLM itself (e.g., *listproc@online.ora.com*, *listserv@l-soft.com*, or *majordomo@greatcircle.com*) or has the same name as the list address with "-request" appended (e.g., *procmail-request@informatik.rwth-aachen.de*). Listproc and LISTSERV Lite always use the MLM name as the request address, SmartList always uses a "-request" address, and Majordomo can do either.

- Problems with the list that require human intervention are reported to the *owner address* for the list. MLMs like Listproc can send copies of bounce messages to the list owner. If the list is moderated, all messages may be passed to the owner for approval. The MLM may indicate the owner address in the headers of the messages it sends, or the address may be the same as the list address with "-request" or "-owner" appended (e.g., *cashews-owner @nuts.com*). The form that is used depends on the MLM. Listproc and Majordomo favor "-owner". LISTSERV Lite uses "-request" for messages to list owners and "-owner" for bounced messages. SmartList uses "-request" as both a request address and owner address; requests it can't handle itself are transparently passed on to the list owner.*

- Majordomo and SmartList use separate addresses, a *digest list address*, and a *digest request address*, for the digested version of a mailing list.

A common mistake of new mailing list subscribers is to send administrative requests to the list address, instead of the request address. As a result, every list subscriber receives the request. MLM software can often prevent this mistake by intercepting messages that look like administrative requests before they are sent out to the entire list.

---

* When *sendmail* sends a message to a mailing list alias, it looks for an "owner-*listname*" alias. If it finds one, it treats that address as the list owner. Many people favor this convention for mailing lists as well.

2

Designing a Mailing List

When you decide to create a mailing list, there are a number of issues that you need to consider, such as the purpose of the list and its moderation status. In this chapter, I provide an overview of the issues involved in creating a mailing list. The chapter also includes a comparison of the features of four MLM software packages, Listproc, Majordomo, SmartList, and LISTSERV Lite, so that you can pick the program that best suits the needs of your mailing lists.

Dramatis Personae

When you set up a mailing list, one important first question you need to consider is who will be responsible for the mailing list? The cast of characters involved in running a mailing list can range from a single person to a multitude. Here are some of the most common roles:

- The *list maintainer*, or *list owner*, is responsible for the operation of the mailing list itself. She has the power to approve subscriptions and is usually the right person to go to when problems with a list arise.

- If the list is moderated, a *list moderator* is responsible for the content of the list's messages. The moderator approves and/or edits messages sent to the list before they are mailed to the subscribers.

- If an MLM is being used to manage the list, the *server administrator* is responsible for the operation of the mailing list server software as a whole. On some systems, the server administrator also sets up mail aliases for the lists—the email addresses to which the MLM software responds.

- The host computer's *postmaster*, *mail administrator*, or *system administrator* is responsible for the operation of the host computer itself. On many systems, the system administrator also sets up the mail aliases for the list.

This chapter and the next five chapters are directed primarily at list maintainers. Chapters 9 through 12 provide information for server administrators.

Mailing List Decisions

Before starting a mailing list, you need to make a number of important decisions. What will the list be called? What is its purpose? What kinds of messages should be sent to the list? A few moments of thought about these issues will save you headaches later on.

Naming the List

What's in a name? Potentially a lot of confusion for your subscribers. When creating a mailing list, choose a name for the list that meets these guidelines:

- To make everyone's mailers happy, the name should use only letters, numbers, dashes (–), and underscores (_). A list name that uses only lowercase letters and doesn't mix dashes and underscores, like *usa-olympic-team*, is easier to remember than one that varies case or punctuation, like *USA-Olympic_Team*.

- The name should be descriptive of the list's topic. If your list is for chess players, *chess-players* is a good name, *chpl* is not. There may be exceptions to this rule, but they're few and far between. For example, if you run a list for covert operatives and allow people to retrieve the names of your lists, *assist* or *pserv* may be less enticing than *secret-agents* as a list name.

- The name should be reasonably short. Very long list names are hard to type.

- The name should be unique. Most importantly, it should not be the name of any of the users of the system, who will wonder why they are no longer receiving their personal mail, but everyone else is.

- It's customary for list names that refer to list members to be plural. Use *chess-players* in preference to *chess-player*.

- On BITNET, list names conventionally ended in "-L"; this convention is less common for lists run by Unix MLMs on the Internet, but is still worth considering. It clearly and concisely identifies the address as that of a mailing list.

List Policy

After you've chosen a name, it's time to decide how the list should be used and to write a *charter* for the mailing list. This charter can announce the list (to a newsgroup or a "list-of-lists") and keep new subscribers informed of the list's purpose and guidelines. The charter should explain the list's purpose, define appropriate and inappropriate postings, and tell users who to contact for help with the list.

The list's purpose

The first thing a charter should do is explain the purpose of the mailing list. Why does the list exist, and who does it serve? Here's an excellent example, from the *sun-managers@ra.mcs.anl.gov* mailing list:

```
The sun-managers mailing list is intended to be a
quick-turnaround list primarily for people who maintain Sun computers.
Its primary purpose is to provide the manager (by "manager" I mean
computer and/or network manager) with a quick communications channel
to other Sun managers, so that s/he can draw on the collective
experience of the large body of Sun system managers.
```

The description of the list's purpose also makes a useful blurb when announcing the list.

Posting guidelines

The charter should also explicitly define what kinds of posts are appropriate and inappropriate for the mailing list. This section of the charter is particularly important reading for new list subscribers. These guidelines are sometimes referred to as the list's *acceptable use policy.*

Although the definitions of appropriate and inappropriate postings vary from list to list, some postings are almost universally considered inappropriate:

- Administrative requests to subscribe or unsubscribe from the list
- Messages that do not address the purpose of the mailing list or that are better served by another mailing list
- Private messages to other subscribers
- Personal attacks on subscribers (i.e., *flames*)
- Excessive or unnecessary profanity
- Commercial postings and advertisements on noncommercial mailing lists

You should also think about whether messages including MIME attachments should be permitted. MIME messages can contain images, spreadsheets, and other binary files that may be of interest to list subscribers. On the other hand, while everyone can read plain text, not everyone uses Microsoft Word. If subscribers do not need to send multimedia files to the list, discouraging binary attachments entirely may be a good idea.

On mailing lists where the messages are questions for the list subscribers, some lists, like *sun-managers*, establish reply rules for questions. A common rule is that replies should be sent to the person who posted the question, not to the list. The querist collects the replies, (hopefully) solves his problem, and then mails a summary of replies back to the list. This reduces the number of messages sent to the list.

Another strategy used by lists that answer subscriber questions is to compile a *frequently asked questions* list, or *FAQ*.* The FAQ contains answers to common questions and documents the collective wisdom of the mailing list. When a list has an FAQ, asking questions already answered by the FAQ is usually inappropriate.

Where to get help

Finally, the list charter should provide the email addresses the subscriber needs to subscribe, send messages, get help from the MLM software, and get help from a human being.

Other List Decisions

After coming up with the list charter, you still face many questions about the list's operation. The answers to these questions should reflect the list's purpose and intended audience. Here are a list of decisions you need to make:

- Is the list *open*, allowing anyone to subscribe, or *closed*, requiring the approval of the list maintainer in order to subscribe? If the list is closed, who is allowed to subscribe to the list?

- Is the list *public*, allowing nonsubscribers to post messages to the list, or *private*, with posting restricted to subscribers? A public list might be appropriate if you want to allow the list to receive informational announcements from nonsubscribers or if subscribers frequently post to the list from different email addresses.

- Is the list moderated? If so, who moderates the list? Is there more than one moderator?

- Is the list distributed as individual messages, as a regular digest of messages, or both? Majordomo and SmartList require the server administrator to set up digested and undigested lists differently and use different addresses for the digested and undigested versions of the list. Listproc and LISTSERV Lite leave this decision to each subscriber, who can choose to receive either individual messages or digests.

- Are the list's messages or digests archived and available for subscribers to retrieve? Are other files available in the archive?

---

* The process of compiling and updating a FAQ can be arduous; some busy mailing list owners delegate the task to a subscriber with more time and energy.

- Is the list to be managed from a single list server, or are there *exploders* or *peer lists* distributed across different servers? Peer lists complicate the management of mailing lists, but allow more efficient use of resources as lists grow larger.

- Does the list exchange messages with a Usenet newsgroup? With a mailing list-news gateway, messages posted to the newsgroup are distributed to the list subscribers, and, in some cases, messages sent to the mailing list are also posted to the newsgroup.

In order to illustrate the creation of a mailing list, we'll create a new list for dog lovers, called *dogfans*, on the host *gshp.com*.* The list is open, private, unmoderated, and undigested. The list is managed by *pepper@gshp.com*. Example 2-1 shows the charter for our list, as it might be sent to a new subscriber.

Example 2-1: The Charter for dogfans@gshp.com

```
Welcome to dogfans!  Please read and save this message, it contains
important information. This welcome message was last updated on
11/18/97 by Pepper.

THE BASICS

The dogfans mailing list is a place for people who love dogs to
discuss the amusing things their pets do and ask questions about
proper upbringing.

This list is not moderated, and not archived. Messages mailed to
the list address are sent to every subscriber. Please read and
understand the rules below about appropriate postings.

WHAT NOT TO POST

Requests to subscribe to or unsubscribe from the list should be
sent to dogfans-request@gshp.com, NOT to the entire list.

Commercial notices from vendors or breeders are NOT appropriate for
this mailing list and should not be posted.

Want-ads, pet-for-sale ads, and lost-pet notices are NOT appropriate
for this mailing list.

When we eventually develop a list of Frequently Asked Questions
(an FAQ), posting questions that are answered by the FAQ will
be inappropriate.
```

---

* That's short for German Short-Haired Pointer, an excellent breed.

Example 2-1: The Charter for dogfans@gshp.com (continued)

```
ADDRESSES

dogfans@gshp.com is the list address. Messages sent to this address
are broadcast to all subscribers.

dogfans-request@gshp.com is the administrative address. Send subscription
requests and other administrivia to this address.

owner-dogfans@gshp.com will reach the human being who manages this list.
```

Subscriptions

Other than the list messages themselves, the primary activity on mailing lists is the subscription and unsubscription of list members. Indeed, automating subscription requests is perhaps the most important function of mailing list management software. Other benefits include restricting posting to subscribers, automating subscriber address changes, and automatically unsubscribing users whose email bounces.

Open and Closed Lists

Open mailing lists are open to subscription by any user. A great advantage of MLM software is that subscriptions to public mailing lists are handled automatically by the software. The user sends a subscription request to the MLM, and the MLM adds the user to the list and sends him a welcome message.

Closed, or "by owner," mailing lists, in contrast, require the list maintainer's approval in order to subscribe to the list. Even so, MLM software can automate some of this process, by forwarding the subscription request to the list maintainer, accepting subscription approvals back from the list maintainer, processing approved subscriptions, and keeping would-be subscribers informed of the standing of their requests.

Public and Private Lists

Whether a list is open or closed, you must decide how to deal with messages sent to the list by nonsubscribers. Listproc and LISTSERV Lite lists can be set up to allow nonsubscriber mailings, to reject them, or to forward them to the list maintainer. Majordomo can allow or reject nonsubscriber mailings. SmartList can allow nonsubscriber mailings, forward them to the list maintainer, or automatically subscribe the sender.

Lists that are primarily for user-contributed informational bulletins should probably be public; even if someone doesn't want to receive the bulletins, he may want to send one. On the other hand, lists that are for ongoing conversations should

The Life Cycle of a List

Brent Chapman, who wrote the Majordomo MLM and manages the *list-managers@greatcircle.com* mailing list, distributed this anonymous essay to the list (April 17, 1995):

Every list seems to go through the same cycle:

1. Initial enthusiasm (people introduce themselves and gush a lot about how wonderful it is to find kindred souls).

2. Evangelism (people moan about how few folks are posting to the list and brainstorm recruitment strategies).

3. Growth (more and more people join, more and more lengthy threads develop, occasional off-topic threads pop up).

4. Community (lots of threads, some more relevant than others; lots of information and advice is exchanged; experts help other experts as well as less experienced colleagues; friendships develop; people tease each other; newcomers are welcomed with generosity and patience; everyone—newbie and expert alike—feels comfortable asking questions, suggesting answers, and sharing opinions).

5. Discomfort with diversity (the number of messages increases dramatically; not every thread is fascinating to every reader; people start complaining about the signal-to-noise ratio; person 1 threatens to quit if *other* people don't limit discussion to person 1's pet topic; person 2 agrees with person 1; person 3 tells 1 and 2 to lighten up; more bandwidth is wasted complaining about off-topic threads than is used for the threads themselves; everyone gets annoyed).

6. (a) Smug complacency and stagnation (the purists flame everyone who asks an "old" question or responds with humor to a serious post; newbies are rebuffed; traffic drops to a doze-producing level of a few minor issues; all interesting discussions happen by private email and are limited to a few participants; the purists spend lots of time self-righteously congratulating each other on keeping off-topic threads off the list).

   OR

   (b) Maturity (a few people quit in a huff; the rest of the participants stay near stage 4, with stage 5 popping up briefly every few weeks; many people wear out their second or third "delete" key, but the list lives contentedly ever after).

usually be private. And lists that are for official announcements, like *ora-news*, shouldn't even let most subscribers post!

Benefits of Public Lists

In a mailing to the *list-managers* mailing list (February 19, 1990), Chris G. Demetriou makes a case for allowing nonsubscribers to post:

For most lists, it causes no harm (great) to allow people to send to the list without subscribing. The only real problems with it (that I can think of 8-) are:

1. SPAM!

2. idiots being jerks, and

3. newbies asking stupid questions without being informed of the FAQ, or whatever.

Usually (2) can be taken care of with reasonable pointers to FAQs wherever the mailing lists are advertised.

On the other hand, there are benefits to having "open-posting" lists:

• allows people who have a quick question that isn't easily answered by list archives or a FAQ to ask it, and not get completely swamped by (for them) irrelevant mail. (This is especially true for high-volume lists.)

• allows people who have a "floating" email address to use the list reasonably... (for instance, I send most of my mail from here (lagavulin), but often from other machines, and most of the mailing lists I'm subscribed to are subscribed to my *berkeley.edu* addresses... 8-) If you restrict postings to people who are subscribed, this becomes harder to deal with properly.

Third-Party Subscriptions and Address Changes

Some MLM packages, like Majordomo, allow a user to submit the email address that she would like subscribed to the list. Others, like Listproc, only subscribe the email address from which the user sends the subscription request, and may, at the list maintainer's discretion, allow the user to change this address later.

While allowing users to send third-party subscription requests is convenient, it creates the possibility that someone might subscribe another person to your mailing list without their knowledge.* Worse, a malicious person might try to subscribe your list to itself, or to other lists.

Address changes can present the same problems, but generally only existing subscribers can change their address. Just as people rarely have the same home address all their lives, people rarely keep the same email address for years on end. People change jobs, graduate from college, and change their Internet service providers. *Sam@here.com* today may be *Sam@gone.com* tomorrow.

MLMs that allow a user to change the address at which she's subscribed can help keep the subscription list current. But many users forget to notify the MLM when they change addresses, and the result is invariably bounced email.

Subscribing with the Web

Instead of forcing people to send carefully formatted email messages in order to join or leave a mailing list, many list administrators prefer to offer a form-based subscription interface using the World Wide Web.

David Baker's LWgate (*http://www.netspace.org/users/dwb/lwgate.html*) is a freely available web gateway to mailing lists. By visiting LWgate, people can view list information, subscribe or unsubscribe to lists, and retrieve files from archives. LWgate can generate requests for lists managed by LISTSERV, Listproc, Majordomo, or SmartList.

A list maintainer can add a list to the NetSpace Mailing List WWW Gateway (*http://www.netspace.org/cgi-bin/lwgate*), or can download the freely available Perl source code and run LWgate locally (with the help of a web administrator).

MajorCool by Bill Houle (*http://ncrinfo.ncr.com/pub/contrib/unix/MajorCool*) is a web interface for sites running Majordomo. Another free gateway is Patrick Fitzgerald's MailServ (*http://iquest.com/~fitz/www/mailserv*), which can generate requests for many less common MLMs.

---

* The victim will find out soon enough, when he receives your welcome message, but will be very confused. If your list is very active, or if the perpetrator has subscribed the victim to many other lists, the accumulated mail might exceed the victim's mail quota and prevent him from receiving messages he really does care about!

Handling Bounced Email

Bounced email is the bane of list maintainers. If the mailing list is properly set up, only the list maintainer receive notifications of bounced email. These notices come in the form of messages from recipients' MTAs (often with addresses such as *mailer_daemon, root,* or *postmaster*). Email delivery can fail for many reasons, but it's particularly important to distinguish between two kinds of bounces:

Hard bounces

Email delivery is never possible. The most common hard bounces occur when a recipient doesn't have an account on the receiving machine ("user unknown") or when the receiving machine doesn't exist ("host unknown"). They can also occur when a recipient's mailbox is full and can't accept any more mail.

Soft bounces

Email delivery isn't possible now, but may be possible later. The most common soft bounces occur when the receiving machine is temporarily out of service or can't be reached ("connection timed out").

If the remote MTA supports the enhanced "delivery status notification" codes specified by RFC 1893, hard bounces can be identified by status codes beginning with "5" and soft bounces by error codes beginning with "4". For example, here's part of a bounce message arising from an unknown user; note the line that contains 550 and the `Status: 5.1.1` line:

```
From MAILER-DAEMON@host.com  Tue Dec  2 16:37:26 1997
From: Mail Delivery Subsystem <MAILER-DAEMON@host.com>
MIME-Version: 1.0
Content-Type: multipart/report; report-type=delivery-status;
        boundary="QAB22212.881102246/host.com"
Subject: Returned mail: User unknown

This is a MIME-encapsulated message

--QAB22212.881102246/host.com

The original message was received at Tue, 2 Dec 1997 16:37:25 -0600
(CST) from sender@someplace.org

   ----- The following addresses had permanent fatal errors -----
baduser@host.com

   ----- Transcript of session follows -----
550 baduser@host.com... User unknown

--QAB22212.881102246/host.com
Content-Type: message/delivery-status
```

```
Reporting-MTA: dns; host.com
Arrival-Date: Tue, 2 Dec 1997 16:37:25 -0600 (CST)

Final-Recipient: RFC822; baduser@host.com
Action: failed
Status: 5.1.1
Last-Attempt-Date: Tue, 2 Dec 1997 16:37:26 -0600 (CST)
```

When a hard bounce occurs, it usually means that the recipient should be removed from the subscribers list because his email account no longer exists. Soft bounces can be handled in one of two ways. On a very busy mailing list, bouncing addresses should probably be removed from the subscribers list. On other lists, some sort of temporary postponement of mail to that user usually suffices.

Moderated Lists

Some lists require more direction than others. Public lists may be plagued by frequently asked questions. Lists focused on controversial topics may be targets for inflammatory postings. Lists with standards for the content or style of postings need to have postings reviewed before they are distributed. One way to handle these lists is through *moderation.*

Messages sent to a moderated mailing list are not automatically distributed to the subscribers; instead, they are passed to the list's moderator. The moderator can post the message to the list verbatim, edit it before posting, incorporate it into a digest, or reject it outright. As a result, moderated mailing lists tend to have a less interactive feeling, but a very high level of substance. Figure 2-1 depicts the flow of a message to a moderated list. Mail to the list is sent to the moderator, who approves or rejects it. Approved mail is sent back to the MLM for distribution.

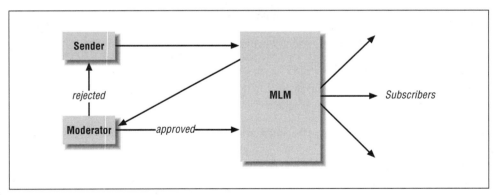

Figure 2-1: Moderated lists

Moderated or Not?

When should a list be moderated? Moderated lists are very effective when:

- The topics are sensitive, controversial, or likely to draw subscribers who are more interested in flaming than contributing to the list. For example, *right_to_die@efn.org*, a list devoted to discussion of views on euthanasia, is moderated.

- The list focuses on announcements by the moderator, or on questions that the moderator is uniquely suited to answer. For example, *delphi-announce @exnext.com* distributes announcements related to Borland's Delphi software.

- The list is used as an electronic journal, with reviewed submissions. For example, *blist@nizkor.almanac.bc.ca* is a list for Holocaust researchers.

- The list members only want to receive mailings that have been deemed worthwhile by the moderator. For example, subscribers to *humornet@bgu.edu* expect to receive jokes the moderators find funny.

On the other hand, unmoderated lists are more appropriate when:

- List traffic is high, and moderation requires too much effort.
- The purpose of the list is conversation and direct discussion.
- The list offers quick response to problems. The *sun-managers@ra.mcs. anl.gov* list for Sun system administrators is one such list.

Some MLMs, like Majordomo, maintain separate lists for digested and nondigested versions of a list. If you use one of these MLMs, you can moderate only one of the lists (usually the digest), and users can choose whether they'd prefer to receive all list mail or just that which has passed through the moderator.

The Moderator's Job

What's it like to moderate a mailing list? Members of moderated lists expect the list messages to meet known standards of content and format. The moderator determines and codifies these standards into a policy for approving, editing, or rejecting list postings. When messages are sent to the list, the moderator applies the list's moderation policy to the messages.

Moderation policy

List moderators decide which list postings are acceptable as they stand, which require editing, and which should be rejected. The list's charter should provide guidelines for making these decisions, but whatever criteria you use, you must apply the criteria firmly and impartially to all postings.

You should also be sure that the subscribers know the moderation criteria. The easiest way to do this is to include the moderation policy in the list's welcome or FAQ message and periodically mail it to the list.

A complete moderation policy includes:

- Criteria used to reject or accept mailings. These include standards of content, formatting, etc. It goes without saying that messages that attempt to contravene the moderator by forging moderator approval should not be accepted.

- Whether and how accepted mailings are edited or modified before being sent on to the list.

- What is done with rejected mailings. It's friendliest to return a rejected message along with a note explaining why it was rejected. This decreases the chance that the author will assume the message wasn't received and thus continue to send copies of the same message.

- How to contact the moderator.

For example, Example 2-2 shows part of the moderation policy posting from the *H-RUSSIA* mailing list.

Example 2-2: A Moderation Policy

```
                        WELCOME TO H-RUSSIA

You have joined H-RUSSIA, an international electronic discussion
group, set up at Michigan State University in order to provide a
forum for scholars of Russian and Soviet history. There are no
geographical or chronological boundaries. Subscription is free, and
as a subscriber you will automatically receive messages in your
computer mailbox. You may save these messages, discard them, copy
them, or print them out. You may also relay them to someone else, so
long as you honor the copyright of the author by including his or her
name and email address and identify H-RUSSIA as the originating list.

H-RUSSIA serves primarily to enable historians and other scholars of
Russia and the Soviet Union to communicate current research and
teaching interests. The nature of those communications depends
largely upon the membership. We will post discussions of research
methods, descriptions of archives and collections, trial balloons of
innovative interpretations, and other research-oriented issues. We
are eager to post questions and observations on teaching Russian and
Soviet studies to graduate and undergraduate students in diverse
settings. Syllabi, recommended readings, suggestions for research
assignments or class discussions are all fair game.

In cooperation with publishers, H-RUSSIA solicits reviews of recently
published books from its members, occasionally with response from the
author posted simultaneously with the review. Our goal is to have
reviews posted within two months of publication, much more quickly
```

Example 2-2: A Moderation Policy (continued)

```
than print journals can manage. We also encourage members to post
abstracts of papers presented at conferences and public seminars.

H-RUSSIA also posts conference announcements (including lists of
sessions), calls for papers, a weekly jobs list, news of interest to
the profession at large and to slavicists in particular,
cross-postings from other lists, information on new software and
internet resources, and a variety of other things that are pertinent
to Russian and Soviet studies.

H-RUSSIA is a moderated list. This means that every posting to
H-RUSSIA will come first to the list editor, who in almost all cases
will forward it to the membership. Postings that are clearly of a
commercial nature, advertising goods and services for profit, will
not be posted. Postings that request information easily found in any
academic library will be returned to the sender with a request that
he or she include a brief description of sources already searched. Ad
hominem attacks, often known as flames, will be returned to sender
with a request for a more substantive posting. The list editor will
not reject postings because they are controversial or because he or
she disagrees with the point of view expressed. Indeed, scholarship
without controversy would be hard to imagine.
```

Turnaround time

An important issue for moderated lists is *turnaround time*: how quickly a message gets approved or rejected by the moderator. If you want your list to retain a conversational feel, turnaround times longer than one day should be avoided.

Multiple moderators and backup moderators

On busy lists, multiple moderators, any one of whom can approve list messages, improve turnaround time. Even on lists with a single moderator, if the moderator must travel or becomes suddenly busy, having a backup moderator who can also approve postings is useful. The alternative is to run the list unmoderated during the moderator's vacation. It's a good idea to let the subscribers know if this is going to happen; some may want to postpone list messages or unsubscribe until the list is moderated again.

SmartList explicitly supports multiple moderators. A message to a moderated list is forwarded to all the moderators, and messages from any moderator are accepted for distribution. Listproc only forwards messages for a moderated list to the list maintainer, but you can emulate multiple moderation by making the list maintainer itself a mailing list of moderators. Majordomo and LISTSERV Lite also expect a single moderator (who need not be the list maintainer), but can be similarly finessed.

Moderating Digests

Many moderators edit all the recent postings to their lists into a *digest*. Moderators of digest lists face some unique problems. In a posting to the *list-managers* mailing list (February 22, 1995), Todd Day noted three problems that can occur when subscribers reply to moderated digests:

l. Subject lines that always say, "Re: blah-blah-digest, V#"

–If your reply is worth a damn, give it a decent subject

2. Too much included text

–Unless you are responding directly to personal views, is it really necessary to say, "On Wed, 22 Feb 1995, Todd Day wrote:"

–Is it really necessary to include full paragraphs of previous text when just one included sentence will do?

–Why include text at all? Why not take the time to write your own summary sentence, like "Regarding previous bitching about included text . . . "

3. Useless signatures.

–I've seen that cute quote before . . . who cares?

–Just sign your name, dammit, unless you want to add an email address that is more stable than the one in your From: line or add a phone number if you've asked someone to call you in your message.

–You are just bulking up the archives and making text searches fail when someone tries to search through them.

–If the address in the From: line is proper, why include your address again at the bottom of your letter?

When I moderate, I edit out anything I wouldn't want to be reading myself. Therefore, I aggressively take out #2 and #3. Too hard to do anything about #1. I personally email the worst offenders. If someone's signature is particularly amusing and somewhat related to the topic of the digest, I'll let it pass, but only once.

Digests

Subscribers to busy mailing lists may receive 10, 20, or even 50 list messages each day. All those messages make it difficult to organize one's email. Some subscribers may not have time to read a list's messages each day, preferring instead to read them en masse on the weekend. Message *digests* are an effective solution to these problems.

A digest is a single email message that contains a series of messages from the mailing list. Instead of receiving 20 individual messages, the subscriber receives a single digest message that contains a table of contents and the 20 messages embedded within it.

Here's what a message digest from the *dogfans* mailing list might look like:

```
From dogfans@gshp.com
Date: Wed, 5 Jul 1995 00:11:03 -0700
Errors-To: pepper@gshp.com
Originator: dogfans@gshp.com
Sender: dogfans@gshp.com
Precedence: bulk
From: dogfasn@gshp.com
To: dogfans@gshp.com
Subject: Dogfans digest 5

                  Dogfans Digest 5

Topics covered in this issue include:

   1) Rawhide vs. Nylon
        by fido@spaniel.com (Fido)
   2) Re: Rawhide vs. Nylon
        by pepper@gshp.com (Pepper)
   3) The movie _Baxter_
        by rex@obedience.edu (Rex)


----------------------------------------------------------------------

Date: Tues, 4 Jul 1995 10:00:01 -0700
From: fido@spaniel.com (Fido)
To: dogfans@gshp.com
Subject: Rawhide vs. Nylon
Message-ID: <199507041000.QAA15420@spaniel.com>

    ... Fido's message text here ...


------------------------------

Date: Tues, 4 Jul 1995 13:23:00 -0700
From: pepper@gshp.com (Pepper)
To: dogfans@gshp.com
Subject: Re: Rawhide vs. Nylon
Message-ID: <AI12J4KI3L24Q4420@gshp.com>

    ... Pepper's message text here ...


------------------------------
```

```
Date: Tues, 4 Jul 1995 21:07:30 -0700
From: rex@obedience.edu (Rex)
To: dogfans@gshp.com
Subject: The movie _Baxter_
Message-ID: <199507042107.QAA15420@obedience.edu>
```

  ... Rex's message text here ...

```
------------------------------

End of Dogfans Digest 5
***********************
```

Digest Formats

Message digests were a natural outgrowth of the increasing volume of mail being handled by mailing lists. If a standard digest format is incorporated into an MLM, the means of reading the digest or "bursting" it into its individual messages is clearly defined.

Unfortunately, there are not one, but three, commonly used, and arguably "standard" message digest formats. Internet RFCs 1153, 934, and 2046 each describe message digests. RFC 1153 documents the digest format that MLMs like Listproc use; it's based on the original LISTSERV digest format. RFC 934 suggests a general format for digests and has been adopted by Majordomo. The later RFC 2046 explains how to encode digests with MIME. SmartList distributes MIME digests. LISTSERV Lite allows subscribers to decide if they prefer RFC 1153 or MIME digests.

RFC 1153: Digests de facto

The example digest at the beginning of this chapter was produced by Listproc. RFC 1153 describes this digest format. These message digests contain four parts:

Digest message headers

These headers are just like the headers of any mail message, except that the Subject header contains the mailing list name, the word "digest," and a digest number or a volume and issue number. The headers are followed by a blank line.

Preamble

The initial part of the digest may contain information about the contents of the digest, administrative notes, etc. Listproc and LISTSERV Lite produce a table of contents in the preamble. The end of the preamble is marked by a blank line, a line of 70 hyphens, and another blank line.

Individual messages

Each individual message in the digest includes headers, a blank line, and the body of the message. The only headers from the original message that should be present are Date, From, To, Cc, Subject, Message-ID, Keywords, and Summary, in that order. The end of an individual message is marked by a blank line, a line of 30 hyphens, and another blank line.

Epilogue

The final part of the digest, after the last individual message, is a two-line epilogue. The first line reads "End of *listname* digest *number*". The second line consists of a row of asterisks underlining the first line.

This traditional digest style is still common. Its major drawback is that it doesn't support messages with MIME-encoded contents, and thus provides no way to send text in other character sets (such as foreign alphabets) or with binary content. A secondary drawback is that messages can't contain lines with a row of 30 hyphens. If a subscriber's signature happens to have such a line, it corrupts the digest. For the same reason, digests of digests don't behave as they should.

RFC 934: A digest standard

The digest format proposed by RFC 934 eliminates the problems with the older RFC 1153 digests.* Its digests aren't quite backward-compatible with older digests, but they are similar enough that most bursting programs can cope with them. Like the older digest format, RFC 934 digests have four parts:

Digest message headers

No restrictions are placed on what the headers may contain, except that they must conform to the RFC 822 standard. The headers end at the first blank line.

Preamble

No restrictions are placed on what may be in the preamble. The end of the preamble is marked by the premessage boundary of the first message.

Individual messages

Each message in the digest begins with a premessage boundary, followed by the headers (including at least Date and From), the body of the message, and a postmessage boundary. The postmessage boundary of one message is the premessage boundary of the following message. Boundaries must begin with a hyphen and a nonspace character. For compatibility with the RFC 1153 digests, message boundaries may be 30 hyphens surrounded by blank lines.

---

* It may seem strange that RFC 934 describes a *newer* digest format than RFC 1153, which was published later. The reason is that RFC 1153 is simply a description (not a proposal) of an already established digest format.

Epilogue

No restrictions are placed on the epilogue.

Embedding messages with rows of hyphens (such as digests) within digests is made possible by a simple convention: when forming a digest, add a hyphen and a space (-) to the beginning of any line that begins with a hyphen. Because lines beginning with a hyphen and a space can't be message boundaries, this convention prevents innocent rows of hyphens from being misinterpreted.

Unfortunately, this convention creates a new problem. Mailing lists devoted to supporting software often distribute patches and bug fixes in a format produced by the Unix *diff* utility, which looks like this:

```
*** hello.c~    Sat Feb 15 23:46:45 1997
--- hello.c     Sat Feb 15 23:47:15 1997
***************
*** 4,8 ****

  main()
  {
!   printf("Hello, world!\n");
  }
--- 4,8 ----

  main()
  {
!   printf("Bonjour, le monde!\n");
  }
```

It's convenient to feed these messages to the *patch* utility, which applies the patch to the source code. *patch*, however, relies on lines beginning with three hyphens. In an RFC 934 digest, these lines are transformed, and begin with a hyphen, a space, and then three hyphens (- ---), which confuses *patch*. If you have a digest-bursting program that automatically removes the "- ", you can avoid this problem. Alternatively, you can turn to the MIME digest format.

RFC 2046: Digests for the MIME age

The MIME specification in RFC 2046 includes a description of how to format messages containing multiple parts. The multipart/digest format is designed explicitly for message digests. Like the other digest formats, a multipart/digest message has four parts:

Message digest headers

Because this is a MIME message, the MIME-Version and Content-Type headers must be included. The Content-Type header looks like this:

```
Content-Type: multipart/digest; boundary="string"
```

The *string* can be any string that is unlikely to occur in any of the individual messages. Strings of random characters are often used. Message boundaries are created by adding two hyphens to the beginning of *string*. The headers end at the first blank line.

Preamble

The preamble doesn't have any MIME type and is usually left out completely (the table of contents is inserted as the first individual message). Sometimes it contains notes to readers who are not using a MIME-compliant MUA and may be confused by the message. The end of the preamble is marked by the first message boundary.

Individual messages

By default, each individual message is a standard (RFC 822) email message. If one of the individual messages is in a different format (for example, a table of contents or an image file), a Content-Type header is given first. The end of each message is marked by a message boundary. The message boundary for the last message, however, has two extra hyphens at its end.

Epilogue

This appears after the final message boundary and may contain anything. Usually, it contains the standard "End of *listname* digest *number*" note and the row of asterisks.

Here's an example of a multipart/digest message:

```
From: pepper@gshp.com
To: dogfans@gshp.com
MIME-Version: 1.0
Subject:  Dogfans Digest, volume 7
Content-Type: multipart/digest;
     boundary="next message"

This message has been formatted with MIME, and a MIME-compliant
mail reader will likely be necessary to read it.
--next message
Content-Type: text/plain
Table of contents:
  Woof or Bark?                      [ fido@spaniel.com (Fido) ]
  Re: Woof or Bark?                  [ rex@obedience.edu (Rex) ]
--next message
From: fido@spaniel.com (Fido)
Subject: Woof or Bark?

   ... Fido's message text here ...
--next message
From: rex@obedience.edu (Rex)
Subject: Re: Woof or Bark?
```

```
    ... Rex's message text here ...
    --next message--
    End of Dogfans Digest, volume 7
    *******************************
```

MIME digests have all the advantages of MIME. They can include any type of message, including binary files, and MIME is a robust email standard. MIME digests also share the major disadvantage of MIME: limited MUA support. Many Unix mail user agents don't cope well with MIME messages, and external MIME decoders, such as the *metamail* program, offer only the most limited functionality.

Bursting Digests

Once you've received a digest, how do you read it? Most digests can be read as a single long mail message, or, if they use the MIME digest format, as a multipart MIME message using *metamail* or *munpack*. But sometimes you may want to "burst" a digest into its individual messages, in order to feed each to a program, or concatenate them into a mailbox file from which you can read, forward, and reply to individual messages.

The *formail* program that comes with the Procmail distribution splits digests if you use the -ds command-line option. If you specify a program name after the option, each message is individually piped to the program. If not, the messages are concatenated together in *mbox* format.

If you don't have *formail*, the Perl script *dburst* can burst a digest from within your MUA and then reinvoke your MUA on the temporary mail folder it creates from the digest. *dburst* is available at *ftp://ftp.oreilly.com/pub/examples/nutshell/mailing_lists*.

Manually Creating Digests

Digests are easily cobbled together by hand, simply by editing together the mail messages to fit one of the formats above. Even if you want to digest messages manually, however, you can simplify the process by using a program like the *digest* script that's included with Majordomo.

To use *digest*, you first set up a configuration file, a header file, and a footer file. Sample files for the *firewalls-digest* mailing list are included with *digest*. *digest* produces RFC 934 format digests.

Automatic Digests with MLMs

Most MLMs can automatically create digests from messages sent to a list. With some MLMs, like Listproc and LISTSERV Lite, any user can choose to receive a list in digest format by using the `set` command. With others, like Majordomo and SmartList, you can offer lists in digested format, undigested format, or both. Users choose to subscribe to either the digested or undigested version of a list.

LISTSERV Lite also allows subscribers to choose to receive a list *index* rather than a digest. An index lists only the author and subject of each message, along with a message number. The subscriber sends commands to LISTSERV Lite to retrieve the messages she wants to read.

Archives

Mailing list management software can do more than distribute email. Most programs can also maintain *archives*, collections of files or messages that can be sent to users on request. Archives can be a potent adjunct to mailing lists. Maybe your mailing list community has built up a really good FAQ, and new subscribers want to get it right away. Maybe you've got image files with pictures of different breeds of dogs that subscribers can use to help decide which one they'd like to have as a pet. Or maybe you'd like subscribers to be able to search the last year's worth of list digests.

What Gets Archived?

Most MLMs can archive the messages or digests sent out on mailing lists they manage. The server organizes archived messages by mailing list and by date, so a subscriber can send the server a request for a message or group of messages that he'd like to retrieve from the archive.

More sophisticated archive systems can also archive files other than list messages. The server administrator or list maintainer adds the files to the archive. Some MLMs can archive binary files and automatically encode them and split them (if they're too large for a single message) before mailing them out. Others can only archive text files, so if you want to make a binary file available, you must manually encode it in a text format (using *uuencode* or MIME encoding) first.

Public and Private Archives

Like mailing lists, archives can be either public or private. Public archives hold files that can be retrieved by anyone. They're ideal for storing FAQs, welcome information, public domain files, etc.

Private archives hold files that can only be retrieved by users or subscribers who know the archive's password. On some closed lists, all subscribers know the password, and the archive contains a complete set of messages sent to the list.

Finding Archived Files

It's not enough to just store messages, digests, or files in an MLM archive; your users need to be able to find the files they want to retrieve. All MLMs can send users a list of public archives and of files that they have permission to retrieve. Most also allow users to search for files that contain a given string or regular expression.

Archive Alternatives

With a little effort, you can bring the convenience of the Web to your archives. LISTSERV Lite includes its own web interface that allows browsing (but not searching) archives. In addition, many programs convert *mbox*-style archives to fully linked hypertext for browsing:

Hypermail—http://www.eit.com/goodies/software/hypermail/hypermail.html
   A popular *mbox* to HTML converter, this program offers multiple indexes (Subject, Author, Date) and threaded views of discussions.

MHonArc—http://www.oac.uci.edu/indiv/ehood/mhonarc.html
   This program offers similar features and handles MIME-encoded messages.

ListWebber II—http://www.lib.ncsu.edu/staff/morgan/about-listwebber2.html
   This program, by Eric Morgan, has a specific purpose: to generate requests to search list archives managed by LISTSERV or Listproc.

Exploders, Peer Lists, and Newsgroups

Large mailing lists can tax the computers they run on. For each mail message sent to a list with 1000 subscribers, the list's host computer may send out 1000 outgoing mail messages.* Digested lists send fewer messages, but whenever a digest is issued, 1000 copies have to go out.

Imagine that your mailing list, *product-support@yoyos.com*, is based in the United States, with 500 subscribers from the United States and 500 from Australia. An efficient way to deliver mail to this list is to have the Australian users subscribe to a

---

* Many MTAs try to reduce the number of individual messages they send out by sending a single message to all recipients who are on the same host, and letting that host's MTA handle the individual delivery. But unless you're running a company mailing list, it's unlikely that many of your subscribers will be from the same hosts.

local list, *product-support-au@yoyos.co.au*, in Australia. Then your list can send 500 messages to the U.S. subscribers, and a single message to the Australian list, which redistributes it to the Australian subscribers. The same principle would apply if your list had a large group of subscribers in another country, say Japan. By distributing the mailing list to *list exploders* on different hosts, you greatly reduce both the load on your system and the international network bandwidth.

Figure 2-2 is a graphic illustration of list exploders. Mail sent to the main list is distributed to the list exploders, which deliver it to the subscribers.

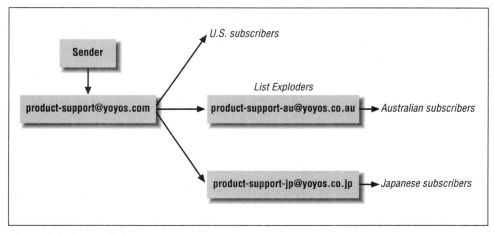

Figure 2-2: List exploders

While list exploders reduce network use and system load, they do have some disadvantages too. Maintaining a network of exploders is more complex than managing a single centralized list, and there are more components that can fail. It may also be more difficult for you or your subscribers to get a list of all the list recipients. Listproc and SmartList (and the full version of LISTSERV) can go a step further by supporting *peer lists*. Peer lists are distinguished from list exploders in that a message can be sent to any of the peer lists, and it is distributed to each other peer list's subscribers. Peer lists can be extremely efficient, particularly when groups of subscribers are isolated by slow or expensive network links; both administrative requests and messages are sent to the local peer list, and the necessary wide-area bandwidth is minimized.

Figure 2-3 illustrates peer lists. Mail sent to any peer is distributed to subscribers of that peer and to the other peers for delivery to their subscribers.

An alternative way to distribute large mailing lists efficiently is to connect them to a Usenet newsgroup. The MLM sends list messages to the subscribers and also posts them to the newsgroup. Instead of subscribing to your mailing list, people

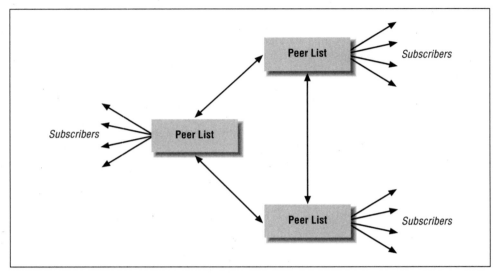

Figure 2-3: Peer lists

can read the newsgroup. Similarly, replies in the newsgroup can be distributed
back to your mailing list. Newsgroup connections require the help of your server
administrator and the news administrator for your organization. The book *Managing Usenet* by Henry Spencer and David Lawrence, published by O'Reilly & Associates, covers the news administrator's role in mailing list gateways. Figure 2-4
shows how a mailing list/news gateway works. Mail sent to the list is posted on
the newsgroup, and messages posted to the newsgroup are received and distributed by the list.

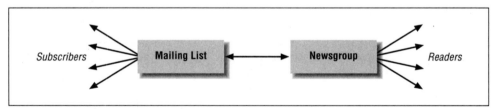

Figure 2-4: Newsgroup gateway

Large Lists

Very large mailing lists require significant resources to distribute. If you're managing a large list, you'll want to be sure your hardware, network connection, and software are up to the challenge. As a server administrator, you may want to consider upgrading your software; as a list manager, you'll want to be sure the server from which your list is run can handle the traffic of a large list.

Listproc is well-designed for running large lists; it acts as its own MTA and delivers mail quickly without exhausting system resources. If you don't use Listproc, however, there are still some things you can do to improve the performance of large lists. *sendmail* users can benefit by upgrading to version 8, the more daring can replace *sendmail* with *qmail*, and anyone can improve list throughput with Keith Moore's *bulk_mailer*.

- Version 8 of *sendmail* is constantly being developed to be more efficient in its handling of large address lists. It is considerably faster than earlier versions of *sendmail* in both network use and queue processing. *sendmail* is available by anonymous FTP from *ftp.sendmail.org* in */pub/sendmail*.

- D. J. Bernstein's *qmail* MTA was designed as a replacement for *sendmail*. It's a secure, reliable, and extremely fast MTA that works well with large lists. If you're accustomed to *sendmail*, however, using *qmail* means thinking about some aspects of mail delivery differently; for example, *qmail* delivers mail to users' home directories, not to a central mail spool directory.* *qmail* allows any user to create her own mailing lists without help from the mail administrator. The latest version of *qmail* is 1.01, and can be found, along with patches to allow Majordomo to work with *qmail*, at *ftp://koobera.math.uic.edu/ pub/software/*. The *qmail* home page, *http://pobox.com/~djb/qmail.html*, lists mirror sites.

- The *bulk_mailer* program accepts a message, an envelope sender, and a list of recipient addresses, groups the addresses into chunks based on hostnames, and invokes multiple *sendmail* processes in parallel. This can reportedly speed up delivery by as much as a factor of three and can be used in the outgoing mail aliases of Majordomo or SmartList (Listproc handles its own SMTP transactions and already organizes its recipients by hostname). *bulk_mailer* is available by anonymous FTP from *cs.utk.edu* in */pub/moore/bulk_mailer*.

---

* You may find this even better than a central spool directory; it makes enforcing quotas easier and avoids problems with delivering mail to NFS-mounted spool directories.

Choosing an MLM

Which MLM is best for you? Here are some of the factors you should consider when choosing an MLM.

Operating System

Obviously, you need to select an MLM that works with the operating system of your host machine. While this book focuses on Unix MLM software, you can find software for most common operating systems. Although Windows NT is gaining adherents among people running MLMs, Unix remains the operating system of choice for most mail hubs. Although Windows and Mac operating systems often provide easier and more appealing user interfaces to their mail systems, Unix MTAs are more mature and generally conform better to the Internet standards than non-Unix MTAs.

Philosophy of the MLM

Each MLM has a social and technical philosophy that underlies its design. The social philosophy determines who controls the server, and list configuration and operation. Listproc requires the server administrator to configure lists; list maintainers can modify little on their own. SmartList can be set up to allow list maintainers who have accounts on the host system to configure their own lists, but doesn't support remote list configuration. Majordomo and LISTSERV Lite, on the other hand, allow list maintainers to remotely configure most features of their lists, making them well-suited for situations where the server administrator doesn't want to be responsible for list configuration. An exception is digests: Listproc, like LIST-SERV Lite, automatically creates digests for any subscriber who requests them, while SmartList and Majordomo require the server administrator to add a new, digested list.

The technical philosophy of an MLM determines how the software operates and interacts with the rest of the host computer system. Listproc is a big system, with many features built in. It runs a continuous background process that checks periodically to see if new messages or requests have arrived. It can even operate as its own MTA, delivering mail directly to subscribers without using the host's MTA. It can be configured to allow subscribers and list maintainers to connect interactively over TCP/IP to the server to manage their subscriptions. SmartList, at the other extreme, is small and simple. Messages are processed individually as they are received, and the host's MTA is used for delivery. Majordomo and LISTSERV Lite fall somewhere in between these extremes: they process messages individually and use the host's MTA, like SmartList, but have fairly extensive features built in, like Listproc. LISTSERV Lite also runs a background process, is highly configurable, and has a web interface for requests. Majordomo distributes messages as they are received, but has extensive configuration features.

Listproc's philosophy of operation gives it an advantage for centrally administered, high-traffic lists with many subscribers. Majordomo comes into its own for sites that host many smaller lists with remote list maintainers. LISTSERV Lite also excels at remote list maintenance and is very efficient in delivery, but is limited to 10 lists of up to 500 subscribers.* SmartList works very well for lists with local list maintainers.

Specific Features

If there are specific MLM features your list needs, be sure that your MLM supports them. No MLM supports every possible feature, but you can often find one that does what you need. Many of these features, such as subscription and bounce handling, moderation, digests, archives, and peer lists, were discussed earlier in this chapter. Some other examples of specific features include:

Programming language the MLM is written in
> If you expect to modify the MLM itself, you'll want one written in a language you know. Listproc is written in C, Majordomo is written in Perl, and SmartList is written in both Perl and *procmail*'s recipe language. Most Unix MLMs also include Bourne shell scripts. LISTSERV Lite doesn't include source code to the server itself.

Restricting submissions
> Most MLMs can restrict submissions to subscribers or allow anyone to send messages to the list. SmartList and LISTSERV Lite also allow submissions from an arbitrary group of other people. Listproc, SmartList, and LISTSERV Lite can ignore messages from specific subscribers.

Loop detection
> SmartList adds an X-Loop header to outgoing messages and refuses to accept messages with such headers. Listproc and LISTSERV Lite use a similar header, but also reject messages that have Message-ID headers corresponding to already delivered messages or whose message bodies have already been sent on the list. Majordomo doesn't attempt to detect mail loops.

Comments, headers, and footers
> Majordomo can attach a header and footer to each message it distributes, so you can be sure that subscribers always know how to unsubscribe or get help.

---

* This limitation is not a technical limitation but a legal one; the Lite version of LISTSERV enforces the limit as a licensing tool, but it's possible to purchase additional "points" from L-Soft and run more and larger lists.

SmartList can attach headers to digests and can be customized to attach headers and footers to all messages. Listproc and LISTSERV Lite can add a Comment header to messages for a list.

Special archive features

Listproc has the most extensive archive control. It stores archived files in compressed format, has a utility for adding new files to archives, can process archive requests in batch at times of low load, and can even fax archived text files if your host supports the feature.

Address translation

Some subscribers may send mail from different addresses than those at which they receive mail. Listproc allows list owners to specify that mail from addresses matching a given regular expression should be treated as if it came from a particular address.

Table 2-1 compares the four MLMs discussed in this book on features that are important to many list managers. "LP" stands for Listproc, "LSL" stands for LISTSERV Lite, "MD" stands for Majordomo, and "SL" stands for SmartList.

Table 2-1: Comparison of MLM Features

Feature	LP	LSL	MD	SL
Uses a daemon process that is always running	Y	Y	N	N
Uses a cron job	N	N	Y	Y
Depends on system's MTA to deliver messages	Y	N	Y	Y
Users can subscribe themselves to lists	Y	Y	Y	Y
Users can subscribe others to lists	N	N	Y	N
Users can choose not to receive own messages	Y	Y	N	N
List owners can approve/reject subscriptions	Y	Y	Y	Y
List owners can require confirmation of subscriptions	N	Y	Y	N
Subscribers whose email bounces can be automatically removed	Y	Y	N	Y
Removed subscribers can be automatically informed and advised	N	N	Y	N
List owners can configure their lists by email	N	Y	Y	N
List owners can configure their lists locally	N	N	N	Y
List owners can be informed of subscriptions, unsubscriptions, etc.	Y	Y	Y	Y
Nonsubscribers can be allowed to post	Y	Y	Y	Y
Submissions can be restricted to subscribers	Y	Y	Y	Y
Submissions can be restricted to an arbitrary group	N	Y	N	Y
Submissions can be rejected from specific subscribers	Y	Y	N	Y
Requests can be restricted to subscribers	Y	Y	Y	Y
Requests can be disabled	Y	N	Y	N

Table 2-1: Comparison of MLM Features (continued)

Feature	LP	LSL	MD	SL
Requests sent to list address are rejected	Y	Y	Y	N
Requests sent to list address are passed to server	N	N	N	Y
Mail loops are detected by adding headers	Y	N	N	Y
Mail loops are detected by Message-ID or Subject header	Y	Y	N	Y
Duplicate message bodies are rejected	Y	Y	N	N
Lists can be moderated	Y	Y	Y	Y
Has strong multiple moderator support	N	N	N	Y
Lists can have a Comment header easily added	Y	Y	N	N
Lists can have header text added to the message	N	N	Y	Digests
Lists can have footer text added to the message	N	N	Y	N
Digests follow LISTSERV (RFC 1153) format	Y	Y	N	N
Digests follow RFC 934 format	N	N	Y	N
Digests follow MIME (RFC 2046) format	N	Y	N	Y
Digests include automatic table of contents	Y	Y	Y	Y
Indexes (table of contents only) can be sent	N	Y	N	N
Lists can be offered as both digested and undigested	Y	Y	Y	Y
Lists can be offered as digest-only	N	N	Y	Y
Users can choose to receive any list as a digest or not	Y	Y	N	N
Archives list messages	Y	Y	Y	Y
Archives other text files	Y	Y	Y	Y
Archives binary files without encoding	Y	N	N	Y
Stores archives compressed	Y	N	N	N
Lists can be peered	Y	N	N	Y
Can post to newsgroups automatically	Y	N	N	N
Supports interactive access or web interface	Y	Y	N	N

Someone Else's MLM

If you don't want the effort of running an MLM server yourself, you may be able to find an existing server that is willing to host your list, either for free (especially if your list is a community service of some kind) or for a fee. This offers you freedom from server administration at the cost of flexibility; you're stuck with the existing server, as configured. Because LISTSERV Lite and Majordomo's list configuration can be set by the list maintainer as well as the server administrator, you may want to pick a host server that runs one of these servers, to give you the most flexibility in maintaining the list.

3

In this chapter:
- *Creating Your List*
- *Writing the Welcome Message*
- *Testing the List*
- *List Administration*

Maintaining Lists with Listproc

List creation and configuration with Listproc are handled by the server administrator, not the list maintainer. Accordingly, this chapter focuses primarily on subscription and submission control, not list configuration, although it does mention features you might want your server administrator to enable or disable for your list.

Appendix A, *Listproc Reference*, includes a reference to all of the Listproc list owner requests, while Chapter 9, *Administering Listproc*, contains everything a server administrator needs to know about Listproc.

Creating Your List

There are three things you need to tell the server administrator in order to have your list added to the Listproc server:

- The email addresses of the primary list owner and any secondary list owners
- The list password
- List options

List Owner Addresses

A Listproc list can have more than one list owner, but one owner is the primary owner. Any owner can issue list maintainer commands, but only the primary owner receives subscription and submission approval requests, and only the primary owner can be notified when people subscribe or unsubscribe from the list.

Listproc recognizes email it receives from the list owners by checking the email address against its list of owner addresses. Accordingly, to get your list created, you have to tell the server administrator the email addresses from which the list administrators send mail. Even if you're the only list owner, you may want to send commands from more than one email address; the server administrator needs to know all of them. If you're planning to use multiple email addresses, you should let the server administrator know at which one you'd like to receive list mail.

The List Password

All of Listproc's list maintainer commands require the list maintainer password in the message. The server administrator may assign this password, but in most cases, you can ask for a particular password when you ask to have the list added. Although it's a good idea to protect this password, Listproc accepts only list maintainer commands from addresses it recognizes as belonging to list maintainers, so the password is really just added security.

List Options

The server administrator needs to know if your list is to be open or closed, public or private, hidden or visible, and moderated or unmoderated. If the list is private, should mail from nonsubscribers be rejected or passed on to you? Because any subscriber may request to receive the list in a digested form, you don't have to decide if the list should be digested.

Other options include automatically archiving list messages (or digests), setting up peer lists, and connecting the list with a newsgroup. If you want these features, ask the server administrator if they're available.

Here's an example of how you might inform the server administrator of your needs:

```
From: pepper@gshp.com
To: topdog@gshp.com
Subject: My new list: dogfans

The dogfans list should be owned by pepper@gshp.com. It should be an
unmoderated, open list that's visible to anyone who asks for the
list of lists that you serve. Mail from nonsubscribers should be
forwarded to me. I'd like to use the password 'milk1bone'. Thanks!
```

Once the server administrator tells you the list has been set up, you're ready to write the welcome message and test out the list.

Writing the Welcome Message

To add a welcome message to your list, you send mail to *listproc* and give the put request in the message body, followed by the welcome message:

```
From: pepper@gshp.com
To: listproc@gshp.com
Subject: setting welcome

put listname list-password welcome
```
Your welcome message here

put replaces the current welcome message with the one you send. If you want to get a copy of your current welcome message, use the edit request:*

```
edit listname list-password welcome
```

Listproc sends a standard welcome message to new subscribers, and includes your customized welcome at the end of the standard message. Here's what the standard message says:

```
You have been added to list dogfans.
The system has recorded your address as
```

email-address

```
and in order for your messages to get posted (if the list accepts
postings), you will have to send them from this address, unless the
list does not require subscription for posting.

If a message is ever rejected, please contact the list's owner:
pepper@gshp.com
```

If the list is set up to assign passwords to each user, the user's password is given and explained here

```
For information on this service and how to use it, send
the following request in the body of a mail message to
listproc@gshp.com:
```

```
            HELP
```

```
All requests should be addressed to listproc@gshp.com
```

It's probably a good idea to set off your customized welcome message from the standard one by beginning your message with a row of dashes or asterisks. In addition to the elements of a welcome message discussed in Chapter 2, *Designing a Mailing List*, a few useful things to mention in a Listproc welcome message include:

---

* put and edit aren't limited to working with the welcome message. You can also use them to change the list of subscribers (subscribers), subscriber aliases (aliases), subscribers to ignore (ignored), the info blurb for your list (info), the file of newsgroup connections (news), and the file of peer list connections (peers). The formats of these files are discussed in Chapter 9.

Mail modes

> List subscribers can choose to receive the list messages individually or as a digest. If they receive individual messages, subscribers can choose whether to receive copies of their own list postings (ACK mode) or not (NOACK mode); digests always include all list postings. Subscribers can send the request HELP SET for information on mail modes.

Subject restrictions

> Listproc rejects messages with subjects that begin with (or contain, in some conditions) words and phrases like "test," "on vacation," and "please ignore," in order to avoid distributing mail from automatic responders. Subscribers should be warned not to send messages with these words in the subject, even if they apply (e.g., "Tests for minerals ignore lead?")

Archive features

> If you're automatically archiving list messages, let the subscribers know. This is a good place to explain the archive search and retrieval commands (detailed in Appendix A) or suggest that subscribers send HELP GET, HELP SEARCH, or HELP INDEX requests for more information.

Testing the List

Once the welcome message has been set up, you're ready to test the list. Start by subscribing yourself to the list (unless your server administrator has done this for you); Listproc does not assume that list owners are also subscribed. You should receive the welcome message when you subscribe.

Test the list by sending some messages and seeing that you receive them. Try subscribing yourself to the list again; Listproc should return an error message.

If your list doesn't work, you'll probably have to contact the server administrator to help you get it working. Once you're happy with it, you can announce it to the world and begin the day-to-day business of list administration.

List Administration

As a Listproc list owner, you will find yourself managing subscriptions and address changes. If the list is moderated, you'll also have to approve submissions.

Subscriptions with Listproc

Listproc lists, by default, are open; anyone can subscribe to the list automatically. With the help of the server administrator, lists can be configured to require approval for subscriptions.

Subscription requests sent to a closed list are forwarded to the list maintainer for approval. The would-be subscriber is notified that list subscription is not automatic, and you receive a message like this:

```
From: listproc@gshp.com
To: pepper@gshp.com
Subject: Subscription approval request

User fido@obedience.edu has requested subscription to list DOGFANS
If you approve, send the following request to listproc@gshp.com:

system DOGFANS <password> fido@obedience.com #SUBSCRIBE DOGFANS Fido

where 'password' is the list's password, as given to you by the
manager of this system.
```

As instructed, send a **system** command back to Listproc to subscribe the user.* If you do not wish to approve the subscription, it is up to you to inform the would-be subscriber of the rejection.

Address Changes

By default, if a subscriber wants to change the address at which she receives list mail, she must unsubscribe from the list by sending an unsubscribe request from her old address, and then resubscribe to the list by sending a subscribe request from her new address.

A list can be customized to simplify this process by allowing variable addresses. When variable addresses are in use, new subscribers are sent a personal list password along with the welcome message. If a subscriber wants to begin receiving the list at a different address, she sends the following request from her old email address:

```
SET listname ADDRESS password new-address
```

A confirmation is sent to the new address. While this system may be more convenient, there's no easy way to distribute list passwords to former subscribers, so variable addressing is best used only when creating a new list.

A more common occurrence is that a subscriber changes email addresses and forgets to notify the list of her new address by sending mail from her old (subscribed) address. By the time she realizes what's happened, she no longer has access to the old address to send an unsubscribe message.

---

* The **system** command can do much more than just approve subscriptions. It allows the list owner to run any list request on behalf of a subscriber as if he were the subscriber.

If a subscriber contacts you in this situation, you can use the `system` command, discussed above, to unsubscribe the subscriber's old address. Alternatively, if the server administrator has enabled Listproc's bounce-checking features, the Listproc server should automatically remove the old address after mail to it bounces a certain number of times.

Moderated Lists

With Listproc, the list owner is always the moderator of a moderated list. Listproc offers two different styles of moderated lists: one uses *catmail*, and the other uses the *config* file. Your server administrator can tell you which type of moderation your list uses.

Moderation with catmail

When a message is sent to a list moderated by *catmail*, the moderator (i.e., list owner) receives a notification from Listproc like this:

```
From: listproc@yourhost
To: pat@gourmet.org
Subject: Notification

Approval request from listproc@yourhost for posting the following
message to moderated list RECIPES. If approved, send the following
request to listproc@yourhost:

APPROVE RECIPES <password> 1

If the message is to be discarded, reply with the following request:

DISCARD RECIPES <password> 1

----------------------- message follows -------------------------
>From subscriber@theirhost Tue Jan  7 23:21:13 1997
Message-Tag: 1
From: Joe Subscriber <subscriber@theirhost>
Subject: Baked Apples
To: recipes@yourhost
```

Body of message here

As the message describes, you (as the moderator) send *listproc* a new message that includes the command to approve or discard the message. Approved messages are posted exactly as sent by the subscriber. Discarded messages are not posted, and the subscriber is not notified.

Listproc can be configured to allow moderators to connect to the Listproc server interactively over TCP/IP with a program called *ilp*. Once connected, a moderator can issue requests as if she'd sent them by email. This can make approving or discarding messages even simpler. *ilp* is discussed in more detail in Chapter 9.

Moderation with config

When a message is sent to a list moderated by *config*, the moderator simply receives a copy of the message, like this:

```
From: Joe Subscriber <subscriber@theirhost>
To: pat@gourmet.org
Subject: Baked Apples

This message was submitted by Joe Subscriber <subscriber@theirhost> to
list recipes@yourhost. If you forward it back to the list, it will be
distributed without the paragraphs above the dashed line. You may edit
the Subject: line and the text of the message before forwarding it
back.

If you edit the messages you receive into a digest, you will need to
remove these paragraphs and the dashed line before mailing the result
to the list. Finally, if you need more information from the author of
this message, you should be able to do so by simply replying to this
note.

----------------- Message requiring your approval ------------------
Sender: Joe Subscriber <subscriber@theirhost>
Subject: Baked Apples
```

Body of message here

To accept the message, you can simply forward it back to the list. No password is necessary because messages from the moderator (list owner) are always accepted. You can also edit the message or incorporate it into a digest. To reject a message, you can simply not forward it back to the list, although you should also reply to the subscriber to explain the rejection.

A drawback of this approach to moderation is that MIME messages are not processed correctly because Listproc does not embed the message to be approved as a MIME attachment. In addition, when forwarding mail back to the list, some mail programs (e.g., *mush*) don't remove the X-Listprocessor header, which causes Listproc to reject the message in an attempt to prevent a mail loop.

In this chapter:
• *Creating Your List*
• *Configuring the List*
• *Writing the Welcome Message*
• *Testing the List*
• *List Administration*

4

Maintaining Lists with Majordomo

Majordomo offers list maintainers almost total control over the configuration of their lists. Accordingly, this chapter is considerably longer than any of the other chapters for list maintainers. It describes the Majordomo list owner commands and the list configuration file. The material assumes that you are using Majordomo 1.94.4, the latest version at the time this book was written.

Appendix B, *Majordomo Reference*, contains a complete reference to the Majordomo requests and configuration file, while Chapter 10, *Administering Majordomo*, covers everything a server administrator needs to know about Majordomo.

Creating Your List

You need to tell the server administrator three things in order to have your list added to the Majordomo server:

• The email address of the list owner

• The initial list password

• Digest options

List Owner Address

Majordomo needs to know the email address of the list owner in order to send error messages, approval requests, and other list maintenance business. Only a single email address can be specified, but if the list owner address is an alias for a group of email addresses, you can have many list owners.

The List Password

All of Majordomo's list maintainer commands require one of the two list maintainer passwords. The server administrator establishes one password (the backup password) when the list is created, so you'll want to tell the server administrator what password you'd like. The backup password is stored separately from the list's *config* file, so that you can use it even if you introduce errors in the *config* file.

Once the list is created, set the administrative list password by editing the list's *config* file. You can also change the backup password with the `passwd` command.

Digest Options

Majordomo lists can be digested. If you want to offer subscribers the choice of receiving list messages in digests or individually, two lists must be created: the ordinary list and a digested list that gets its messages from the ordinary list. A subscriber chooses whether to subscribe to the ordinary list or its digested counterpart, but she always sends her postings to the ordinary list.

If you want digesting, be sure to let the server administrator know. He'll have to set up both lists and arrange for the digested list to get messages sent to the ordinary list.

If you'd like to have list messages automatically archived, or if you need the list connected to a newsgroup, ask the server administrator if these features are available. The server administrator has to do some additional configuration to make these features work.

Majordomo lets you control other list options, like whether the list is to be open or closed, public or private, hidden or visible, and moderated or not. In other words, you don't have to tell the server administrator about these options because you can set them yourself.

Here's an example of how you might inform the server administrator of your needs:

```
From: sombrero@casa.mx
To: serveradmin@hats.com
Subject: My new list: haberdashers

Thanks for setting up the haberdashers@hats.com mailing list for
me. I understand that you run majordomo. Here's what you'll need to
set up the list.

The haberdashers list should be owned by sombrero@casa.mx. I'd like to
offer both a digested (haberdashers-digest) and an undigested
```

```
(haberdashers) version. I'd like to use 'fez' as the initial password.
Thanks!
```

Once the server administrator tells you the list has been set up, you're ready to configure the list, write the welcome message, and test out the list.

Configuring the List

You configure your list by requesting a copy of the list's configuration file, *list-name.config*, editing the file, and mailing it back to Majordomo. If you've requested a digested list, you'll need to request and edit the *config* files for both the digested list and its undigested counterpart.

Requesting the config File

Request a copy of the *config* file by sending a message to *majordomo* with the `config listname list-password` command:

```
To: majordomo@hats.com
From: sombrero@casa.mx
Subject: config request

config haberdashers fez
```

The *config* file is then mailed to you. Save it to a file and then edit the file to configure your list.

Editing the config File

The *config* file offers you a great deal of control over how your list operates. Because there are so many *config* directives, I'm only going to cover the most important ones here, to show you how to set up some common list configurations. A complete list of *config* file directives can be found in Appendix B.

config file basics

Lines in the configuration file that begin with a pound sign (#) are comments. Other lines define the values of list options. Most list options take string values, numbers, or filenames, and are of the form *option = value*. Others take lists of strings or regular expressions* and are defined like this:

```
option    << END
```
Values are listed here, one per line or this might be a paragraph value

---

* Regular expressions are a flexible way of specifying patterns of text that are used by many Unix programs (e.g., *grep*, *emacs*, and *perl*). For a comprehensive guide to regular expressions, see O'Reilly & Associates' *Mastering Regular Expressions* by Jeffrey E. F. Friedl.

To include a blank line, use a line with a single hyphen:
```
-
```
Normally, multiple spaces   like this are treated as a single space
If it's important to preserve them, start the line with a hyphen:
```
-1     2      3      4      5
```
To get a single hyphen at the beginning of a line, double it:
```
-- is a hyphen
```
The definition ends with the line END
```
END
```

For example, here's part of the standard sample configuration file that is created for every new list:

```
    # comments                 [string_array] (undef) <config>
    # Comment string that will be retained across config file rewrites.
comments               <<   END

END

    # date_info              [bool] (yes) <majordomo>
    # Put the last updated date for the info file at the top of the
    # info file rather than having it appended with an info command.
    # This is useful if the file is being looked at by some means other
    # than majordomo (e.g., finger).
date_info              =    no
```

Here's how you could modify these options to include a comment and to put the last updated date for the info file at the top of the file itself:

```
    # comments                 [string_array] (undef) <config>
    # Comment string that will be retained across config file rewrites.
comments              <<   END
This is a sample configuration file.
-
It's used to illustrate how to set options of various sorts.
END

    # date_info              [bool] (yes) <majordomo>
    # Put the last updated date for the info file at the top of the
    # info file rather than having it appended with an info command.
    # This is useful if the file is being looked at by some means other
    # than majordomo (e.g., finger).
date_info              =    yes
```

Setting the list password

As I mentioned earlier, Majordomo lists have at least two passwords: the backup password the server administrator initially assigns to the list, and the administrative password you set in the *config* file.* Either password can authorize list maintainer requests to Majordomo. The backup password, stored apart from the *config* file, is

---

* You can also change the backup password by sending a `passwd` *listname current-backup-password desired-backup-password* request to Majordomo. ·

useful if you make an error in your *config* file, and Majordomo can't read it. Using the backup password, request a copy of your *config* file to fix the problem.

The administrative password is set in the *config* file by the `admin_passwd` option. It defaults to `listname.admin`, which is easy to guess, so you should definitely change it.

List visibility and subscriber privacy

When a user sends a `lists` request to Majordomo, the MLM responds by sending back descriptions of the lists that the server manages. In the *config* file, you can set the list description and control to whom your list is visible.

The `description` option sets a single string that describes the mailing list in Majordomo's response to the `lists` request.

The `advertise` and `noadvertise` options control the visibility of the list in response to a `lists` request. To represent a list of email addresses, these options use arrays of regular expressions as values, like this:

```
advertise       << END
/@.*.myhost.com/
/sarah@friendly.org/
END
noadvertise     << END
END
```

Each line in the list is a regular expression, enclosed by slashes.

Lists are always visible to their subscribers. For nonsubscribers, if the email address of the sender of a `lists` request matches a regular expression in `noadvertise`, the list doesn't appear in Majordomo's response. If the sender is not excluded by `noadvertise`, the list appears if the sender's address *does* match a regular expression in `advertise`. Either or both of these options may be left undefined by including no regular expressions between `<< END` and `END`. Undefined options are effectively disabled.

In the example above, the list is only visible to requests that come from *.myhost.com* addresses or from *sarah@friendly.org*. To make a list totally invisible to nonsubscribers, define `noadvertise` like this:

```
noadvertise     << END
/./
END
```

`noadvertise` takes precedence over `advertise`.

You can also control who can issue the `who` command to retrieve a list of subscribers for a list. The `who_access` option takes one of three values:

`open`

Allows anyone to issue a **who** command.

`list`

Allows only list members to issue a **who** command.

`closed`

Prevents anyone from using the command (except that the list's owners can override `closed` access by using the **approve** command). For example:

```
approve listname password get filename
```

Similar *command_access* options are available for the **get**, **index**, **info**, **intro**, and **which** commands.

The format of list messages

A number of options provide control over the format of list messages. If you define the `subject_prefix` option, its value is prepended to the subject line of outgoing list messages (unless it already appears in the message subject).* The `subject_prefix` can be a single word or one of three special values:

`$LIST`

Expands into the name of the mailing list. This is often valuable, as it allows subscribers to easily determine which messages in their mailbox came from your list.

`$SENDER`

Expands into the sender's address from the message's From header.

`$VERSION`

Expands into the Majordomo version number.

In addition to modifying the subject header, you can define paragraphs of text that are inserted in the header (`message_headers` option), at the beginning of the message body (`message_fronter` option), or at the end of the body (`message_footer` option) of each message or digest distributed to the list. If the list isn't digested, you can use the $LIST, $SENDER, and $VERSION strings in these paragraphs, and they are properly expanded. If the list is digested, you can use the special string _SUBJECTS_ in the `message_fronter` to include a table of contents for a digest.

If Majordomo finds two consecutive blank lines in one of these paragraphs, it ignores whatever follows. When writing header or footer paragraphs, be sure to leave only single blank lines between paragraphs.

---

* `subject_prefix` makes sense only for undigested lists. Digests automatically receive a subject.

Here's an example of the use of the list-formatting options:

```
subject_prefix = $LIST
message_headers    <<END
X-Majordomo-Version: $VERSION
END
message_footer    <<END
----------------------------------------------------------------
This is the $LIST mailing list, managed by Majordomo $VERSION.
-
To send a message to the list, email $LIST@hats.com.
To send a request to majordomo, email majordomo@hats.com and put
your request in the body of the message (use request "help" for help)
This list is maintained by owner-$LIST@hats.com
END
```

Controlling subscriptions

A particularly important configuration option, `subscribe_policy`, controls who can subscribe to the list without the approval of the list owner. It can take one of these values:

auto

> Means that anyone can subscribe to the list without approval. Further, third-party subscriptions are allowed; anyone can ask to subscribe an address different than that in his From header.*

auto+confirm

> Works like auto, but Majordomo sends an authentication number to the subscriber, which he must send back to Majordomo to complete the subscription. This prevents people from subscribing others unwittingly and protects the list from addresses with typos in them.

open

> Allows anyone to subscribe themselves to the list without approval. Attempts to subscribe other addresses require approval.

open+confirm

> Works like open, but also requires confirmation. This is the default subscription policy.

closed

> Required list owner approval for every subscription request.

---

* This is a dangerous option; it's all too easy for someone to subscribe the list to itself, creating a mail loop, or to subscribe an unwitting and unwilling victim to an unwanted list. Consider using auto+confirm instead.

`closed+confirm`
> Works like `closed`, but also requires confirmation.

Either the `auto+confirm` or `closed+confirm` subscription policy is probably suitable for 95% of all lists.

A similar option, `unsubscribe_policy`, controls who can unsubscribe from the list without the approval of the list owner. Its values are:

`auto`
> Anyone can unsubscribe anyone without approval.

`open`
> Anyone can unsubscribe themselves without approval.

`closed`
> All unsubscriptions require approval.

Almost all lists should use the `open` unsubscription policy.

In addition to setting a subscription policy, you can control whether the welcome file is sent to new subscribers with the `welcome` option. You can also control whether you receive notices of subscriptions and unsubscriptions with the `announcements` option.

Controlling submissions

To prevent nonsubscribers from sending messages to the list, set the `restrict_post` option to the name of the list, like this:

```
restrict_post = haberdashers
```

Moderated lists

It's easy to make a Majordomo list moderated. Only three options must be set:

- The `moderate` option must be set to `yes`.
- The `moderator` option should be set to the address of the list moderator, if the moderator is someone other than the list owner.
- The `approve_passwd` option must be set to the password the moderator uses to approve messages sent to the list. It defaults to *listname*.pass, which is easily guessable, so it should be changed.

Digested lists

The following options control the operation of digested lists:

`digest_name`

> The digest's subject line contains the value of `digest_name` followed by the volume and issue numbers. `digest_name` defaults to the name of the mailing list.

`digest_volume`, `digest_issue`

> `digest_volume` gives the next digest volume number; `digest_issue` is the next issue number. `digest_issue` is automatically updated as each digest is produced. `digest_volume` must be updated manually when a new volume should be issued; when you update `digest_volume`, you must also reset `digest_issue` to 1.

`digest_maxdays`, `digest_maxlines`, `maxlength`

> `digest_maxdays` and `digest_maxlines` control how many days can pass between digests and how long (in lines) a digest can grow before being distributed. `maxlength` controls how long (in characters) a digest can grow before being distributed.

`reply_to`

> The `reply_to` option sets the value for the Reply-To header of outgoing messages. Digested lists with undigested counterparts use this option to direct replies to the digested list back to the undigested list. For example, if you've set up both *haberdashers* and *haberdashers-digest* lists, the `reply_to` option should be left unset in the *haberdashers config* file and should be set to *haberdashers@hats.com* in the *haberdashers-digest config* file.

More information about setting up digested lists is available in the Majordomo FAQ and the *README.digest* file that comes with Majordomo.

Installing the New config File

After modifying a list's configuration file, you can install the new file by sending the `newconfig` command to Majordomo. The syntax for `newconfig` is:

```
newconfig listname password
config file contents here
EOF
```

Writing the Welcome Message

Once you've configured the list, it's time to write the welcome message. Majordomo calls its welcome message an "intro" message,* and you can set it with the `newintro` command:

---

* Majordomo also allows you to have an "info" message that's sent in response to an `info` request and used in place of the intro message if you don't have one. The `newinfo` command sets up an info message and works just like `newintro`.

```
newintro listname list-password

Welcome to mylist!
  ...Welcome message continues here...
EOF
```

Updating Lists from Majordomo 1.93 or Earlier

Majordomo 1.94 added some options to the list configuration file and
removed others. A quick way to convert older list configuration files is to use
Majordomo's `writeconfig` command, which rewrites a list's configuration
file to include all of the current variables and comments:

```
writeconfig listname password
```

You can then edit the rewritten configuration file (using `config` and `new-
config`) to take advantage of the new features.

What belongs in a welcome message for a Majordomo list? In addition to the usual
ingredients of a welcome message, you should probably let subscribers know that
if the list is offered in digested and undigested forms, they must subscribe to the
form they want. You might include a paragraph like this in the welcome message
for an undigested list:

```
This is the undigested version of this mailing list. You can, instead,
choose to receive this list as weekly digests. To do so, send email
to majordomo@hats.com, and write the following in the message body:
        unsubscribe haberdashers
        subscribe haberdashers-digest
```

Similarly, the digested list welcome message might include:

```
This is the digested version of this mailing list. You will receive a
weekly digest containing all the messages sent to the list each week.
You can, instead, choose to receive each message individually.  To do
so, send email to majordomo@hats.com, and write the following in
the message body:
        unsubscribe haberdashers-digest
        subscribe haberdashers
```

Testing the List

Once the welcome message has been set up, you're ready to test the list. Start by
subscribing yourself to the list (unless your server administrator has done this for
you); Majordomo doesn't assume that list owners are also subscribed. You may be

asked to confirm the subscription. Once you do, you should receive the welcome message back.

Test the list by sending some messages and seeing that you receive them. Make sure their headers and body look the way you expect. To test a digested list, send messages to its undigested counterpart, then send Majordomo this command:

```
mkdigest listname list-password
```

The `mkdigest` command forces Majordomo to issue a digest so you can see what the digest looks like.

If your list doesn't work, get the *config* file and see if you can figure out what the problem is, or contact the server administrator to help you get it working. Once you're happy with it, you can announce it to the world and begin the day-to-day business of list administration.

List Administration

Majordomo lists can be managed remotely by sending list owner commands along with the list owner password. For example, you can subscribe or unsubscribe someone with the `approve` command:

```
approve list-password subscribe listname address
approve list-password unsubscribe listname address
```

When unsubscribing a user, the **address** must be given exactly as it appears in the list's subscriber file. Majordomo also includes two Perl scripts, *approve* and *bounce*, that list owners can use to ease list maintenance.

Approving Subscriptions and Messages

With Majordomo, you approve subscriptions to a closed list and approve messages for a moderated list in the same way. When Majordomo receives a request or a message that requires approval, it forwards a copy to the list owner. Subscription requests have APPROVE in the subject line; messages have BOUNCE in the subject line, along with the reason for the "bounce" and a copy of the message in the body.

If you're on a Unix system and have the *approve* script, you can pipe these messages to *approve*, which automatically approves subscriptions or messages. If your mail reader doesn't have a "pipe message to a program" function, you can save the message to a file and feed it to *approve* from your shell, like this:

```
% approve < filename
```

approve uses a file named *.majordomo* in your home directory. Each line of this file describes a mailing list's name, password, and request address, separated by tabs (not spaces). Here's an example:

```
haberdashers    909one majordomo@hats.com
happy-list      joyjoy majordomo@smile.grin.org
```

If you can't use *approve*, you can approve subscriptions and messages manually. When a subscription requires approval, the message you receive gives explicit instructions for subscribing the user:

```
From: majordomo@smile.grin.org
To: happy-list-approval@smile.grin.org
Subject: APPROVE happy-list
Reply-To: majordomo@smile.grin.org


--
irie@somewhere.net requests that you approve the following:

    subscribe happy-list irie@somewhere.net

If you approve, please send a message such as the following back to
majordomo@smile.grin.org (with the appropriate PASSWORD filled in, of
course):

    approve PASSWORD subscribe happy-list irie@somewhere.net

If you disapprove, do nothing. Thanks!

majordomo@smile.grin.org
```

If you don't want to approve a subscription request, it's better that you do something, contrary to Majordomo's recommendation. It's a good idea to reply to the sender of the request and explain why the subscription is being rejected, so the subscriber doesn't wonder what's going on.

Manually approving messages on a moderated list is almost as easy, and it is the only way to add moderator comments. When the list receives a message requiring approval, Majordomo forwards a copy to you:

```
From: owner-happy-list@smile.grin.org
To: owner-happy-list@smile.grin.org
Subject: BOUNCE happy-list@smile.grin.org: Approval required

From irie@somewhere.net Wed Jul  3 21:00:18 PDT 1996
Date: Wed Jul  3 21:00:18 PDT 1996
From: irie@somewhere.net
To: happy-list@smile.grin.org
Subject: These are a few of my favorite things

Dreadlocks on rude boys and whiskers on kittens...
```

If you don't want to approve the message, it's courteous to mail a note to the original sender and explain why. If you approve the message, send the message back to the list, adding the following line to the message header or the first line of the message body:

```
Approved: password
```

There are two ways to add the header:

- If your mail system lets you bounce messages and edit their headers, bounce the message back to the list, adding the Approved header and leaving only the From, To, and Subject headers from the original message. The forwarded message should look like this:

```
From: irie@somewhere.net
To: happy-list@smile.grin.org
Subject: These are a few of my favorite things
Approved: joyjoy

Dreadlocks on rude boys and whiskers on kittens...
```

Or save the message to a file, edit it until the headers look like those above, and give it to *sendmail* directly:

```
% /usr/lib/sendmail -oi -t < msgfile
```

Notice that when the Approved header appears in the message header, the other message headers should contain the original message sender, subject, etc. Compare that with the next method.

- If you can't modify your message headers, send a new message to the list and add the Approved header as the very first line of the body of your message. Follow it with a copy of the approved message including its headers. Here's what such a message should look like:

```
To: happy-list@smile.grin.org
From: listowner@smile.grin.org
Subject:

Approved: joyjoy
From: irie@somewhere.net
To: happy-list@smile.grin.org
Subject: These are a few of my favorite things

Dreadlocks on rude boys and whiskers on kittens...
```

Notice that the first set of headers are from the list's owner; the original message headers follow the Approved line and are used when Majordomo distributes the mail. Many mail programs have a "forward message" command that allows you to edit the message body before forwarding it; this can also be used to approve messages.

No matter how you approve messages, don't worry about accidentally sending the password to the whole list. If Majordomo accepts the approval password, it strips out the Approved line; if it doesn't, it doesn't allow the message to be sent to the list at all.

Handling Bounces

Majordomo can help handle bounced email to subscribers, though the process is not as automatic as Listproc's. Majordomo notifies you when a message to a subscriber of your list bounces. You can use the *bounce* script, distributed with Majordomo, to unsubscribe list members whose email is bouncing. Their addresses are removed from the mailing list and added to a special list called *bounces* (if the Majordomo administrator has created one). Each night, Majordomo tries to send mail to each of the addresses on the *bounces* list with instructions on how to resubscribe to the list.

The *bounce* program automates the process of removing users from lists and optionally adding them to the *bounces* list. Because it can be very hard to automatically determine the address that caused the bounce, the *bounce* script works differently than *approve*:

```
% bounce [-unsub] [-expire [-maxage days]] listname user@gone.com
```

The basic *bounce* command unsubscribes the address `user@gone.com` from `listname` and adds it to the *bounces* list. You must have an entry in *.majordomo* for both `listname` and *bounces* for this to work.

The `-unsub` command-line option unsubscribes the address but doesn't add it to the *bounces* list. This is also the default behavior if the *bounce* script is named (or linked to) *unsub*.

The `-expire` option removes addresses from the *bounces* list that have been present for more than 21 days. A different number of days can be used by including `-maxage days` in the command. This command is usually used by the Majordomo administrator, but he may ask you to expire addresses that originate from your list.

If you can't run the *bounce* script, you can bounce addresses manually by sending mail to Majordomo with these commands:

```
approve listname-passwd unsubscribe listname user@gone.com
approve bounces-passwd subscribe bounces user@gone.com (yymmdd listname)
```

The first command unsubscribes the user from the current list. The second subscribes the user to the *bounces* list, with a comment that shows the date (e.g., `97061` for June 10, 1997) and the name of the list she was on.

5

Maintaining Lists with SmartList

The server administrator, not the list maintainer, configures lists run by SmartList. In fact, the list owner has relatively little control over a list. As such, this chapter focuses primarily on subscription and submission control, rather than list configuration, although it does mention features you might want your server administrator to enable or disable for your list.

Appendix C, *SmartList Reference*, contains a complete reference to all of the SmartList requests and configuration options, while Chapter 11, *Administering SmartList*, covers everything that a server administrator needs to know about SmartList.

Creating Your List

There are three things that you need to tell the server administrator in order to have your list added to the SmartList server:

- The email address of the list owner and any moderators

- The list password

- List options

List Owner and Moderator Addresses

The server administrator needs to know the email address at which you want to receive messages sent to the list owner. You'll also have to include this address in any list owner commands you send to SmartList.

If your list is moderated, you can have as many moderators as you like; SmartList handles multiple moderators elegantly. Just tell the server administrator the email addresses of all of the moderators.

The List Password

The list password is also sent along with list owner commands; without the password, you can't maintain the list. Tell the server administrator what you'd like to use as a password.

When SmartList processes a list owner command, it sends a notification back to the list owner's address. So, if someone else learns the list password and sends a command, you'll be notified, but it's probably better to pick a good password from the beginning.

List Options

Because SmartList configuration rests with the server administrator, you have to let him know if you want your list to be moderated, digested, or archived. You need to say whether subscriptions should require your approval or be automatic. You also need to tell him who should be allowed to post to the list: subscribers only, a subset of subscribers (for example, only you), or anyone.

Here's an example of how you might inform the server administrator of your needs:

```
From: sally@happy.fun.org
To: jolly@happy.fun.org
Subject: My new list: lightbulb-jokes

The lightbulb-jokes list should be owned by sally@happy.fun.org.  It
should be an unmoderated, open list that anyone can subscribe to
without approval. Only subscribers should be allowed to post to the
list.  I'd like to use the password 'filament'. Thanks!
```

The server administrator sets up two addresses for your list: *listname* and *listname-request*. *listname* is the address for sending submissions (e.g., *lightbulb-jokes@happy.fun.org*). *listname-request* is the address for sending list requests and list owner commands (e.g., *lightbulb-jokes-request@happy.fun.org*).

Once the server administrator tells you the list has been set up, you're ready to write the welcome message and test out the list.

Writing the Welcome Message

With SmartList, you can have multiple welcome messages sent to new subscribers and can also customize the message people receive when they unsubscribe. Unfortunately, to add a welcome message to your list, you need to send it to the server administrator and ask him to install it.

What special information should go in welcome messages for SmartList lists? You should be sure the subscribers know that the address for list commands is *listname-request*; people familiar with other list servers may be expecting a centralized address that manages all of the lists, rather than separate *-request* addresses for each list.

Also, SmartList expects its requests to appear in the Subject header, rather than the body of the message. This can be confusing to people who use other list servers as well.

Even if you don't ask to have your list messages permanently archived, SmartList archives the last couple of postings to the list. You should make subscribers aware of this. Suggest that they send an **archive help** request for information about using the archive.

Finally, SmartList includes a copy of the subscription request message at the end of your welcome message. This lets the subscriber check to be sure they really intend to subscribe from that address. Conclude your welcome message with a brief explanation of what's attached.

Here's some paragraphs that you might include in the welcome message for the *lightbulb-jokes*:

```
This list is maintained by SmartList. SmartList operates differently
than other mailing list software you may be familiar with in a couple
of important ways:
* Commands to the list server should be sent to:
        lightbulb-jokes-request@happy.fun.org
  SmartList monitors this address and executes commands it receives.
* Commands to the list server are put in the Subject: header of the
  message, *not* the body of the message.

For example, to get help with the archiving features of SmartList,
send a message to lightbulb-jokes-request@happy.fun.org, with a
Subject: of "archive help". (By the way, SmartList temporarily
archives the last few list messages, so you might want to send that
command and find out how to work with the archive.)

The message that you sent to subscribe to this list is given below,
for your reference:
```

Testing the List

Once the server administrator installs your welcome message, you can test the list. Subscribe yourself to the list (SmartList does not do this by default). Check that you receive your welcome message.

Send a few messages to the list and make sure you receive them. Try subscribing yourself again; SmartList should return an error message.

If the list doesn't work, you'll have to contact the server administrator to help you get it working. Once it's operational, you can tell the world about it and get on to list administration.

List Administration

As a SmartList list maintainer, there's not a lot of work to be done. Your primary responsibility is to manage subscriptions. If the list is moderated, you also have to approve submissions.

Subscriptions with SmartList

SmartList handles the most common subscription woe—bouncing mail—automatically. It removes users whose mail bounces a specified number of times. If a user is removed from your list, SmartList sends a message to notify you.

SmartList list owners can remotely subscribe or unsubscribe users; search for an email address in the *dist* file, which contains subscription addresses, and retrieve the entire *dist* file. List owner commands are sent to the list's request address by including an X-Command header in the message headers. The format of the header is:

```
X-Command: owner's-email-address list-password command
```

The server administrator may change the header to be called something other than X-Command, so you should be sure to find out what the server is actually using.

The subscription commands list owners can use are:

subscribe *address*
> Subscribes a user to the list.

unsubscribe *address*
> Unsubscribes a user from the list.

checkdist *address*
> Searches the list of subscribers (the *dist* file) for addresses that match *address* and returns the eight closest matches. This command is useful when you receive mail from *sam@overhere.b.com* asking that his mail be sent to *sam@b.com*, when in fact he subscribed from another workstation, *sam@elsewhere.b.com*. Using checkdist sam@b.com returns *sam@elsewhere.b.com*; you can then unsubscribe the incorrect address and resubscribe the correct one.

showdist
> Retrieves the *dist* file.

`showlog`

> Retrieves the list's log file. The log file contains short summaries of message headers for requests sent to SmartList. The `wipelog` command clears the log file.

The results of a command are sent back to the list's owner with the header changed to X-Processed. For example, here's an email message the list owner might send to SmartList to subscribe *newuser@host.com*:

```
From: sally@happy.fun.org
To: lightbulb-jokes-request@happy.fun.org
Subject: subscribing a new user
X-Command: sally@happy.fun.org filament subscribe newuser@host.com
    The message body can contain anything
```

SmartList sends the welcome message to *newuser@host.com* and sends a confirmation of the command back to the list owner:

```
From: lightbulb-jokes-request@happy.fun.org
To: sally@happy.fun.org
Subject: subscribing a new user
X-Processed: sally@happy.fun.org filament subscribe newuser@host.com
    The message body can contain anything
```

SmartList comes with a script called *doxcommand*, which the server administrator can provide. The script simplifies sending commands to SmartList. First, you have to edit the script to set the list's request address, maintainer address, and password, as well as the name for the X-Command header if it's been changed. *doxcommand* accepts a command as its only argument; it calls *sendmail* to send an appropriately formatted message to the list's request address. Here's how *sally* could subscribe *newuser@host.com* using *doxcommand*:

```
% doxcommand subscribe newuser@host.com
```

Moderated Lists

When mail arrives for a moderated list, SmartList sends each moderator a copy of the message that looks like this:

```
From recipes-request@yourhost  Sun Mar 31 23:47:51 1996
X-Envelope-From: subscriber@theirhost  Sun Mar 31 23:47:49 1996
From: Joe Subscriber <subscriber@theirhost>
Subject: Baked Apples
To: recipes@yourhost
    Message body
```

Unfortunately, the message looks a lot like a genuine list message. A distinguishing feature is that it lacks an X-Mailing-List header. To approve the message, any moderator resends it to the list with an **Approved:** *moderator-address* header added. Resending the message without modifying its headers isn't easy in most MUAs, however.* Example 5-1 shows a Perl script called *smartlist-approve* that makes it easier. Just pipe the message to `smartlist-approve` *list-address* (e.g., `smartlist-approve recipes@yourhost`).

Example 5-1: The smartlist-approve Script

```perl
#!/usr/bin/perl
#
#
# smartlist-approve: a filter to take an email message sent to a
#                    smartlist moderator when a message is sent to the
#                    list and repost it to the list with a Approved:
#                    header.
#
# By Alan Schwartz <alansz@cogsci.berkeley.edu> 1996
#
#
# Usage: pipe mail message to
#    smartlist-approve <list address>
#
# Example:  cat message | smartlist-approve recipes@gourmet.org
#

# Set this to point to where your sendmail program is located:
$sendmail='/usr/lib/sendmail';

# Set this to your email address as a moderator
$email='myaddress@myhost';

die "Usage: $0 <list-address>\n" unless ($list = $ARGV[0]);
die "Unable to call $sendmail\n" unless open(OUT,"|$sendmail $list");

# Print out the headers, except any escaped >From header
while (<STDIN>) {
  last if /^$/;
  print OUT unless /^>From/;
}

# Add the Approved: header and a blank line
print OUT "Approved: $email\n\n";

# Print the rest of the body
print OUT <STDIN>;
close OUT;
```

SmartList keeps track of the last few messages sent, and thus prevents multiple approvals from resulting in multiple copies of a message being sent to the list.

---

* *elm*, for example, can either "bounce" a message, which preserves its headers, but doesn't let you add on the Approved: header, or "forward" a message, which makes it appear to come from you.

6

Maintaining Lists with LISTSERV Lite

LISTSERV Lite allows the list maintainer to perform much of the configuration and customization of a mailing list. The server administrator sets up the list initially and must set up list archives, but other list configuration can be handled by the list maintainer. L-Soft International, Inc., the company that currently develops and licenses LISTSERV, provides a comprehensive guide to LISTSERV for list maintainers.* You can retrieve it from your *listserv* server by sending the request `GET LISTOWNR.MEMO`. This chapter focuses on the most common list configurations and management situations.

I have followed the convention of the LISTSERV Lite manuals by writing list requests in uppercase. In fact, however, LISTSERV Lite is not case-sensitive. A `LISTS` request can also be given as `Lists`, `lists`, or even `LiStS`.

Appendix D, *LISTSERV Lite Reference*, contains a complete reference to the LISTSERV Lite list owner commands, while Chapter 12, *Administering LISTSERV Lite*, covers everything a server administrator needs to know about LISTSERV Lite.

Creating Your List

You need to tell the server administrator three things in order to have your list added to a LISTSERV Lite server:

- A one-line description of the list
- The email addresses of the primary list owner and any secondary list owners
- Archive and digest options

---

* L-Soft's list owner's manual is written with LISTSERV Classic in mind; some of the features it describes aren't available on sites running LISTSERV Lite. When in doubt, ask your server administrator.

One-Line Description

Each LISTSERV Lite list has a one-line description that is included in the standard LISTSERV welcome message and in the response to the `LISTS` request.

List Owner Addresses

A LISTSERV Lite list can have more than one list owner. However, one owner is the primary owner. Any owner can issue list maintainer commands, but the primary owner is the default moderator for moderated lists and receives administrative messages and error messages generated by the list. Secondary owners come in two flavors. Ordinary secondary owners can issue list maintainer commands and receive administrative email like primary owners. "Quiet" secondary owners can issue list maintainer commands, but don't receive administrative email.

LISTSERV Lite recognizes email it receives from list owners by checking the email address against its list of owner addresses. Accordingly, to get your list created, you have to tell the server administrator the email addresses from which the list administrators send mail. Even if you're the only list owner, you may want to send commands from more than one email address; the server administrator needs to know all of them. If you're planning to use multiple email addresses, you should let the server administrator know at which one you'd like to receive list mail. That address should be the primary owner; your other addresses can be quiet secondary owners.

Archive and Digest Options

The only list feature you can't control is how the list is archived. If you want to archive your list, you have to let the server administrator know. You also have to tell him:

How frequently new archive files should be generated
    All of the archived messages can be kept in a single file, each message can be archived in a separate file, or messages can be organized into files by year, month, or week.

Who should be able to access archived messages
    You have considerable flexibility in this decision. Archive access can be public or restricted to any combination of list owners (of your list or other lists), list subscribers (of your list or other lists), and individual email addresses.

Whether to allow web access to your list archives
    If your server administrator is running the LISTSERV Lite web interface, you can make your list archives and subscription options available on the Web.

Your archives must be public and must be archived yearly, monthly, or weekly in order to make them available.

If you don't want archiving, but want to allow subscribers to receive the list in digested form, you have to let the server administrator know. If archiving is turned off, digests are disabled by default. You should also let him know how often the digest should be distributed: daily, weekly, or monthly.

Here's an example of how you might inform the server administrator of your needs:

```
From: santa@northpole.org
To: rudolph@northpole.org
Subject: My new list: nice-children

I'd like to have you set up a "nice-children" list. The description is
"List for nice children to get to know one another." It should be owned
by santa@northpole.org, and mrsclaus@northpole.org should be a "quiet"
owner. I'd like the list archived by year, and the archives should be
public and accessible on the web server.
```

Once the server administrator tells you the list has been set up, you're ready to configure the list, write the welcome message, and test out the list.

Personal Passwords and Confirmation

LISTSERV Lite has two levels of security for commands. The first is based on passwords. LISTSERV Lite's list maintainer commands may require a password in the message. To get a personal password, send email to your local *listserv* address with the request PW ADD *password*:

```
To: listserv@northpole.org
From: santa@northpole.org
Subject: I need a password

pw add jnglbell
```

To use your password, add PW=*password* to the end of commands that you send to *listserv*. Because you include your password in email messages sent to LISTSERV Lite to maintain the list remotely, the password is easily compromised, and should not be the same as your account password or any other important password.

The second level of security is confirmation notices. LISTSERV Lite may send you a message asking you to confirm a command it receives from you. This prevents someone who learns your password from forging your email address and issuing commands with your password; it's much easier to forge an address than to intercept the confirmation message LISTSERV Lite sends back. To confirm a command, simply follow the instructions in the confirmation notice; typically, you're asked to reply to the confirmation notice with the single word ok.

Configuring the List

You configure a list by requesting a copy of the list's header file, *listname.LIST*, editing the file, and mailing it back to *listserv*.

Requesting the Header File

Request a copy of the header file by sending a message to *listserv* that contains the following GET command:

```
GET listname.LIST (HEADER PW=personal-password
```

The header file is mailed to you, and the list is locked. Locking the list prevents other list owners from requesting the header file and prevents users from subscribing to the list until you've finished your configuration. If you decide not to change the list configuration, send *listserv* the request UNLOCK *listname* to unlock the list.

Editing the Header File

The header file offers you a great deal of control over how your list operates. Because there are many keywords, I'm only going to cover the most important ones here, to show you how to set up some common list configurations. A complete list of header file keywords is available by sending the command GET LISTKEYW.MEMO to *listserv*.

Header file basics

When you use GET to retrieve the header file, LISTSERV Lite responds by sending back both the command to store the new header file and the current header file itself. For example, the reply from LISTSERV Lite might look like this:

```
From: "L-Soft list server at NORTHPOLE (1.8c)" <LISTSERV@NORTHPOLE.ORG>
Subject:       File: "NICE-CHILDREN LIST"
To: Santa Claus <santa@NORTHPOLE.ORG>

PUT NICE-CHILDREN LIST PW=XXXXXXXX
* List for nice children to get to know one another
*
* Owner= santa@northpole.org
* Notebook= Yes,/home/listserv/archives/nice-children,Yearly
```

The first line in the message body is the PUT command, which updates the list header file (replacing the XXXXXXXX with your personal password). All the lines thereafter are lines of the header file.

Each line in the header file must begin with an asterisk (*). The first line is the description of the list. Subsequent lines may contain keywords and their values. Keywords end in an equal sign (e.g., `Owner=`) and are followed by the value of the keyword.

LISTSERV Lite has reasonable defaults for most keywords. The server administrator can create your list with a small number of keywords, and then you can add those that you need in order to change LISTSERV Lite's default behavior.

Controlling subscriptions

The `Service` keyword defines your list's "service area." People outside the service area can't subscribe to the list. Its value is a comma-separated list of host-names; wildcards are allowed. For example, to allow access to all machines in the *myhost.com* domain, use a line like this:

```
* Service=myhost.com,*.myhost.com
```

The `Subscription` keyword controls how users subscribe to the list. It can take one of four values:

`Open`
> Anyone can subscribe to the list without approval.

`Open,Confirm`
> Works like `Open`, but LISTSERV Lite sends a confirmation notice to the subscriber, which he must send back to *listserv* to complete the subscription. This prevents people from subscribing others by forging their email addresses; it also prevents the subscription of one-way or broken email addresses. This is the recommended subscription option for open lists.

`By owner`
> Subscription requests are forwarded to the list owner for approval. This is LISTSERV Lite's default subscription mode.

`Closed`
> No subscriptions are allowed. Requests to subscribe are rejected rather than forwarded to the list owner.

For more fine-grained control, use the `Filter` keyword to prevent email addresses that match one of a list of patterns from subscribing to the list. Here's how you'd prevent users from *naughty.com* from subscribing:

```
* Filter= Also,*@*NAUGHTY.COM
```

The `Default-Options` keyword sets the default mail options for new subscribers. Its value is a comma-separated list of mail * options—the same options

used by the `SET` command (see Appendix D). For example, to cause new subscribers to receive copies of their own postings, you could use:

```
* Default-Options=Repro
```

List visibility and subscriber privacy

When a user sends a `LISTS` request to LISTSERV Lite, the MLM responds by sending back descriptions of the lists the server manages. The first line of the header
file sets the description of the list. You can also control whether your list is visible
to a `LISTS` request at all.

The `Confidential` keyword determines whether a list appears in response to
the `LISTS` request. If set to `Yes`, the list is hidden; the default is `No`. You can hide
the list from hosts that are out of its service area by setting `Confidential` to
`Service`.

Users can issue a `REVIEW listname` request to ask for a copy of the list of subscribers. If you want to protect (or expose) your subscriber list, you can set the
`Review` keyword. It takes one of four values:

Public
    Permits anyone to review the subscriber list.

Service
    Permits anyone within the list's service area to review the subscriber list.

Private
    Permits list subscribers to review the subscriber list. This is the default.

Owners
    Permits only list owners to review the subscriber list.

The format of list messages

LISTSERV Lite offers some flexibility in how the headers of list messages appear.
The To header always contains the list address, which simplifies responding to the
list or filtering email from the list.

The `Reply-To` keyword determines how the Reply-To header is formatted. It
consists of two values, separated by a comma. The first value can be either a specific address or one of the following values:

List
    Sets Reply-To to the list address

Sender
    Sets Reply-To to the sender's address

`Both`

> Sets Reply-To to both addresses (which may fail for some MTAs)

The second value determines how to handle messages that already have a Reply-To header:

`Respect`

> Leave the existing header.

`Ignore`

> Remove it and replace it with the desired Reply-To header.

To set up headers so that subscribers can choose to reply either to the sender or to the list, try:

```
* Reply-To= Sender,Respect
```

The `Subject-Tag` keyword sets a single word to be inserted (in brackets) at the beginning of the Subject header for mail distributed to the list subscribers. Subscribers can turn this feature on or off with the `SET` request. `Subject-Tag` defaults to the name of the list.

Controlling submissions

To prevent nonsubscribers from sending messages to the list, set the `Send` keyword to `Private`, like this:

```
* Send= Private
```

The default value for `Send` is `Public`. You can also set it to `Owner` to allow only the list owner to send messages to the list or `Owner,Confirm` to allow only the list owner to send messages and to require confirmation to prevent someone from forging messages as the list owner. This would be suitable for an announcements-only list.

Moderated lists

`Send` is also used to cause a list to be moderated. To set up a moderated list, you must give `Send` the value `Editor`, `Editor,Hold`, or `Editor,Hold,Confirm` and assign a moderator using the `Editor` keyword:

```
* Send= Editor,Hold
* Editor= santa@northpole.org
* Editor= mrsclaus@northpole.org
```

When `Send` contains the `Editor` value, mail that doesn't come from one of the addresses listed in the `Editor` keyword is forwarded to the first `Editor` listed. That moderator edits the message, if necessary, and then resends it to the list. If the `Hold` value is included for `Send`, the moderator can simply reply to *listserv* with `ok` to approve a message. If `Confirm` is also included, all mail must be approved by the primary moderator (using `ok`), even if it comes from another moderator. This prevents people from posting messages by forging a moderator's address.

A useful variation is:

```
* Send= Editor,Hold
* Editor= santa@northpole.org
* Editor= (NICE-CHILDREN)
```

This gives anyone already on the *nice-children* list permission to send messages to the list without approval, but forwards non-subscriber messages to the person listed as the first `Editor`, usually the list owner.

Digested lists

A subscriber to a LISTSERV Lite list can request to have messages sent in digest form. As list owner, you determine whether and how digests are made available.

Note that if your list isn't being archived, digests are disabled by default. In this case, you need the help of the server administrator in order to enable digests.

The `Digest` keyword controls the operation of digests. To disable digests:

```
* Digest= No
```

To enable digests, the syntax is:

```
* Digest= Yes,Same[,frequency,[time,[Size(lines)]]]
```

The optional *frequency* can be `Daily`, `Weekly`, or `Yearly`. The optional *time* specifies the time of day at which to distribute digests:

- For daily digests, *time* is a two-digit hour (00–23) or hour and minute (00:00–23:59).

- For weekly digests, *time* is a weekday (Monday–Sunday).

- For monthly digests, *time* is a day of the month (1–31).

The `Size(lines)` value limits the size of the digest to *lines* lines long. If a digest gets longer than *lines* lines, it is issued immediately.

The default value of `Digest` is `No` if the list is not archived. If the list is archived, the default is to issue digests of no more than 10,000 lines daily at midnight:

```
* Digest=Yes,Same,Daily,00,Size(10000)
```

Storing the New Header File

After you modify a list's header file, you can store the new header file by sending it back to *listserv* in a PUT request. The syntax for using PUT on a header file is:

```
PUT listname.LIST PW=personal-password
Header file contents here
```

LISTSERV Lite responds to your PUT request by telling you the header file has been successfully stored or by pointing out problems with the file.

Writing the Welcome Message

To add a welcome message to your list, use the PUT request to store a file called *listname*.*welcome*:

```
From: santa@northpole.org
To: listserv@northpole.org
Subject: setting welcome

PUT nice-children.welcome PW=personal-password
Your welcome message here
```

PUT replaces the current welcome message (if any) with the one you send. If you want to get a copy of your current welcome message, use the GET request:

```
GET nice-children.welcome PW=personal-password
```

LISTSERV Lite sends a standard informational message to new subscribers, and it also sends your customized welcome message as a separate email message with a Subject of "Usage guidelines for *listname*." Here's what the standard informational message says:

```
Your subscription to the listname list (description) has been accepted.

Please save this message for future reference, especially if this is
the first time you subscribe to an electronic mailing list. If you
ever need to leave the list, you will find the necessary instructions
below.  Perhaps more importantly, saving a copy of this message (and
of all future subscription notices from other mailing lists) in a
special mail folder will give you instant access to the list of
mailing lists that you are subscribed to. This may prove very useful
the next time you go on vacation and need to leave the lists
temporarily so as not to fill up your mailbox while you are away!  You
should also save the "welcome messages" from the list owners that you
will occasionally receive after subscribing to a new list.

To send a message to all the people currently subscribed to the list,
just send mail to listname@listhost. This is called "sending
mail to the list", because you send mail to a single address and
LISTSERV makes copies for all the people who have subscribed.  This
```

address (*listname@listhost*) is also called the "list address".
You must never try to send any command to that address, as it would be
distributed to all the people who have subscribed. All commands must
be sent to the "LISTSERV address", LISTSERV@*listhost*. It is
very important to understand the difference between the two, but
fortunately it is not complicated. The LISTSERV address is like a FAX
number that connects you to a machine, whereas the list address is
like a normal voice line connecting you to a person. If you make a
mistake and dial the FAX number when you wanted to talk to someone on
the phone, you will quickly realize that you used the wrong number and
call again. No harm will have been done. If on the other hand you
accidentally make your FAX call someone's voice line, the person
receiving the call will be inconvenienced, especially if your FAX then
re-dials every 5 minutes. The fact that most people will eventually
connect the FAX machine to the voice line to allow the FAX to go
through and make the calls stop does not mean that you should continue
to send FAXes to the voice number. People would just get mad at you.
It works pretty much the same way with mailing lists, with the
difference that you are calling hundreds or thousands of people at the
same time, and consequently you can expect a lot of people to get
upset if you consistently send commands to the list address.

You may leave the list at any time by sending a "SIGNOFF
listname" command to LISTSERV@*listhost*. You can also tell
LISTSERV how you want it to confirm the receipt of messages you send
to the list. If you do not trust the system, send a "SET
listname REPRO" command and LISTSERV will send you a copy of
your own messages, so that you can see that the message was
distributed and did not get damaged on the way. After a while you may
find that this is getting annoying, especially if your mail program
does not tell you that the message is from you when it informs you
that new mail has arrived from *listname*. If you send a "SET
listname ACK NOREPRO" command, LISTSERV will mail you a short
acknowledgment instead, which will look different in your mailbox
directory. With most mail programs you will know immediately that this
is an acknowledgment you can read later. Finally, you can turn off
acknowledgments completely with "SET *listname* NOACK NOREPRO".

Following instructions from the list owner, your subscription options
have been set to "MIME" rather than the usual LISTSERV defaults. For
more information about subscription options, send a "QUERY
listname" command to LISTSERV@*listhost*.

Contributions sent to this list are automatically archived. You can
get a list of the available archive files by sending an "INDEX
listname" command to LISTSERV@*listhost*. You can then
order these files with a "GET *listname* LOGxxxx" command.

This list is available in digest form. If you wish to receive the
digested version of the postings, just issue a SET *listname*
DIGEST command.

```
Please note that it is presently possible for other people to
determine that you are signed up to the list through the use of the
"REVIEW" command, which returns the e-mail address and name of all the
subscribers. If you do not want your name to be visible, just issue a
"SET listname CONCEAL" command.

More information on LISTSERV commands can be found in the LISTSERV
reference card, which you can retrieve by sending an "INFO REFCARD"
command to LISTSERV@listhost.

-----------------------------------------------------------------------
This server is running the Free Edition of LISTSERV(R) Lite for unix
(SunOS 4.1.3_U1). The Free Edition supports up to 10 lists of up to 500
subscribers each, and is available for free download from
http://www.lsoft.com/free-edition.html. It may not be sold or used for
commercial purposes.
-----------------------------------------------------------------------
```

Because LISTSERV Lite provides such an extensive standard welcome message, your custom welcome message can focus exclusively on issues related to your list's content and procedures.

You can also store a file called *listname.farewell* that is sent to people who unsubscribe from the list.

Testing the List

Once the welcome message has been set up, you're ready to test the list.* Start by subscribing yourself to the list (LISTSERV Lite doesn't assume that list owners are subscribed). Depending on how you've configured the list headers, you may be asked to confirm your subscription. When the subscription process is complete, you should receive the list's informational and welcome messages.

Test the list by sending some messages and see if you receive them. Try subscribing yourself to the list again; LISTSERV Lite should return an error message.

If your list doesn't work, you'll probably have to contact the server administrator to help you get it working. Once you're happy with it, you can announce it to the world and begin the day-to-day business of list administration.

List Administration

As a LISTSERV Lite list owner, you will find yourself managing subscriptions and address changes. If the list is moderated, you'll also have to approve submissions.

---

* In fact, *santa@northpole.org* recommends "making a list and checking it twice."

Subscriptions with LISTSERV Lite

LISTSERV Lite lists, by default, are closed. Subscription requests sent to a closed list are forwarded to the list maintainer for approval. The would-be subscriber is notified that list subscription is not automatic, and you receive a message like this:

```
From: "L-Soft list server at NORTHPOLE (1.8c)" <LISTSERV@NORTHPOLE.ORG>
Subject:        NICE-CHILDREN: virginia@KIDSITE.EDU requested to join
To: Santa Claus <santa@NORTHPOLE.ORG>

Tue, 14 Oct 1997 12:05:53

A request for subscription to the NICE-CHILDREN list (List for nice
children to get to know one another) has been received from Virginia
O'Hanlon <virginia@KIDSITE.EDU>.

You can, at your discretion, send the following command to
LISTSERV@NORTHPOLE.ORG to add this person to the list:

        ADD NICE-CHILDREN virginia@KIDSITE.EDU Virginia O'Hanlon

PS: In order to facilitate the task, this message has been specially
formatted so that you only need to forward it back to
LISTSERV@NORTHPOLE.ORG and fill in the password to have the command
executed. Note that while the formats produced by the forwarding
function of most mail packages are supported, replying will seldom
work, so make sure to forward and not reply.
-------------------------------------------------------------------
// JOB PW=XXXXXXXX
ADD NICE-CHILDREN virginia@KIDSITE.EDU Virginia O'Hanlon
// EOJ
```

You can either forward the message back as instructed (replacing **XXXXXXXX** with your personal password), or you can send a new message to *listserv* with the **ADD** request. Note that in most cases, the **ADD** request should be written to include your personal password:

```
ADD NICE-CHILDREN PW=password virginia@KIDSITE.EDU Virginia O'Hanlon
```

A few other points are important. The **ADD** command must include either a full name (at least two words long) or an asterisk (*) at the end. If an asterisk is used in place of the full name, LISTSERV Lite checks other lists for the subscriber's email address and full name and replaces the asterisk with the full name it finds. If it can't find one, the MLM uses "(No Name Available)" as the full name.

ADD circumvents any subscription confirmation message, but sends the new subscriber the informational and welcome messages for the list. If you want to add a subscriber without sending the subscriber any messages, use **QUIET ADD** instead of **ADD**.

If you don't wish to approve a subscription, it's up to you to inform the would-be subscriber of the rejection.

Address Changes

By default, if a subscriber wants to change the address at which she receives list mail, she must unsubscribe from the list by sending an unsubscribe request from her old address and resubscribe to the list by sending a subscribe request from her new address.

A more common occurrence is that a subscriber changes email addresses and forgets to notify the list of her address by sending mail from her old (subscribed) address. By the time she realizes what's happened, she no longer has access to the old address to send an unsubscribe message.

If a subscriber contacts you in this situation, you can use the **DELETE** command to unsubscribe the subscriber's old address. **DELETE** works much like **ADD**:

    DELETE *listname subscriber-address* PW=*personal-password*

Similarly, you can use **QUIET DELETE** to remove a subscriber without sending the farewell message.

If you can't find the exact subscriber address, you can issue the **SCAN** request:

    SCAN *listname string* PW=*personal-password*

SCAN causes LISTSERV Lite to mail back a list of subscribers whose email addresses or full names include *string* in them.

If bounce handling is turned on, the LISTSERV Lite server automatically removes email addresses if mail to them bounces for four days or more than 100 times. These defaults can be changed by the server administrator.

Moderated Lists

LISTSERV Lite moderators (called "editors" in the header file) receive messages that require approval. If the list's header file includes **Send= Editor**, the moderator receives a notification like this:

```
From: Donner <donner@northpole.org>
To: nice-children@NORTHPOLE.ORG
Subject: Comet and Cupid

This message was originally submitted by donner@NORTHPOLE.ORG to the
NICE-CHILDREN list at NORTHPOLE.ORG. If you simply forward it back to
the list, using a mail command that generates "Resent-" fields (ask
your local user support or consult the documentation of your mail
program if in doubt), it will be distributed and the explanations you
```

```
are now reading will be removed automatically. If on the other hand
you edit the contributions you receive into a digest, you will have to
remove this paragraph manually. Finally, you should be able to contact
the author of this message by using the normal "reply" function of
your mail program.

---------------- Message requiring your approval (2 lines) ----------

Comet and Cupid say hello!
```

The moderator approves the message by bouncing it back to *listserv*, possibly after editing it. For many moderators, this proves to be a problem: many MUAs have a "bounce" feature that adds the required Resent- headers, but few allow you to edit the posting before bouncing it.

An alternative is to set the `Send` keyword to `Editor,Hold`. When a subscriber sends a message to the list, the moderator receives notification of the message, but can approve it by simply replying to the message with `ok`. Here's what the notification looks like:

```
From: "L-Soft list server at NORTHPOLE (1.8c)" <LISTSERV@NORTHPOLE.ORG>
Subject:       NICE-CHILDREN: approval required (370E7C67)
To: Santa Claus <alansz@NORTHPOLE.ORG>

This message was originally submitted by donner@NORTHPOLE.ORG to the
NICE-CHILDREN list at NORTHPOLE.ORG. You can approve it using the "OK"
mechanism, ignore it, or repost an edited copy. The message will
expire automatically and you do not need to do anything if you just
want to discard it. Please refer to the list owner's guide if you are
not familiar with the "OK" mechanism; these instructions are being
kept purposefully short for your convenience in processing large
numbers of messages.

---------------- Original message (ID=370E7C67) (14 lines) ----------
Received: (from donner@localhost)
        by NORTHPOLE.ORG (8.8.7/8.8.7) id MAA11983
        for NICE-CHILDREN; Tue, 14 Oct 1997 12:56:13 -0500 (CDT)
From: Donner <donner@NORTHPOLE.ORG>
Message-Id: <199710141756.MAA11983@NORTHPOLE.ORG>
Subject: Comet and Cupid
To: NICE-CHILDREN@NORTHPOLE.ORG
Date: Tue, 14 Oct 1997 12:56:12 -0500 (CDT)

Comet and Cupid say hello!
```

7

Maintaining Lists with sendmail

While most of this book discusses the features of MLM software, there's a lot that can be done with *sendmail* alone. This chapter details the operation of the *sendmail aliases* file and looks at examples that use *sendmail* to manage mailing lists and serve files.

You can't maintain a list under *sendmail* without knowing something about how *sendmail* works. Although this chapter is directed at list maintainers, on most systems you'll need the help of the system administrator to set up lists and other mail services. For a complete description of *sendmail*, check out O'Reilly & Associates' *sendmail*, Second Edition, by Bryan Costales and Eric Allman.

The sendmail Toolkit

If you plan to provide mailing list or archive services without using an integrated MLM package, you can save yourself a lot of work by having the right tools. Here's some programs that are invaluable in creating *sendmail*-based mail services:

sendmail v8

> If your host computer isn't already using version 8 of *sendmail*, it probably should be. This latest version is being actively developed and includes important security features and enhancements. At the time of this writing, the current version was 8.8.8. *sendmail* is available at *ftp://ftp.sendmail.org/pub/ sendmail*. You will need your system administrator to install this.

Perl

> Larry Wall's Perl programming language is designed for text-processing and is well-suited for writing scripts to process mail messages. The latest version is 5.004, available from *http://www.perl.com/CPAN/src/5.0*.

procmail

> *procmail* is a powerful mail filter that uses its own scripting language and can perform a variety of mail tasks. One of the programs in the package, *formail*, is a filter that adds, removes, renames, or replaces headers from mail messages; it's incredibly handy.

deliver

> *deliver* is a general-purpose mail filter that uses shell scripts to control delivery of mail. Because it does file-locking when delivering mail to files, it's particularly useful when using versions of *sendmail* other than version 8. You can get it as a shell archive in six parts at *ftp://ftp.uu.net/usenet/comp.sources. reviewed/volume01/deliver/*. You'll need the six *part* files (00-05) and the four *patch* files (07-10).

The aliases File

sendmail's *aliases* file (usually */etc/aliases* or */usr/lib/aliases*) defines email addresses for which *sendmail* accepts mail that aren't account names already on the local system. The format of the file is:

```
alias: expansion[,expansion[,expansion...]]
```

There are four kinds of things that can appear on the right side of an alias in the *aliases* file:

- An email address to forward mail to:

    ```
    chuck: charlie@peanuts.ora.com
    ```

- A file to save mail to, beginning with a slash (/):

    ```
    trouble-file: /staff/trouble.mbox
    ```

- A command to feed mail to, beginning with a vertical bar (|):

    ```
    printer: |/usr/ucb/lpr
    ```

- A file, beginning with *:include:*, that contains any combination of email addresses, filenames, and pipe commands:

    ```
    trouble: :include:/staff/trouble.alias
    ```

For example, the file */staff/trouble.alias* could contain:

```
charlie@peanuts.ora.com
sally@peanuts.ora.com
/staff/trouble.mbox
```

You can create simple mailing lists using files of email addresses, and you can implement many more powerful functions using pipes. When you combine *sendmail's* *aliases* file with tools like Perl scripts, *formail*, and *cron*, you can create powerful mail services.

Whenever you modify the *aliases* file, you should run the *newaliases* command. *newaliases* instructs *sendmail* to check the aliases file for errors (such as alias loops) and to convert it to a format that *sendmail* can read quickly.

Who Am I?

The *sendmail* daemon is normally run as *root*. For security reasons, the daemon gives up its root privileges when it processes pipe aliases.

Unfortunately, you can't always be sure which user and group it changes its ID to. For aliases that pipe mail to commands, the rules in *sendmail* version 8 are:

- If there's a controlling user (i.e., if the sender of the mail is a local user on the system), change to that user's ID and group ID.

- Otherwise, change to the user and group ID given in *sendmail's* configuration file (usually *daemon* or *nobody*).

Though it may be impossible to predict the user who is running the program in a pipe alias, you can ensure that the right user is running the program by making the program setuid to that user (or by writing a setuid wrapper if the program is a shell script). A setuid program is always run with the same user ID. All four MLMs discussed in this book use setuid programs in their aliases. A sample setuid wrapper program is included at the end of this chapter.

Another trick that works with *sendmail* version 8 is to use an `:include:` file that contains the pipe command. *sendmail* version 8 changes its ID to the owner of the included file when processing the addresses in the file, so the pipe is executed as that user (unless the owner is *root*).

Mailing Lists

The `:include:` alias format makes it easy to create simple, user-maintained mailing lists. To create a mailing list called *alphabet* owned by user *kermit*, add these aliases:

```
alphabet: :include:/home/kermit/alphabet-subscribers
owner-alphabet: alphabet-request
alphabet-request: kermit
```

kermit should create the file *alphabet-subscribers* in his home directory and add the email addresses of subscribers. Since `:include:` files can also include full paths to files and pipes to commands, just like the *aliases* file, *kermit* could keep an archive of all the list messages by including a */home/kermit/alphabet-archive* entry in the *alphabet-subscribers* file and creating an empty file with that name.

The *owner-alphabet* alias is important; if *sendmail* has trouble delivering messages to the *alphabet* list (for example, if a message bounces because a subscriber's address no longer exists), it delivers the error message to the owner alias, if one is defined, rather than to the message sender, who usually can't fix the problem. To handle problems with *owner-* aliases themselves, include this alias:

```
owner-owner: postmaster
```

If mail to *owner-alphabet* fails, the *postmaster* is informed.

For fancier handling of list headers, you can pipe incoming messages through a filter and then back to *sendmail* to distribute. For example, you could use *formail* to add a Comment header and set the Errors-To, Precedence, and To headers:

```
alphabet: "|/usr/local/bin/formail
        -A 'Comment: Alphabet list. Report problems to kermit@muppets.org'
        -I 'Errors-To: kermit@muppets.org'
        -I 'Precedence: bulk'
        -I 'To: alphabet@muppets.org'
         | /usr/lib/sendmail -oi alphabet-outgoing"
alphabet-outgoing: :include:/home/kermit/alphabet-subscribers
```

A message sent to this mailing list by *grover@sesame.org* would have headers like this:

```
From: grover@sesame.org
Subject: Big, bigger, biggest
To: alphabet@muppets.org
Comment: Alphabet list. Report problems to kermit@muppets.org
Errors-To: kermit@muppets.org
Precedence: bulk
```

Mailing Lists Without Root Access

One inconvenient aspect of setting up mailing lists with *sendmail* is that root access is typically required to edit the *aliases* file. That's good, because *sendmail* aliases can pipe mail to commands, and may run those commands as *daemon* or (in older versions) even as *root*. But it makes it difficult to allow users to create their own mailing lists without assistance.

One solution is to use a set of setuid programs to allow users to create and remove mailing lists. The *mklist* system provided at *ftp://ftp.oreilly.com/pub/examples/nutshell/mailing_lists* is such a system. It consists of three parts:

mklist

> Creates subscriber files for mailing lists. Subscriber files are kept in a special directory (for example, */etc/aliases.inc*) and are owned by the list owner, who

adds subscriber addresses to the files. Depending on the setup of your system, *mklist* may need to be setuid *root.*

rmlist

Deletes subscriber files from the special directory. Again, it may need to be setuid *root.*

Makefile

Builds the system and incorporates newly created lists into the *aliases* file. It's run from *root*'s *crontab* every 15 minutes, and if a subscriber file has been created since the last run, it calls *inclist. inclist* is a Perl script that rebuilds the *aliases* file from the subscriber files.

The *mklist* system is designed for hosts that manage their own *aliases* files; it probably requires some changes to work correctly on an NIS client that receives its *aliases* file in part from an NIS server.

Digested Lists

It's possible to offer digested lists using *sendmail.* The basic strategy is to save list mail to a file and then periodically to run a script to convert the file into a digest and mail it out.

If you're using *sendmail* version 8, delivering mail to files is straightforward. But other versions of *sendmail* don't perform file-locking when they deliver to files, so the file's contents may be corrupted if two messages are received at once. An alternative is to use *deliver* to deliver the messages to the file since *deliver* performs file-locking. You can use *deliver* by piping messages to:

```
deliver -b filename
```

The *mkdigest* script produces a digest from a file of mail messages in any of the styles discussed in Chapter 2, *Designing a Mailing List.* It also creates a table of contents automatically and incorporates header and footer files that you specify. Find *mkdigest* at *ftp://ftp.oreilly.com/pub/examples/nutshell/mailing_lists.*

You'll still have to add headers to the resulting digest, either by hand, with *formail,* or with another script. A complete digested list setup might consist of these aliases:

```
nobody: /dev/null                    You probably have this one already
mylist-subscribers: :include:/home/me/subscribers
mylist-digest: /home/me/received-mail
mylist-digest-request: me
owner-mylist-digest: mylist-digest-request
owner-mylist-subscribers: mylist-digest-request
```

With most versions of *sendmail*, you have to create the file *received-mail* in a directory that is world-searchable. With some versions, you may also have make *received-mail* setuid to yourself so that *sendmail* uses your permissions to add to the file, instead of its default permissions.

Messages sent to *mylist-digest* are stored in the *received-mail* file. To mail a digest from this file, you might use a shell script like:

```
#!/bin/sh
# Path should include formail, mkdigest, and date
PATH=/usr/bin:/usr/local/bin
chdir /home/me
# Don't produce a digest if the file is size 0 or non-existent
if [ -s received-mail ]; then
  mkdigest -t < received-mail | \
  formail -a Message-ID: -a "To: mylist-digest@myhost" \
  -a "From: mylist-digest-request@myhost" \
  -a "Subject: Digest of mylist for `date`" \
  | /usr/lib/sendmail -oi mylist-subscribers,nobody \
  && cp /dev/null received-mail
fi
```

This script uses *formail* to add headers to the beginning of the message. You could use *sed* or some other program instead. To produce weekly digests, add a line like this to your *crontab* file:

```
0 0 * * 1 /home/me/shellscript
```

Digests produced using the scripts above look like this:

```
From mylist-digest-request  Mon May 12 14:52:40 1997
Date: Mon, 12 May 1997 14:52:41 -0700 (PDT)
Message-ID: <"rx6jq2.0.Q42.fywbn"@myhost>
To: mylist-digest@myhost
From: mylist-digest-request@myhost
Subject: Digest of mylist for Mon May 13 14:52:40 PDT 1996

Table of Contents:

    This is the first message of the week       Me <me@myhost>
    Second message                              Me <me@myhost>


------------------------------

Date: Mon, 12 May 1997 14:52:13 -0700 (PDT)
From: Me <me@myhost>
To: mylist-digest@myhost
Subject: This is the first message of the week
Message-ID: <199705122152.OAA08457@myhost>

This is the first message received this week.

------------------------------
```

```
Date: Mon, 12 May 1997 14:52:29 -0700 (PDT)
From: Me <me@myhost>
To: mylist-digest@myhost
Subject: Second message
Message-ID: <199705122152.OAA08466@myhost>

This is the second message received this week.

-----------------------------
```

Email File Servers

Another handy application for email is to provide information in response to messages to a special alias. For example, you might want email sent to *product-list@nuts.ora.com* to return a list of nutty products. Or you might want a more extensive archive server that responds to email commands by providing a requested file, searching a database, or whatever.

Sending a Canned Reply

You can send a file in response to an email message simply by calling *formail* from your *aliases* file:

```
owner-product-list: sam
product-list: "|/usr/local/bin/formail -r | /bin/cat - /path/to/file
               |/usr/lib/sendmail -t -oi"
```

formail's -r option generates an auto-reply header from an incoming mail message that can reply to the sender. If you use -rk, the body of the sender's message is included, with each line prefixed with >. The header (which includes a blank line at the end) is concatenated with the file and piped on to *sendmail* to deliver. *sendmail* is called with the -t option (use the To header in the message to decide where to deliver the message) and the -oi option (don't consider the message over if you come across a line containing just a single period).

Another option is to use the *canned_reply* Perl script provided at *ftp://ftp.oreilly. com/pub/examples/nutshell/mailing_lists*.* The *canned_reply* script handles mail problems by emailing the list owner about the problem and including a copy of the incoming message so the list owner can reply to the sender.

---

* The *canned_reply* script was written by Jerry Peek and originally appeared in O'Reilly & Associates' *Managing Internet Information Services*.

Processing Commands

A more powerful file server would be able to return more than just one file, depending on what the user wanted. We can extend *canned_reply* to scan the Subject header of the message for a `get filename` command and return */etc/replies/filename* if it exists, or a default file if the Subject header doesn't contain a `get` command. Such a script, called *bottled_reply*, is available at *ftp://ftp.oreilly.com/pub/examples/nutshell/mailing_lists.*

You could similarly extend the file server to process other commands or to parse commands in the body of the message.

A setuid Wrapper

A *wrapper* is a program that runs another program, after insuring that the environment is correct for the other program. A common use of a wrapper is to set the correct user or group ID before the real program is executed. Another important function might be to clear environment variables that aren't relevant to the program's operation. Because many systems don't allow setuid shell scripts (and because setuid shell scripts are security risks on some systems that do allow them), a wrapper can be the only safe way to change the user by whom a shell script is run.

An example of the source code in C for a simple wrapper is shown in Example 7-1. To use the wrapper, compile the program and use *chown* and *chmod* to set the wrapper's user and group ID and the setuid and/or setgid permission bits. Then replace calls to your shell script or other program with calls to the wrapper, giving your script's name and arguments as arguments to the wrapper. For example, if you normally run your script as:

```
% myscript filename
```

Using this setuid wrapper, you would run it instead as:

```
% wrapper myscript filename
```

I prefer to give each wrapper I write a name that reflects the user it's supposed to change ID to. For example, if I compiled a wrapper and made it setuid *pepper*, I might call it *aspepper*, so I would run my script with:

```
% aspepper myscript filename
```

Example 7-1: A setuid Wrapper in C

```
#include <stdio.h>

/* A very simple wrapper.
 * Usage: wrapper program-to-run arguments
```

Example 7-1: A setuid Wrapper in C (continued)

```
 * We'll change to our effective uid/gid and run the program.
 * We completely wipe out the environment when we run the new program.
 * This is safe, but might be annoying - maybe you want TERM preserved
 * or something; see Majordomo's wrapper.c for a more complex wrapper.
 */

int
main(argc, argv)
    int argc;
    char * argv[];
{
    if (argc < 2) {
        fprintf(stderr, "Usage: %s program [<arg> ...]\n", argv[0]);
        exit(1);
    }

    setgid(getegid());
    setuid(geteuid());

    if (execve(argv[1], argv+1, NULL) < 0) {
        perror("wrapper");
    }
}
```

8

In this chapter:
• User Errors
• Bounced Email
• Mail Loops
• List Abuse

Troubleshooting
Your Lists

Most of the time you spend managing a mailing list will be spent handling bounced email. In this chapter, we'll look at examples of list problems ranging from the simple to the complex. This chapter sits between the list manager and server administrator sections of the book because these troubleshooting issues often apply to both list managers and server administrators.

User Errors

User errors are often easy to anticipate and resolve. Subscribers send misspelled commands to the list's request address or confuse the request address and the list address. Some MLMs automatically handle these mishaps; with others, the list owner is responsible for educating the subscribers. A good rule of thumb in the latter case is to respond immediately to the user with a description of his mistake and instructions about the proper way to use the list server.

Bounced Email

List owners and MLM managers quickly grow accustomed to messages from mailer daemons containing lines like these:

```
Deferred: Connection Reset By Peer During Client Greeting With foo.org.
Deferred: Connection Timed Out With bar.net.

550 Host Unknown (Name Server: noplace.edu: Host Not Found)
550 sarah@somehost.com... User unknown

Disk Quota Exceeded
Unknown Mailer Error

554 Service Unavailable
```

```
Local Configuration Error
Mx List For myhost1.gov. Points Back To myhost2.gov.
```

The numbers at the beginning of the messages are SMTP reply codes. A complete list of codes and their meanings can be found in RFC 821.

You can usually ignore messages that mention deferrals. These indicate temporary conditions that prevent mail delivery, and the undelivered mail should be queued for a later attempt. The other messages can often be categorized as one of four problems:

- Bad email addresses are those for which the hostname doesn't exist or those for which the user doesn't exist at the host. If the user subscribed himself at a particular email address, he may have made a typo in his username or hostname. A subscriber may have changed email addresses without unsubscribing from the list, or the host from which he subscribed may have been renamed. Usually, you won't be able to contact the user by email. You should remove bad email addresses from subscriber lists if your MLM doesn't do it for you automatically.

  Unfortunately, two other conditions can resemble a bad email address. Domain Name Service (DNS) servers are systems that translate hostnames to Internet addresses. If your local DNS name server is down or not responding, mail is returned with "unknown host" errors because your system can't translate the hostname. If the remote user's system is down for a long period of time,* mail to the user bounces, although the address may work again at a later date.

- Problems with a user's account abound. A user may have set up a mail forwarding loop between two of her accounts, may be forwarding her email to a program that she doesn't have permission to execute, or may have exceeded her disk quota for mail. Typically, it won't be possible to contact the user by email. Users who are over-quota usually correct the situation themselves given time. In other cases, temporarily remove the user from the subscriber list and contact the postmaster at the user's site, explaining the problem. You may be able to track down another email address for the user by using the *finger* command; on some systems, fingering a user reports where she forwards her mail and fingering her host while she's connected shows the site from which she connects. Or you could try searching her out on the Web.

- Problems with the user's MTA are less common, but not unheard of. Messages such as "Service Unavailable" or "Local Configuration Error" signal problems with the MTA at the user's site. Messages that refer to MX (mail exchanger) entries indicate a problem with the DNS database at the user's site. In these

---

* In an MTA context, a "long" period of failed delivery usually ranges from 3 to 10 days.

situations, you can try to contact the postmaster by email. If that fails, you may be able to find the postmaster's phone number by fingering *root* at the host or by searching the Internic WHOIS database, which lists names and phone numbers of people responsible for domain names.

- Problems with your MTA are something you hope you don't encounter. If you can send and receive ordinary email messages, your MTA should be suitable for managing a small mailing list. Fixing your MTA's configuration is beyond the scope of this book.

Mail Loops

Despite your MLM's best efforts, a combination of unforeseen events can conspire to produce the dreaded mail loop, in which your MLM sends the same message to the list repeatedly. If you notice looping mail (and 12 copies of the same message in your mailbox is a giveaway), here are the steps to take:

1. Stop the MLM. The first priority is to interrupt the mail loop, which usually requires turning off the MLM software. If you're not the server administrator, you'll need to contact him. Stopping an MLM that runs a separate server process, like Listproc and LISTSERV Lite, is easy; simply stop the server (`start -k` for Listproc, `lcmd stop` for LISTSERV Lite). MLMs that process messages as they arrive, like Majordomo and SmartList, are more difficult to suspend. The list aliases can be commented out. Making the list moderated can keep the messages from piling up for subscribers other than the moderator(s), and sometimes refusing to approve a copy of the message stops the loop. Replacing the program to which mail is piped with a shell script that returns an exit status of 75 causes incoming list mail to be temporarily refused (the sending host queues the message and retries delivery later.)* But the mail will be delivered later, making the next step imperative.

2. Discover the cause of the loop. This may require some detective work. Is the mail looping between the list server and a user's address, the list server and a system's mailer daemon, or between the list server and itself?

   Often the problem lies at the subscriber's end. Most MLMs have some form of loop prevention. One common method involves adding a special header to outgoing email (e.g., X-Loop) and refusing to deliver incoming mail with the same header. Another method involves keeping track of Message-IDs that have already been seen. An MLM can also keep track of checksums for bodies of messages it has already processed and then refuse to deliver messages

---

* Chapter 10, *Administering Majordomo*, contains an example of such a shell script.

whose bodies match a stored checksum. Finally, MLMs often ignore messages with a Precedence header of `bulk`.

Is the other end of the loop stripping out or modifying these headers before sending the message back? If the subscriber went on vacation and left an automatic reply program answering his email, the program should send mail with `bulk` precedence, and refrain from sending the automated reply more than once to the same address. The *vacation* program, distributed with most Unix systems, typically conforms to these requirements, but home-grown auto-reply systems may not.

3. Fix the problem. If the problem is with a particular remote user, unsubscribe her from the list and contact the user (and possibly their postmaster, if the mailer daemon is at fault).* If you don't use an MLM with loop detection, you can implement your own header-based loop detection by using *formail* to add an X-Loop header to outgoing messages and checking for the header with a Perl script. For example, here's how you might add loop detection to a mailing list that uses the alias *simplelist*. Change the aliases in */etc/aliases* from:

```
simplelist: :include:/maillist/simplelist.subscribers
```

to:

```
simplelist: "|/maillist/loopcheck simplelist simplelist-outgoing"
simplelist-outgoing:
  "|formail -A 'X-Loop: simplelist'
  |/usr/lib/sendmail -oi simplelist-subscribers"
simplelist-subscribers: :include:/maillist/simplelist.subscribers
```

And install the *loopcheck* program shown in Example 8-1. *loopcheck* is available at *ftp://ftp.oreilly.com/pub/examples/nutshell/mailing_lists*.

Example 8-1: A loopcheck Perl Script

```
#!/usr/local/bin/perl
#
# Called as 'loopcheck listname outgoing-alias' with an email message
# on standard input.
# Check for an X-Loop: listname header
# If it finds one, the message is tossed to the postmaster
# If it doesn't, the message is sent on to the outgoing-alias
#
# By Alan Schwartz, 1997
```

---

* Unsubscribing a user (or setting her mail mode to POSTPONE in Listproc) prevents the MLM from sending her another copy of the looping message. Another tactic is to keep the user's mail from reaching the MLM. Jerry Peek, who used to run the Listproc server for O'Reilly and Associates, suggests stopping Listproc loops by adding the user to the *.ignored* file for the list or the server itself, which keeps Listproc from accepting the user's mail. Nathan Brindle notes that the LISTSERV SERVE *address* OFF command does the same thing.

Example 8-1: A loopcheck Perl Script (continued)

```
#

# Where is sendmail?
my $sendmail = "/usr/lib/sendmail";

die "Usage: loopcheck listname outgoing-alias\n" unless @ARGV == 2;

my $listname = shift(@ARGV);
my $alias = shift(@ARGV);

# Read the message headers, checking for X-Loop: listname
$loop = 0;
while (<STDIN>) {
  push(@header,$_);
  last if /^$/;
  $loop = 1 if /^X-Loop: $listname/o;
}

if ($loop) {
  # This message is looping. We'll send it to the postmaster instead.
  open(MAIL,"|$sendmail -oi postmaster") or
    die "Unable to pipe to sendmail\n";
  print MAIL <<END_OF_MESSAGE;
To: postmaster
From: Loopcheck <nobody>
Subject: Mailing list loop detected

The loopcheck program received a message for the list $listname
that already had an X-Loop: header from that list. The message
is reprinted below. It has not been distributed to the list.

@header
END_OF_MESSAGE
  print MAIL <STDIN>;
  close(MAIL);
} else {
  # The message is ok
  open(MAIL,"|$sendmail -oi $alias") or
    die "Unable to pipe to sendmail\n";
  print MAIL @header;
  print MAIL <STDIN>;
  close(MAIL);
}
```

List Abuse

Mailing lists are a wonderful resource, but they are also subject to abuse. Three common concerns of list managers and server administrators are subscription terrorism, address harvesting, and junk mail, or spam.

A Third-Party Loop

I'd been running a mailing list with Listproc for some months when suddenly a subscriber's message began going out to the list again and again. The subscriber wasn't using an automatic reply program and had sent only one copy of the message! The culprit turned out to be a malfunctioning SMTP gateway. Another list subscriber received his email at a site with an SMTP gateway that converted incoming Internet mail to its local mail system. But the gateway ignored the SMTP RCPT command, which indicates the recipient of the message; instead, it used the To header to determine where to deliver the message. Because Listproc sets the To header to the address of the mailing list, the SMTP gateway delivered our messages back to Listproc. Listproc has many ways to prevent mail loops, but this gateway defeated them all:

- Listproc checks the Message-ID header of messages and refuses to distribute those which match earlier messages. But the SMTP gateway stripped off Message-ID headers.

- Listproc adds an X-ListProcessor-Version header to its outgoing messages, and refuses to distribute messages that already contain the header. But the SMTP gateway stripped off the X-ListProcessor-Version header also.

- Listproc keeps track of the checksums of distributed message bodies and refuses to accept messages with the same checksums. But the SMTP gateway defeated even this check. Traditionally, a single period on a line by itself signals the end of an email message; while few mailers still honor this convention without being told, the gateway didn't take chances. When delivering messages containing a single period at the beginning of a line, it added an extra period to prevent a mailer from misinterpreting the line. Unfortunately, it added the extra period to *any* line starting with a period, not simply lines with single periods. It happened that the original subscriber's message contained a line of five periods, so the SMTP gateway added another period to the line with each bounce. The addition of the extra period changed the checksum of the message and prevented Listproc from detecting the mail loop.

Ferreting out the chain of events responsible for this loop required careful comparisons of the looping messages as received by Listproc (to discover the unusual To line and the extra periods). It also required a few tests with the SMTP gateway to verify its bad behavior. During this time, I turned off Listproc to prevent the loop from continuing. Once the cause was clear, I set that subscriber's mode to POSTPONE, sent him (and his postmaster) email, and restarted the server. Finally, I let the other subscribers know what had been happening; they were as surprised as I!

Subscription Terrorism

An active mailing list can generate a lot of email. Imagine what would happen if you were subscribed to 50, 100, or 400 mailing lists. You'd soon run out of space in your mailbox as unwanted list messages poured in, preventing you from receiving important email. What if you had never used a mailing list before and didn't know how to unsubscribe?

Subscription terrorism refers to the practice of subscribing a victim to a multitude of mailing lists without her knowledge. The terrorist can perform this attack by forging his email subscription requests so they appear to be from the victim, or by using web-based subscription interfaces.

Majordomo and LISTSERV Lite provide good protection from subscription terrorism with confirmation codes. These MLMs can be configured so that subscription requests generate a confirmation message; when the victim receives the confirmation message, she can ignore it and avoid being subscribed. In addition, the confirmation message can tip her off to the attack.

SmartList and Listproc provide no such protection. List managers and server administrators using these MLMs must be alert to the possibility of subscription terrorism and act quickly to remove users who don't know how to unsubscribe from the list. If subscription terrorism is of particular concern, SmartList and Listproc can both be configured to require list manager approval of subscriptions; the list manager can send out confirmation messages manually.

Address Harvesting

Many unscrupulous companies would like nothing more than to get a large list of valid email addresses to which to send unsolicited advertisements. Your subscriber list is a prize source of such addresses, and if your MLM offers `lists` and `who` requests, it may be simple to retrieve the subscriber addresses for each of your mailing lists.

Most MLMs offer some protection against address harvesting. The `lists` and `who` requests can usually be disabled or restricted to subscribers on either a per-list or server-wide basis. Listproc and LISTSERV Lite subscribers can control whether their email address is concealed from `who` requests on each list.

Junk Mail

If someone wants to send junk mail (or spam) to thousands of people, why should he collect thousands of individual addresses when he can broadcast his mail to mailing lists? How can you prevent your mailing list from being abused by junk mailers?

Most MLMs can run private lists, which do not accept email from nonsubscribers. In order to send junk mail to a private list, the mailer would have to be subscribed himself. Moderated lists prevent junk mail even from subscribers, at the cost of the moderator's time.

It's possible to configure Majordomo, Listproc, and SmartList to reject messages with subjects that match a given pattern (such as "MAKE MONEY FAST"). Majordomo and SmartList can also check message bodies. The commercial version of LISTSERV Classic includes a number of built-in "spam-filters."

9

Administering Listproc

Listproc is a very powerful MLM. It is most suitable for large lists with heavy traffic, but offers many features that even smaller lists can take advantage of. In this chapter, we'll examine the installation, configuration, and operation of the free version of Listproc, Listproc 6.0c. in detail. This version is no longer under active development and is beginning to show its age; its quirks are notable.

After Listproc 6.0c was released, development of Listproc was taken over by the Corporation for Research and Educational Networking (CREN). At the time of this book's writing, CREN members could license one copy of CREN Listproc 8.0 for free; license fees for additional copies or non-CREN members ranged from $2,000–2,500 per year. Information about CREN Listproc is available on the Web at *http://www.cren.net/www/listproc/listproc.html.*

Recently, Anastasios Kotsikonas, Listproc's author, left CREN and has announced the imminent release of Listproc 6.0d, which incorporates many of the Listproc 8.0 features in a free package.

What's Different in CREN Listproc?

Some differences between Listproc 6.0c and CREN Listproc 8.0 are:

- Easier setup, installation, and creation of new lists. Many options previously set during compilation are now set at run-time. Better logging options are available.

- Multithreaded to handle multiple lists more efficiently.

- List owners can be notified of ignored and queued messages. They can completely control welcome and signoff messages. List configuration that could only be performed by the server administrator can now be performed by the list owner. List owners can turn mail distribution and request processing for their lists on and off.

- Headers are now compliant with RFC 822. Multiline headers and quotes in From headers work correctly. MIME is supported. Resent- headers are supported. Generally, more control over outgoing mail headers. Digests are in MIME format.

- Users may subscribe to archives and be notified when files in the archive change.

- Better handling of connections to moderated newsgroups.

- Listproc 6.0c includes an interactive ListProcessor client (*ilp*) that Unix subscribers can use to maintain their subscriptions and search list archives in real time. CREN Listproc also includes graphical interactive ListProcessor clients for the X Window System and Microsoft Windows.

- List owners can require confirmation of subscriptions.

- Many other small bug fixes and efficiency improvements. Detection of more possible mail loops.

Overview of Operations

Before we dive into the installation and use of Listproc, you may find it useful to have a basic understanding of how Listproc operates.

Listproc expects users to communicate with the list server at the *listproc@host* address. The Listproc server administrator sets up mail aliases for each mailing list and for *listproc*. When mail is sent to a list or Listproc, it's piped to the *catmail* program, which adds the message to a file of unprocessed messages for the list or requests for Listproc.

The server administrator uses the *start* program to start (or stop) the Listproc server daemon, *serverd*. *serverd* periodically checks the unprocessed message and request files. If it finds unprocessed messages, it spawns the *list* program to process the messages and deliver them to the mailing list's subscribers. If it finds unprocessed requests, it spawns the *listproc* program, which handles administrative requests.

Listproc can be accessed interactively over the Internet by using the *ilp* client. If interactive Listproc is enabled, a second *serverd* process listens for TCP connections on port 372, and services interactive requests.

Figure 9-1 shows the relationships between the Listproc programs.

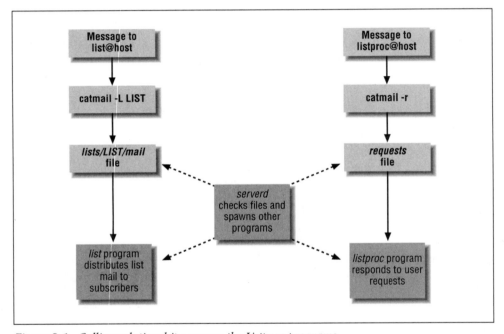

Figure 9-1: Calling relationships among the Listproc programs

Preparing to Install Listproc

Listproc is arguably the most powerful and flexible of the MLMs described in this book, but its power comes at the price of a complex installation and configuration process.

Root access is required for some of the Listproc installation. Notably, the Listproc server daemon *serverd* is usually run from the system startup files (*/etc/rc.local* on BSD systems and files in */etc/init.d* on System V systems), and editing these files requires root access. Root access is also usually required to add mailing list aliases to *sendmail's* *aliases* file.

WARNING   As the Listproc *README* file warns, Listproc relies heavily on file-locking. If your system can't perform reliable file-locking over NFS, don't install Listproc on an NFS-mounted filesystem.

Setting Up the Server User

Listproc requires a separate account, *server*, which runs its processes. The server account can be created the way you'd create any new account on your system. Listproc is installed into the server's home directory, which is referred to as HOME-DIR in the Listproc manual pages. This chapter assumes that you're going to install Listproc into the */usr/server* directory. The entry in */etc/passwd* for the server user should look something like this:*

```
server:PAfXAdnOwXg.6:75:75:Listproc:/usr/server:/bin/csh
```

It's also helpful to establish a *listproc* group. The */etc/group* entry should look something like:

```
listproc:*:75:server
```

The server account can be set up to use any shell; choose your favorite. Whichever you choose, the shell's initialization file (*.profile* for */bin/sh* or *.cshrc* for */bin/csh*) should define the environment variable ULISTPROC_UMASK, which controls the file permission mask Listproc uses when creating files. Either 066 or 026 should work fine. The initialization file should also set a command path that includes paths to the programs *awk, cut, grep, paste, telnet,* and *uptime.* The *grep* program must support the -i (ignore case) and -v (print nonmatching lines) switches. If Listproc is going to be posting to newsgroups, */usr/lib/news/inews* must exist, or be a link to an *inews* program elsewhere. *inews* is distributed with major Unix news server packages, including C News and INN.

In order to take advantage of Listproc's ability to restrict requests when system load is high, your *uptime* program must produce output that looks like this:

```
12:45pm up 5 days, 16 mins, 4 users, load average: 0.00, ...
```

---

* If your system uses shadow passwords, the encrypted password won't appear in */etc/passwd*. The other fields should be similar.

Getting Listproc

Once the server account is established, log in as *server* and download the Listproc source code from *cs-ftp.bu.edu* by anonymous FTP. As of this writing, the file to get is */pub/listserv/listproc6.0c.940712.0.sh.Z*.

Listproc is distributed as a compressed shell archive. To unpack it, use the *uncompress* and *unshar* (or *sh*) programs:

```
% uncompress listproc6.0c.940712.0.sh.Z
% unshar listproc6.0c.940712.0.sh
```

The */pub/listserv/utils* directory at *cs-ftp.bu.edu* contains useful scripts and programs for Listproc administrators. While you're downloading Listproc itself, go ahead and download all the files in the *utils* directory.

Guide to the Files

Listproc is a complex system; it comprises many directories and files. Figure 9-2 shows the basic structure. There's nothing special about */usr/server*; you can install Listproc into any directory as long as you use that directory in place of */usr/server* in the instructions below.

Here's a quick look at what each directory contains:

/usr/server
> Contains links to the Listproc programs, as well as the *config* and *owners* files and mailboxes for requests received by *listproc*.

/usr/server/archives
> Each archive has a subdirectory under */usr/server/archives* to hold the archived files and indices.

/usr/server/doc
> Holds the Listproc manual pages.

/usr/server/gateway
> Contains code for an interactive Listproc proxy gateway. Use of the gateway is beyond the scope of this book.

/usr/server/help
> Contains the help files that *listproc* can return in response to a `help` request.

/usr/server/lists
> Each list has a subdirectory under */usr/server/lists*. A list directory contains the subscriber file, welcome message, mail sent to the list address, and mail delivered to the subscribers, etc.

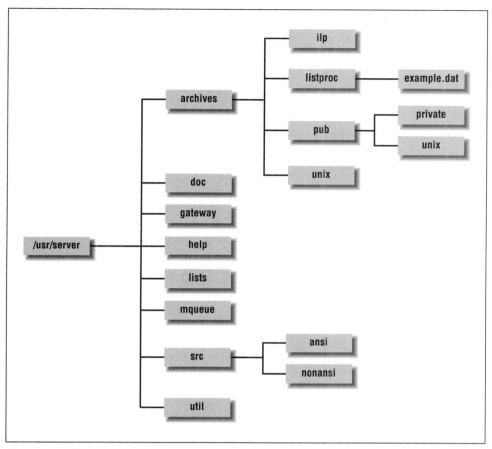

Figure 9-2: The Listproc directory structure

/usr/server/mqueue

Listproc uses */usr/server/mqueue* internally, to queue up outgoing messages. This allows it to resume gracefully after a system or program crash.

/usr/server/src

Contains the source code for Listproc.

/usr/server/util

Holds some utilities and patches that are distributed with Listproc.

Appendix A, *Listproc Reference*, contains a detailed reference to the files in each directory.

Compiling and Installing

Here are the steps required to compile and install Listproc. More information can be found in the Listproc *README* and *src/README* files and the server manual page, *doc/server.nr*:

1. Edit and run the *systest* script for suggestions about compiling and installing Listproc.

2. Edit *src/Makefile* to define compilation options.

3. Run the *setup* script to build and install the system.

Edit and Run systest

The *systest* script tests the features of your system. It reports on your computer's ability to use some of Listproc's more advanced features and suggests options to use when compiling and configuring Listproc.

Before you run *systest*, you must decide which C compiler you're going to use to compile the programs. You can save a lot of hassle by using a compiler that understands ANSI C, like the GNU C compiler, *gcc*. ANSI C compilers are standard in some Unix operating systems (e.g., Irix, Ultrix, and Linux), but are optional extras in others (e.g., SunOS and Solaris). *systest* tells you if your compiler is ANSI-compliant.*

If you're planning to use a compiler that doesn't understand ANSI C, you have to use the *unproto* program to remove ANSI features from the Listproc source code. *unproto* can be obtained by anonymous FTP from *cs-ftp.bu.edu* in */pub/unproto*.

Once you've chosen a C compiler, edit the *systest* script and find the line that reads:

```
CC="cc"
```

Change this line to specify the compiler you're going to use to build Listproc, as well as any compilation flags. (The comments at the top of the file *src/Makefile* summarize compiler flags for the native compilers on many operating systems.) For example, if you intend to build Listproc with GNU *gcc* (which requires the `-fwritable-strings` flag to compile Listproc), change the line to read:

```
CC="gcc -fwritable-strings"
```

Then run the *systest* script. It may be a good idea to print out the results. Example 9-1 shows an example of output from *systest*.

---

* If you know that your compiler understands ANSI C, but *systest* tells you it doesn't, your compiler may not be defining the `__STDC__` symbol. Try adding the flag `-D__STDC__=1` to your compiler.

Example 9-1: Running systest

```
% ./systest
        Testing your system's suitability to run ListProcessor 6.0 ...

NOTICE: Make sure you redefine the CC variable in this script to use the
same compiler and flags you will be using to compile the system.

The system has been ported to the following Unixes:
SUN IBM SGI DEC HP Convex Stardent KPC NeXT SCO Apollo Sequent DG i860 OSF
i386
Good, the system has already been ported to your SUN.

--- Looking for required utilities:
echo: found
cut: found
paste: found
wc: found
cat: found
tr: found
sum: found
awk: found
mv: found
cp: found
rm: found
grep -i: works OK
uuencode: found
compress: found
zcat: found
uncompress: found
tar: found
egrep: found
tail: found
uptime: found
ps: found: BSD version; use the 'option bsd_ps' in the config file
chmod: found
chown: found
sort: found
uniq: found

--- Special compilation options:
*** Do NOT compile with the -DHAVE_SELECT_H flag
*** Do NOT compile with the -DHAVE_ULIMIT_H flag
*** Compile with -DHAVE_SETJMP_H
*** Compile with -DHAVE_TZFILE_H
*** You may wish to compile with -DSYSLOG=facility to use syslog(3) for
reports

--- Looking for specific header files:
The system can go interactive: yes
TCP/IP present: yes (system mailmethod should be used if using SMTP)

--- Looking for inews: /usr/lib/news/inews not found: see src/Makefile
--- Looking for UCB mail: found; nothing you have to do
```

Example 9-1: Running systest (continued)

```
--- Testing the compiler: It's an ANSI-C compiler; good
If you decide to use gcc, use the -fwritable-strings flag
See src/Makefile for compilation options

--- Testing the system: It's got BSD flavor; *** Compile with -Dbsd
system() works OK
*** Consult doc/server.nr for more information on your SUN system
Non-blocking I/O support: yes
File locking support: yes
```

Edit src/Makefile

Using the output of *systest* and the information in the "PORT SPECIFIC" section of *doc/server.nr*, edit *src/Makefile* to fit your system. The most difficult part of compiling Listproc is setting the variables in *src/Makefile*. Here's a rundown on them:

CC The CC variable should be set to the compiler and compilation flags you want to use to build Listproc. The comments at the top of *src/Makefile* suggest definitions of CC for many systems. If you're using GNU *gcc*, set CC to gcc -fwritable-strings.

DEFINES

Listproc recognizes dozens of values that can be included in the DEFINES variable to tune the compilation for a particular system or to enable optional features of Listproc. *systest* recommends defining (or not defining) some of these. In Example 9-1, *systest* recommended using -Dbsd, -DHAVE_SETJMP_H, and -DHAVE_TZFILE_H, but not using -DHAVE_SELECT_H or -DHAVE_ULIMIT_H. *systest* also tells you if -DNO_LOCKS, -DNEED_VSPRINTF, or -DNO_TCP_IP must be included.

The optional features that can be set with DEFINES are covered below, after the rest of the *Makefile* variables.

OPTIMIZATION

If you want to use a symbolic debugger, like *dbx* or *gdb* with Listproc, OPTIMIZATION should include the -g flag. If not, setting OPTIMIZATION to -O causes most compilers to produce optimized code. If you're using *gcc* as your compiler, you can have the best of both worlds by setting OPTIMIZATION to -g -O.

CPP, SRC, and COMP

If you're using a compiler that understands ANSI C, you don't have to change these definitions at all. If not, you must compile and install the *unproto* program, and then uncomment the appropriate SRC and COMP definitions. *systest* tells you if your system's C preprocessor understands the #elif directive; if it doesn't, define CPP as the location of the C preprocessor that comes with *unproto*.

HOMEDIR

> HOMEDIR should be defined as the directory where Listproc is installed, the home directory of the *server* user. By default, this is */usr/server*.

LDFLAGS and LIBS

> These variables define the flags and libraries to pass to the linker when compiling the software. Because Interactive ListProcessor requires BSD-style sockets and signals, non-BSD systems may have to specify a BSD-compatibility library in the LIBS variable (e.g., -lbsd, -lucb, or -lsocket). On some systems, a special library may be necessary to resolve Internet hostnames using the domain name service (-lresolv).

DEFINES options

Many features of Listproc are customized by setting the DEFINES variable in *src/Makefile* before compiling. Here's the lowdown on the options you can use:

Syslog

> If you want Listproc to log information using the standard *syslog* system, add -DSYSLOG=*facility* to DEFINES, where *facility* is one of the *syslog* facilities to identify what's being logged. Common choices for *facility* are LOG_MAIL, LOG_USER, or one of the local facilities LOG_LOCAL0 through LOG_LOCAL7.

Interactive ListProcessor (ilp)

> By default, the Listproc server is built to support interactive connections across the Internet by listening for connections to TCP port 372. If you want to use a port other than 372, add -DILP_PORT=*port-number*. To limit the number of simultaneous *ilp* connections, add -DMAX_CONNECTIONS=*number*; the default is five connections at a time. If you get errors when you try to compile, try adding -DNO_ABORT_OP to DEFINES.* If you don't want to allow interactive connections at all, define -DDONT_GO_INTERACTIVE.

Headers

> By default, Listproc includes an Errors-To header in its messages. While this header isn't part of the RFC 822 standard, it's useful to some older mail systems. If you don't want Errors-To headers, define -DNO_ERRORS_TO. Listproc can include the list's address and the current message number in the subject of messages it distributes. To do so, define -DLIST_ ALIAS_IN_SUBJECT.

---

* This prevents Interactive ListProcessor from recognizing CTRL-C as an abort; some systems have trouble with this.

MTA peculiarities

By default, Listproc uses the MTA running on the local host to deliver email. But if your host doesn't run an MTA or if there's an MTA on a central mail host you'd rather use, define `-DSENDMAIL_HOST=\"hostname\"`. The backslashes before the quotation marks are required.

When Listproc connects to an MTA to deliver mail, it follows the SMTP convention of beginning with a `HELO`. Some mailers, like *Zmailer* and *sendmail* versions 8.7 and later, require `HELO hostname` instead. If your mailer does, define `-DZMAILER`. To find out if your MTA needs `-DZMAILER`, try these commands:

```
% telnet localhost 25
Trying 127.0.0.1...
Connected to localhost.domain.com
Escape character is '^]'.
220 mailhost.domain.com ESMTP Sendmail 8.7.3/8.7.3; Sun 14 Jan 1996
20:51:43 -0800 (PST)
helo
501 helo requires domain address
```

If the response to your `helo` begins with the number `250`, you don't need to use `-DZMAILER` (but it won't hurt if you do.) Otherwise, as in this case, you do. The documentation for `-DZMAILER` in *src/Makefile* that claims that *sendmail* doesn't require `-DZMAILER` is obsolete for *sendmail* versions 8.7 and later. If you don't have TCP/IP, and you define this, you must specify your machine's hostname and local address by editing *src/defs.h* (search for the strings `HOSTNAME` and `LOCAL_ADDR`).

If your MTA doesn't add a Date: header line and you need one, define `-DNEED_DATE`. You may not know if you need this until you try compiling without it and find that your list messages arrive undated. Don't define this if you use *sendmail*.

Automation features

If you define `-DERROR_MAIL_ANALYSIS=1`, Listproc examines bounce messages it receives from mailer daemons and tries to determine why the mail bounced. If the bounce was due to an unknown user or host, or if mail won't be deliverable for more than seven days, Listproc moves the subscriber from the list's *.subscribers* file to its *removed.users* file. If the bounce was due to a temporary condition, and mail won't be deliverable for more than seven days, Listproc changes the subscriber's mail mode to `POSTPONE`.

If you define `-DERROR_MAIL_ANALYSIS=9`, Listproc tries to remove or `POSTPONE` other subscribers from the same host as well. Despite the information in the *src/Makefile*, values between 1 and 8 are treated as if you'd set `ERROR_MAIL_ANALYSIS` to 1.

The seven-day grace period can be changed by defining -DGRACE_PERIOD=*seconds*. For example, a grace period of three days (259,200 seconds) can be set with -DGRACE_PERIOD=259200.

If -DLIST_CHECKING_FOR_REQUESTS is defined, Listproc examines messages sent to the list address to see if they appear to be Listproc requests for lists the local Listproc knows about, and returns such messages to the sender with an explanation. Because misaddressed requests are so common, this option is very useful.

Maximum values

By default, you can create 10 lists. To increase the number of lists you can create, define -DMAX_LISTS=*number*. The *number* should be one more than the number of lists you plan to create. For example, -DMAX_LISTS=41 allows a maximum of 40 lists. Because higher numbers do increase the size of the *serverd* process somewhat, it's best not to define this number higher than necessary; you can always change it and recompile later.

Listproc pauses for 30 seconds after sending every 10 messages to give the MTA time to deliver the messages. Mailings to a list of 1000 users take 50 minutes to deliver at this rate. To change the number of messages to send before pausing, define -DMAX_EMAILS=*number*.

If for some reason you expect list mail to have very long lines (longer than 1024 characters), you should define -DMAX_LINE=*max-char-per-line* to prevent Listproc from overrunning its buffers and crashing.

Program locations

Listproc uses the UCB *mail* program when it sends notices to list owners and the server administrator. It assumes that *mail* can be found in */usr/ucb/mail*. On many systems, *mail* is located elsewhere and may be named *Mail*. To make matters worse, some versions of Unix, like Irix 5.2, have both */usr/bin/mail* and */usr/sbin/mail*. The former is the UCB *mail* program. The latter is the older Unix *mail* program, sometimes called *binmail*. One way to determine which *mail* you're using is to try the -s *subject* command line; UCB *mail* allows it while *binmail* doesn't:

```
irix% /usr/sbin/Mail -s "Subject" alansz < /dev/null
irix% /usr/bin/mail -s "Subject" alansz < /dev/null
Subject... User unknown
```

To tell Listproc where to find UCB mail, define -DUCB_MAIL=\"*path-to-mail*\". Note that there must be backslashes before the quotation marks.

If you're planning to gateway a mailing list to a Usenet news group, Listproc has to know where to find the *inews* program. It assumes that *inews* is in

/usr/lib/news/inews, but you can give an alternative location with
-DINEWS=\"*path-to-inews*\". Again, the backslashes are required before
the quotation marks.

Miscellaneous

Finally, there are some definitions that *systest* probably should tell you about,
but doesn't. If your system doesn't support the *waitpid* system call, you can
force Listproc to use *wait3* instead by defining -Dunknown_port. If your
wait3 expects a union **wait** argument rather than an **int**, also define
-DWAIT3_NEEDS_UNION.

If your system's *setpgrgp* system call expects arguments, define -DSETP-
GRP_NEEDS_ARGS.

If your MTA expects lines to end with carriage-return line-feed pairs (\r\n)
rather than line feeds (\n), define -DUSE_CARRIAGE_RETURN_LINEFEED.

Here's what a completed DEFINES section for a SunOS 4.1.4 system using *sendmail* 8.8.8 might look like:

```
DEFINES=-DHAVE_SETJMP_H -DHAVE_TZFILE_H -DSETPGRP_NEEDS_ARGS \
        -Dbsd \
        -DINEWS=\"/usr/local/bin/inews\" \
        -DLIST_CHECKING_FOR_REQUESTS \
        -DMAX_LISTS=41 -DSYSLOG=LOG_LOCAL0 \
        -DGRACE_PERIOD=84600 \
        -DERROR_MAIL_ANALYSIS=1 -DZMAILER
```

Run the setup Script

To compile Listproc, run the *setup* script. *setup* insures that everything is in place,
performs the compilation in the *src* subdirectory, and installs the Listproc components where they belong. If you plan to run the Interactive ListProcessor daemon,
and want it to use its assigned port number (372), you need to enter the root password when *setup* asks for it. If you're not going to offer interactive connections, or
if you're going to use a nonprivileged port number (above 1024), the root password is not necessary for this part of the installation.

WARNING   Don't run *make* in the *src* subdirectory! If you ever need to rebuild
Listproc, run *setup* instead to ensure that all the components are correctly installed.

Example 9-2 shows some of what a first-time *setup* run looks like.

Setuid Start?

The *start* program, which starts and stops the Listproc server daemon, *serverd*, is usually run when the system is booted from */etc/rc.local* (on BSD Unix systems) or from a file in */etc/init.d* (on System V systems).

Because *start* should always be run by the server user, startup scripts must often resort to a complex command like:

```
/bin/su server -c "/usr/server/start -cr"
```

This uses the *su* program to run *start* as user server.

Another alternative is to make the *start* program setuid to server, by using the *chmod* command:

```
% chmod u+s /usr/server/start
```

Then, the startup file can simply run *start*:

```
/usr/server/start -cr
```

If you choose to make *start* setuid, you should know that the setuid bit is cleared any time you recompile the system. To avoid that, edit *src/Makefile* and find the line that begins `install:`. At the end of the entry for install, change the line that reads:

```
@(cd $(HOMEDIR); chmod u+s catmail)
```

to:

```
@(cd $(HOMEDIR); chmod u+s catmail start)
```

Now *start* is setuid when you run *setup*.

Example 9-2: Running setup for the First Time

```
           ListProcessor system setup script
           ----------------------------------

                       Version 6.0


The system will now be built under /usr/server,
as requested in src/Makefile; if you want to build it under another
directory you may alter the HOMEDIR path in src/Makefile now.
Proceed [y]? y
Remaking flocks
Remaking queued
Remaking peer
Remaking news
Remaking config
```

Example 9-2: Running setup for the First Time (continued)

```
Remaking help/TOPICS
Remaking help/listproc
Remaking src/ansi/defs.h
Remaking src/nonansi/defs.h
Remaking archives/listproc/DIR
Remaking archives/listproc/INDEX
Remaking archives/pub/unix/DIR
Remaking archives/pub/unix/INDEX
Remaking archives/pub/private/DIR
Remaking archives/pub/private/INDEX
Remaking archives/pub/DIR
Remaking archives/pub/INDEX
Remaking archives/unix/DIR
Remaking archives/unix/INDEX
Remaking archives/ilp/DIR
Remaking archives/ilp/INDEX
Creating directory /usr/server/lists
Creating directory /usr/server/mqueue
Looks like you cannot compile with the -DHAVE_SELECT_H flag; run systest.
Looks like you cannot compile with the -DHAVE_ULIMIT_H flag; run systest.
Compile with -DHAVE_SETJMP_H if you already have not done so.
Compile with -DHAVE_TZFILE_H if you already have not done so.
You may wish to compile with -DSYSLOG=facility to use syslog(3) for reports.
Do you wish to use unproto for compilation [n]? n
gcc -fwritable-strings -c -g -O -I/usr/server -I/usr/server/src
-DHAVE_SETJMP_H  -DHAVE_TZFILE_H
-DERROR_MAIL_ANALYSIS=9  -DUCB_MAIL=\"/usr/ucb/Mail\"
-DUSE_CARRIAGE_RETURN_LINEFEED signals.c
etc...
Installing listproc
Installing list
Installing serverd
Installing start
Installing tlock
Installing farch
Installing pqueue
Installing catmail
Installing ilp
Installing rev
Installing fwin
Installing semset
```

```
Now serverd will have to be setuid to root if it is to run in interactive
mode and use a privileged port. Please enter the root password below if so:
Password:   no password entered
Sorry
serverd unchanged
```

```
NOTICE: the canned archives/ilp directory contains everything a user will
need for live connections; you may wish to copy it to your own archives now.
```

Example 9-2: Running setup for the First Time (continued)

```
Finally, if this is an upgrade from 6.0 or earlier, run the script
upgrade_to_6.0c
ListProcessor System ready.
```

You are now ready to configure the server for operation. Before you do, though, read the file *src/REGISTRATION*. It contains information about how to register your Listproc installation and how to join the *unix-listproc@avs.com* mailing list (served, of course, by Listproc!).*

Configuring the Server

Listproc offers a bewildering array of configuration options. As you create new lists or offer new features to list subscribers, you'll find yourself continuing to return to the *config* file, the *owners* file, and the *help* directory.

We will now look at the Listproc configuration files and *help* directory. The manual page for *server* also documents server configuration, which you can find in the "SYSTEM SETUP" section.

The config File

The *config* file is the heart of Listproc configuration. Each line in the file controls an aspect of the server's operation. A sample *config* file is distributed with Listproc, but you'll need to edit it extensively. Each configuration directive must be given on a single line; don't use an editor that wraps long lines when editing the *config* file. A line that ends with an ampersand (&) is considered to continue on the next line, however, so long lines can be broken up. Any line beginning with a pound sign (#) is treated as a comment and ignored.

In most cases, directives are simply followed by their value, like this:

```
manager topdog@gshp.com
```

Unless otherwise noted, you can assume that this is the syntax you should use to set a directive. I'll indicate when a different syntax is required.

Now let's look at some of the most important and common things you need to do.

Tell Listproc who's boss

The **manager** directive sets the email address of the person responsible for the Listproc server. Use a full email address, including a fully qualified domain name

---

* At the time of publication, this was the correct address for the *unix-listproc* list. However, plans were underway to move the list to *emailsol.com*; if *listproc@avs.com* doesn't recognize the list, try *listproc@emailsol.com*.

(i.e., *kiwi@fruit.ora.com* rather than simply *kiwi* or *kiwi@fruit*). The manager receives messages from Listproc when problems occur.

Tell Listproc its own address

The `server` directive gives the request address of the MLM and some options to use when the *listproc* program is run. It's specified like this:

```
server listproc@your-host options
```

Here are the most common options:

-a *LISTNAME*
: This option makes a list closed. Subscriptions to closed lists are forwarded to the list owner for review. The *LISTNAME* should be in uppercase. Multiple `-a` options can be given to make more than one list closed.

-c *LISTNAME*
: This option conceals a list. A concealed list doesn't appear when a user sends a `lists` request. As with `-a`, the *LISTNAME* should be in uppercase and multiple `-c` options can be used.

-d *request*
: This option disables a request. Users can't use disabled requests. Multiple requests can be disabled. For example, you might want to disable the `recipients` request to protect your subscribers' privacy.

You can also restrict requests to times of low usage, cause requests to be executed in batch, and turn on debugging features. See Appendix A for details.

Here's an example of a complete server directive. The list *closed* is closed, the list *hidden* is concealed from the `lists` request, and the `recipients` request is disabled.

```
server listproc@gshp.com -a CLOSED -c HIDDEN -d recipients
```

Tell Listproc how to send email

The `mailmethod` directive controls how Listproc delivers email. It's important that Listproc sends messages with the right SMTP From header. The SMTP From header for a message on a list should be:

```
From listname@your-host
```

Messages from *listproc* itself should have this SMTP From header:

```
From listproc@your-host
```

Each of the methods you can specify achieves this in a slightly different way:

system

With this method, Listproc opens a TCP socket to an SMTP server (usually the local *sendmail* daemon) and transfers outgoing mail using SMTP. This is the most reliable and efficient method; it works on almost all systems that have TCP/IP capability.

telnet

If the `system` method doesn't work for some reason, but your system has a working *telnet* program, the `telnet` method can be used. It uses the *telnet* program to connect to an SMTP server.

env_var

Finally, as a last resort, the `env_var` method can be used. It's specified as:

```
mailmethod env_var LOGNAME mail-program
```

where **mail-program** is usually either */bin/rmail* (on UUCP systems) or */usr/lib/sendmail -ba*, though other mail delivery programs may work as well. This method works by resetting the environment variable **LOGNAME** to the name of the list (or *listproc*) and then using a mail program that gets the user's name from **LOGNAME** to deliver the mail.

Another useful directive is `precedence`, which sets the value of the Precedence header that Listproc adds to outgoing messages. The default precedence is `bulk`, which instructs the MTA to give lower priority to processing the message, and prevents vacation programs from replying to mailing list messages. However, some mail programs preserve Precedence headers in replies, so users replying to list messages may find their replies rejected by Listproc, which rejects incoming bulk messages to help avoid mail loops. One solution to this problem is to define a new precedence level in your MTA and use that with Listproc. *sendmail* users, for example, might add this line to their *sendmail.cf* file:

```
Plist=-50
```

Now you can use the `precedence list` in your Listproc *config* file.

Set some useful options

The `option` directive sets some miscellaneous system-dependent options. The *systest* script suggests setting some of these. Others are matters of taste or local policy. You can use this directive more than once to set multiple options. Some of the more useful options that *systest* doesn't mention include:

ignore_invalid_requests

By default, when Listproc receives a request it doesn't understand, it stops processing the rest of the message. If the `ignore_invalid_requests` option is set, Listproc simply ignores invalid requests and continues checking the message for valid requests.

`relaxed_syntax`

If the `relaxed_syntax` option is set, Listproc accepts user requests with more than the expected number of arguments. By default, Listproc rejects such requests.

`post_mail` or `gate_mail`

When a mailing list is connected to a Usenet newsgroup, messages can be sent to the newsgroup in two ways. If the `post_mail` option is set, messages are sent to the newsgroup by using *inews*. The path to *inews* is given in *src/Makefile*'s `INEWS` define. If the `gate_mail` option is set, messages are emailed to a news gateway rather than posted with *inews*.

The owners File

The *owners* file tells Listproc the email address of the server administrator, the list owner(s) for each list, and what kind of email they each prefer to receive.

The server administrator

The entry for the server administrator in the *owners* file looks like this:

```
email-address server [admin-preferences]
```

The *admin-preferences* specify when the server administrator is sent copies of outgoing mail from the server. Possible preferences include:

CCGET

Send the administrator a copy of responses to `get` requests.

CCINDEX

Send the administrator a copy of responses to `index` requests.

CCLISTS

Send the administrator a copy of responses to `lists` requests.

CCRELEASE

Send the administrator a copy of responses to `release` requests.

CCHELP

Send the administrator a copy of responses to `help` requests.

CCERRORS

Send the administrator a copy of error messages sent by the server in response to bad or rejected requests.

CCALL
Send the administrator copies of all of the above.

Multiple preferences can be specified:

```
topdog@gshp.com        server CCLISTS CCERRORS
```

List owners

List definitions in the *config* file include the email address of the primary list owner. In order for the list to operate correctly, this email address must also be added to the *owners* file. In addition, secondary list owners can be specified. The format for a list-owner entry in *owners* is:

```
email-address listname [owner-preferences]
```

Owner preferences include:

CCSET
Send the owner a copy of all **set** requests.

CCSUBSCRIBE
Send the owner a copy of all **subscribe** requests.

CCUNSUBSCRIBE
Send the owner a copy of all **unsubscribe** requests.

CCRECIPIENTS
Send the owner a copy of all **recipients** requests.

CCINFORMATION
Send the owner a copy of all **information** requests.

CCSTATISTICS
Send the owner a copy of all **statistics** requests.

CCRUN
Send the owner a copy of all **run** requests.

CCPRIVATE
Send the owner a copy of all **recipients**, **statistics**, and **run** requests that are rejected because the list is closed and the request came from a non-subscriber.

CCERRORS
Send the owner a copy of error messages generated when messages are rejected.

CCALL
Send the owner copies of all of the above.

Preferences are optional, and multiple preferences can be specified:

```
pepper@gshp.com          dogfans CCSUBSCRIBE CCUNSUBSCRIBE
kirk@enterprise.starfleet.gov tribbles
```

Only the primary list owner can use owner preferences, and therefore only the primary list owner can be informed when someone subscribes, when there is a list error, etc. Furthermore, if the list is moderated, the primary owner is the moderator of the list. Both primary and secondary owners can use list-owner commands to remotely maintain the list.

A list's primary owner can, however, be another mailing list that contains the addresses of all the moderators. By using a mailing list as the primary owner and listing each moderator as a secondary owner of the list, a list can have an arbitrary number of moderators. Because the primary owner is a mailing list, each moderator receives copies of messages to approve and requests sent to the list. Because each moderator is a secondary owner, any of them can approve a message by forwarding it to the list. It's no problem if two moderators approve the same message; Listproc rejects later submissions of identical messages.

The Help Files

Files in the *help* directory are help files that Listproc can return in response to a `help` request. Read them over: if any seem unclear or too terse for your users, you can customize them simply by editing them.

You can also create your own help files. For example, you might want to write a help file with information about your organization. Help files can be either plain-text files or executable scripts. If you choose to use scripts, they should begin with `#!`*full-path-to-program*.

The *TOPICS* file lists the available help topics and their associated files:

```
approve        /usr/server/help/approve
discard        /usr/server/help/discard
edit           /usr/server/help/edit
fax            /usr/server/help/fax
etc
```

To remove a help topic, simply remove its line in the *TOPICS* file. To add a help topic, add a line with the topic's name and the full path to its file.

Starting and Stopping the Server

The *start* program starts and stops the Listproc server daemon and insures that lock files are properly set up. When starting the server, *start* also reads the *config* and *owners* files, and reports errors. If *start* finds no errors, it creates subdirectories under *list* for any newly defined lists. Finally, *start* executes *serverd*.

WARNING	The *start* program should always be run by the server user. If it's run by any other user, it may create files that are unreadable or unwritable by the server user, which causes endless trouble. Because the only user besides *server* who should be able to access the server account is *root*, take special care not to run *start* as *root*. One way to insure that *start* is always run by *server* is to make it setuid *server*.

Running *start* without any command-line arguments causes the server to be started. If *serverd* is already running, *start* asks if you wish to kill it and restart. If new list subdirectories should be created, *start* asks if you wish to create them. Three command-line arguments modify this behavior:

-c Don't ask for confirmation before killing old *serverd* processes or creating new list directories.

-k Kill *serverd* processes and exit. This allows you to stop the server.

-r Don't report *start*'s actions to *stdout*. This switch has no effect if Listproc was compiled to use *syslog* for logging. It is useful (along with -c) when starting Listproc from the host system's boot files.

The listproc Alias

In order for users to send requests to your server, you must add a *listproc* alias to your MTA's *aliases* file. The *listproc* alias should pipe the message to *catmail* with the -r and -f flags:

```
listproc: "|/usr/server/catmail -r -f"
```

If you use *sendmail*, don't forget to run *newaliases* after changing the *aliases* file.

Adding Lists

Now you're ready to start adding lists to the server. The list owner may let you know how she wants the list to operate, or you may have to make some of the decisions yourself. Here's a step-by-step look at how to add a list, using the *dog-fans* list from Chapter 3, *Maintaining Lists with Listproc*, as an example.

Define the List in the config File

The first step in adding a list is to define it in the *config* file using the `list` directive, as well as other optional directives. The following sections explain how to set up common list configurations.

Establishing the list

The `list` directive establishes the list and must precede any other directives that refer to the list. The syntax of `list` is:

```
list listname list-address owner-address password options
```

listname should be the name used to define the list's alias for the local MTA. *list-address* is the list's full email address. *owner-address* is the full email address of the primary list owner, and *password* is the list's password.* Finally, a number of options control how mail to the list is handled. Here are some of the most useful options:

-f Normally, Listproc rejects messages from people who aren't subscribed to the list and returns a copy to the sender. The `-f` option causes the rejection message to be forwarded to the list owner instead of the sender.

-s This option allows nonsubscribers to send email to the list. Lists of product announcements, for example, might benefit from vendors sending announcements without subscribing to the list.

-m *number*

This option controls the number of recipients per message. By default, Listproc sends out messages with one recipient per message. The recipient's address is listed in the To header. It is more efficient and often more useful to send out messages to multiple recipients at once, and to have the To header contain the list address. The `-m` option causes messages to be sent out to *number* recipients at a time, and changes the To header to read:

```
To: Multiple Recipients of List <dogfans@gshp.com>
```

-P The `-P` option sets the Reply-To header of outgoing list messages to the address of the message sender. By default, Listproc sets the Reply-To header to point back to the list address, which causes most MUAs to always send replies to the whole list. By using both the `-m` and `-P` options, you can create headers that allow subscribers to choose to reply to either the list or the message sender.

-M The `-M` option is one way to create a moderated mailing list.† Mail sent to lists defined with `-M` is forwarded to the primary list owner, who can then forward

---

* Because the list owner must include the list password in email messages sent to Listproc to maintain the list remotely, the password is easily compromised, and should not be the same as the list owner's account password, the server account password, or any other important password.

† The other way is to give the -m flag to *catmail* in the alias for the list in your MTA's aliases file. Using *catmail* for moderation sends the list owner a copy of the message and instructions on how to approve or discard the message by sending commands to Listproc. This can reduce bandwidth, as the owner doesn't have to forward the entire message back to Listproc. However, the owner can't post an edited version of the message as easily.

it back to the list (possibly after editing it). Mail from any list owner is sent directly to the list.

Here's what the `list` directive for *dogfans* looks like:

```
list dogfans dogfans@gshp.com pepper@gshp.com -m 10 -P -s
```

The list allows subscribers to reply to either the message sender or the list (`-m 10 -P`), and allows anyone to mail the list (`-s`).

Preserving headers

The `header` directive specifies headers that should be preserved from the original sender's message. Headers defined here are case-sensitive. `header` has an unusual syntax. It looks like this:

```
header listname {
        header
        header
        ...
}
```

Here's how you'd use the header directive to preserve MIME headers on incoming mail:

```
header dogfans {
        MIME-Version:
        Mime-Version:
        Mime-version:
        Content-Type:
        Content-type:
        Content-ID:
        Content-id:
        Content-Description:
        Content-description:
        Content-Transfer-Encoding:
        Content-transfer-encoding:
}
```

Setting default mail modes

The `default` directive sets default behaviors for list subscribers. Its syntax is similar to `header`:

```
default listname {
  option = value
  option = value
  ...
}
```

There must be a space both before and after the equal sign. The options and their values are:

address

>   The `address` option may be set to `fixed` or `variable`. When the address
>   option is set to `fixed`, a user can't change the address she subscribes with.
>   She must unsubscribe from her old address and resubscribe at her new
>   address. When the address option is set to `variable`, a user can use the fol-
>   lowing command to change her address:
>
>   ```
>   set listname address subscriber-password new-address
>   ```
>
>   This option also causes Listproc to notify a new subscriber of her list password
>   and how to change it. The default is `fixed`.

conceal

>   The `conceal` option may be set to `yes` or `no`. By default, subscriber email
>   addresses can be seen by issuing a `recipients` or `statistics` request.
>   Subscribers who prefer not to reveal this information can ask Listproc to con-
>   ceal their email addresses. The `conceal` option determines whether sub-
>   scribers are concealed by default or not. Its value can be `yes` to conceal new
>   subscribers or `no` to not conceal new subscribers, which is the default.

mail

>   The `mail` option controls how new subscribers receive list messages. Values
>   include `ack` (subscribers receive copies of their own messages), `noack` (sub-
>   scribers do not receive copies of their own messages), `digest` (subscribers
>   receive list digests instead of individual messages), and `postpone` (sub-
>   scribers receive no messages). The default is `noack`, which can be confusing
>   for some users; if you use it, be sure to explain in your list's welcome message
>   that subscribers should not expect to see their own messages to the list.

password

>   The `password` option can set a single list password that is assigned to all
>   new subscribers if Interactive ListProcessor or variable addresses are enabled.
>   Without this option, Listproc assigns a different random nine-digit number to
>   each subscriber.

For the *dogfans* list, subscribers should receive their own messages and should be
concealed by default. Here's what the *dogfans* `default` directive looks like:

```
default dogfans {
        mail = ack
        conceal = yes
}
```

Adding an X-Comment header

The `comment` directive defines a comment to be included in the X-Comment header in each outgoing list message. Here's how it looks:

```
comment dogfans #Mailing list for dog fans. Send requests to listproc
```

The comment must be given all on a single line. The pound sign (#) is required in the directive, but doesn't appear in the X-Comment header. List comments are also shown in response to a `lists` request; accordingly, the comment should reflect the list's purpose or function.

Controlling digests

The `digest` directive determines how often a list digest is sent to subscribers who choose to receive digests. It looks like this:

```
digest listname number-of-lines number-of-hours
```

Listproc sends digests when the length of the digest exceeds *number-of-lines* or when *number-of-hours* have passed since the last digest. For example, to have *dogfans* digests sent when they are longer than 660 lines or older than two days:

```
digest dogfans 660 48
```

Putting it all together

It's a good idea to group all of the directives relating to the same list together in the *config* file. Here's the complete definition of the *dogfans* mailing list:

```
# Definition of dogfans list
list dogfans dogfans@gshp.com pepper@gshp.com -m 10 -P -s
header dogfans {
        MIME-Version:
        Mime-Version:
        Mime-version:
        Content-Type:
        Content-type:
        Content-ID:
        Content-id:
        Content-Description:
        Content-description:
        Content-Transfer-Encoding:
        Content-transfer-encoding:
}
default dogfans {
        mail = ack
        conceal = yes
}
```

```
comment dogfans #Mailing list for dog fans. Send requests to listproc
digest dogfans 660 48
```

If you want the list to be closed or concealed, you also have to change the
server directive, as explained in the discussion of server configuration above.

Define the List Owner in the owners File

Next, edit the *owners* file and define the list's owner(s). The entry for the *dogfans*
list should look like this:

```
pepper@gshp.com dogfans CCSUBSCRIBE CCERRORS
```

The owner for the list is *pepper@gshp.com*, and the list owner receives copies of
welcome messages to new subscribers and error messages related to the list.

Restart the Server

Run *start* to restart the server. If the list is correctly defined, the server creates the
list's subdirectory in *list*. Watch *start*'s output or the *syslog* file, to be sure that the
list was correctly set up; if it wasn't, the output tells you what was wrong. Common mistakes include forgetting to put the list owner in the *owners* file and
putting *config* directives that mention the list before the **list** directive.

Customize the Files in the List's Subdirectory

Edit the files in the *list/listname* directory to fit the list. In particular, the *.wel-
come* file should contain the list's charter, and the *.info* file should contain a line of
information about the list to send in response to an **information** request. If the
list is to be remotely maintained, you can leave this step for the list owner, who
can use the **edit** and **put** requests to create these files.

Other important files include:

.subscribers

> This file contains the list of subscribers. Lines in the file look like this:
>
> ```
> FIDO@OBEDIENCE.EDU ACK 999999999 YES Fido
> ```
>
> The first string is the subscriber's email address. The second gives the sub-
> scriber's mail mode: **ACK**, **NOACK**, **DIGEST**, or **POSTPONE**. The third string is
> the subscriber's password, initially a random nine-digit number. The fourth
> string is the subscriber's conceal mode: **YES** or **NO**. The rest of the line is the
> subscriber's full name.

.aliases

> This file contains rules for aliasing subscriber addresses. Listproc recognizes
> subscribers by their email address; if the address matches an address in the

.subscribers file, it's a subscriber's address. Some subscribers, however, may send mail from multiple machines and different addresses. The *.aliases* file allows you to associate patterns of addresses the subscriber might use with his address in *.subscribers*. Lines in the file look like this:

```
^FIDO@.*\.OBEDIENCE\.EDU FIDO@OBEDIENCE.EDU
```

The first string is a case-insensitive regular expression pattern that is matched against the sender's address (in this case, the pattern is "an address that begins with *fido@*, followed by any number of characters, and then *.obedience.edu*"). If the sender's address matches the pattern, it's rewritten to the second string, which should be an address in the list's *.subscribers* file.

.ignored

> This file contains a list of regular-expression patterns. Messages sent from addresses matching a pattern in the *.ignored* file are ignored; this effectively prevents these users from sending mail to the list.

Add Aliases for the List to the MTA

Edit your MTA's *aliases* file to define an alias for the mailing list. The alias must pipe the message to the *catmail* program, with appropriate flags. Here's what the entries in the *sendmail aliases* file should look like for the *dogfans* list:

```
dogfans: "|/usr/server/catmail -L DOGFANS -f"
dogfans-request: listproc
```

The first alias directs mail for *dogfans* to be piped to the *catmail* program (assuming that *listproc* is installed in */usr/server*). The `-L list` flag indicates which Listproc list the mail should be sent to. `-f` is required to prevent lines in the message body which begin with the word "From" from being interpreted as the beginning of a new message. The case of the list name (lowercase for the alias, uppercase after the `-L`) is important.

Directing *dogfans-request* to point to the *listproc* alias is not strictly necessary if your subscribers know that the request address is *listproc@gshp.com*, but it's convenient because many would-be subscribers may assume that the list is managed by whoever or whatever answers to the address *dogfans-request*. An alternative is to set that alias to the list owner, who can inform people about the *listproc* request address as well as handle other problems and issues.

When using Listproc, don't set up an *owners-dogfans* alias. Delivery to the *catmail* program should always succeed, and bounced messages and other problems with the list are either handled automatically or forwarded to the list owner by Listproc.

If you're using *sendmail*, remember to run *newaliases* after modifying the *aliases* file.

Inform the List Owner

Finally, tell the list owner the list's name, password, and address. Remind the owner to subscribe to the list, and to use the `edit` and `put` requests to design the *.welcome* file if you haven't done that already.

Archives

Listproc is not only a list server, but also a file server. Listproc archives can contain mail messages, other text files, or even binary files. Archived files can be stored in compressed format to conserve disk space. When Listproc sends files, it automatically decompresses, uuencodes, and/or splits them into mailable chunks if necessary. Archives can be password-protected.

The files in an archive must have lowercase filenames. Archive directories can use upper- and lowercase, though *farch* only creates archives with lowercase names.

Creating archives by hand isn't difficult, but requires a good understanding of the Listproc archive system. Listproc archives have index directories under */usr/server/archives*. Each archive contains a file called *INDEX* that lists the names, index directories, and optional passwords for itself and any subarchives, and a file called *DIR* that lists files in the archive and their locations.

The master list of archives is */usr/server/archives/listproc/INDEX*. Whenever you create a new archive, it must be added to this list. If you want to set up a hierarchy of subarchives,[*] they must be listed in order of descent from the master archive (i.e., subarchives are listed first, followed by subsubarchives corresponding to each subarchive, in the same order, etc.). Because every archive with subarchives must also list them in its own *INDEX* file, you're likely to find a relatively "flat" archive structure easier to maintain than a multilevel hierarchy.

An archive's *DIR* file lists the files that are available from the archive, in the following format:

```
filename parts bytes-in-part1 [bytes-in-part2...] directory [comment]
```

The `filename` must be lowercase. If it ends in *.Z*, Listproc assumes the file is compressed and decompresses it with *zcat* before sending it. If `parts` is 1, only `filename` is sent; if `parts` is larger, files named `filename1`, `filename2`, etc., are sent. A negative value for `parts` indicates a binary file whose parts must be uuencoded before delivery. After the number of parts, the size of each part in bytes is given. On most Unix systems, the *wc* command can get this information.

---

[*] A subarchive doesn't have to be a subdirectory of its parent archive. The subarchive structure is purely a logical hierarchy, and doesn't have to reflect the actual layout of files on the disk.

The *directory* should be a full path to the archive directory. Comments can extend over multiple lines if each line ends with a backslash (\).

There are three ways that a Listproc archive can be created and populated with files: using the *config* file `archive` directive, creating the archive manually, and using the *farch* program.

Archiving List Messages Automatically

The `archive` directive in the *config* file can set up various kinds of automatic archiving. It can archive all of the messages sent to a list, only messages with Archive-Name or Volume-Number headers, or only message digests. It looks like:

```
archive listname archive-dir format [index-dir] [archive-password] [digest]
```

Messages in `listname` are automatically archived in `archive-dir`, which must be a full path to a directory writable by the server user. The files *DIR* and *INDEX* are kept in the `index-dir`, which is a relative path under */usr/server/archives*. If you include an `archive-password`, requests for files from the archive must be accompanied by the password. A password of – is the same as no password. If you use the `digest` keyword, only digests of the mailing list are archived.

The *server* manual page suggests that you can leave out the `index-dir` or use a default directory by using –. This doesn't really work well; it overwrites the *archives/listproc/DIR* file with the new list's directory. The manual page also suggests that `index-dir` should be a relative path under *listproc*, for example *listproc/mylist*. While that works fine, it's often simpler to use the list's name as the index directory, rather than making it a subdirectory of *listproc*. If the archive directory is */usr/server/archives/mylist*, and the index directory is *mylist*, all the archived files and the *DIR* and *INDEX* files are stored together, which is convenient. Another variation is to make the archive directory a directory accessible by FTP or gopher, and keep the *DIR* and *INDEX* files in a similarly named directory under */usr/server/archives*.

The `format` specifies how the files in the archive are named. Format can include lowercase letters, numbers, and some special sequences:

`%m` Month of the year, a number from 01–12.

`%h` Month name, Jan.–Dec.

`%d` Day of the month, a number from 01–31.

`%y` The last two digits of the year.

`%j` Day of the year, a number from 001–366.

%a   The value of the Archive-Name header, if any, which may appear in either the mail headers or the body of the message. Because digests might have multiple Archive-Name headers, %a can't be used when archiving digests.

%#   The digest number, if digests are being archived.

%1   The first word of the body of the message.

%v and %n
      Volume and issue numbers. To use %v and/or %n, the message should begin with a "Volume <#> Number <#>" line.

When using the sequences %a, %v, or %n, Listproc only archives messages that fit the required format (an Archive-Name header or a Volume-Number line.) You can use these to archive only files sent to the list, while leaving ordinary messages out of the archive.

The Subject header of an archived message is stored along with the archive file-name, size, and location in the archive's directory file, *DIR*. (If a message is archived with the same filename as an earlier message, it's appended to the file, but only the first message's Subject header is listed in the archive file's description. There's code commented out in *src/list.c* (line 2956) that might change this behavior to give each archived message a unique filename by appending a period and a number.)

Here's how you can tell Listproc to archive digests from the *dogfans* list by digest number. The archive itself is stored in */ftp/dogfans/archives*, a directory under the *gshp.com* anonymous FTP archive. The archive's index is kept in */usr/server/archives/dogfans*:

```
archive dogfans /ftp/dogfans/archives dogfans-digest-%# dogfans - digest
```

When Listproc is restarted with *start*, it automatically creates the directories required for any newly defined archives and begins archiving mail.

Archiving Files Manually

Imagine that you want to create a public archive of pedigrees. Here are the steps to create the *pedigree* archive manually; and to make the files *fido.txt*, *rex.txt*, and *pedigree.doc* (a binary file for a word processor) available:

1. Change to the archive directory and create the directory for the new archive:

   ```
   % cd /usr/server/archives
   % mkdir pedigree
   ```

2. Edit *listproc/INDEX*, the master archive index file, and add this to the end:

```
pedigree /usr/server/archives/pedigree
```

If you were creating a private archive, you'd also add the archive password to the end of this line. If you're using subarchives, and this archive were a sub-archive, you'd add the same line to the end of each of its ancestor archives' *INDEX* files.

3. Create *pedigree/INDEX*, the pedigree archive index file, and add the same line to the top of the file. The first line of an *INDEX* file should always point to the archive itself.

4. Put the three files to be made available into the *pedigree* subdirectory.

5. Figure out the size in bytes of each file. Here's how to do it with *wc*:

```
% wc -c fido.txt rex.txt pedigree.doc
  3045 fido.txt
  2954 rex.txt
 17800 pedigree.doc
 23799 total
```

6. Create *pedigree/DIR* and list each file in it:

```
fido.txt 1 3045 /usr/server/archives/pedigree Fido's pedigree
rex.txt 1 2954 /usr/server/archives/pedigree Rex's pedigree
pedigree.doc -1 17800 /usr/server/archives/pedigree Word pedigree
```

7. Test your archive by sending mail to listproc with commands like:

`index pedigree`	*List the files in the archive*
`get pedigree fido.txt`	*Get one*
`get pedigree pedigree.doc`	*Should arrive uuencoded*
`search pedigree Rex`	*Search for text files containing "Rex"*

Simpler Archiving with *farch*

The *farch* program simplifies the creation and management of Listproc archives. It can create new archives, and add or remove files from archives, automatically splitting, uuencoding, tarring, and/or compressing files. *farch* doesn't archive files with names that are already in the archive's file list. *farch*'s syntax is:

```
farch [options] file(s)
```

Creating the *pedigree* archive with *farch* is as easy as:

```
% farch -a pedigree -D "Rex's pedigree" rex.txt
New archive pedigree; creating all directories and necessary files
rex.txt:
        - file not split, compressed
        - archived in pedigree
        - directory: /usr/server/archives/pedigree
```

```
% farch -a pedigree -D "Fido's pedigree" rex.txt
fido.txt:
        - file not split, compressed
        - archived in pedigree
        - directory: /usr/server/archives/pedigree
% farch -a pedigree -B pedigree.doc        -B for binary
pedigree.doc:
        - file not split, compressed
        - archived in pedigree
        - directory: /usr/server/archives/pedigree
```

If you later decide to remove *fido.txt*, you can do that just as easily:

```
% farch -a pedigree -r fido.txt
fido.txt: removing parts: 1
```

Here are all of *farch*'s command-line options:

-a *archive*

Specifies which archive is used for the command. If a new subarchive is being created, the parent archive is created as well, if it doesn't already exist. If no archive is given, the master archive (*archives/listproc*) is assumed.

-p *password*

Assigns *password* to be the archive's password when creating a new archive.

-d *directory*

Puts the output files into *directory*. By default, files are put into the archive's directory. *directory* is created if necessary.

-D *description*

Use *description* as the file's comment in the archive's file list when adding a file. If *description* contains spaces, it must be surrounded by single or double quotes.

-s *kilobytes*

Files above *kilobytes* kilobytes in size are split into parts automatically when archived, unless the −n switch is given. The default maximum size is 64 KB.

-n Don't split files, even if they exceed the maximum size.

-b Assumes that the input files are binary and should be uuencoded before archiving. The uuencoded files may be split, subject to the −s and −n switches.

-B Assume that the input files are binary, but don't uuencode or split them.

-t *tarfile*

Use *tar* to combine the files into a single *tarfile*, uuencode it (unless −B is also given), compress it (unless −Z is also given), and archive *tarfile*.

When creating tarred archives, use only relative pathnames to the input files (e.g., *source/*.c* rather than */developer/source/*.c*) to ensure that they can be untarred by any user.

-Z Do not compress the files in the archive. Archives are compressed by default.

-u Update files already in the archive, and preserve their comments in the file list, unless -D *description* is given.

-r Remove the files from the archive.

Interactive ListProcessor

One of Listproc's unique features is its ability to accept interactive connections. Using the Interactive ListProcessor client program, *ilp*, users can subscribe or unsubscribe from lists, change their subscription parameters, and search and retrieve files from archives. List owners can issue administrative requests just as they would over email. The manual page for *ilp* explains how to use the *ilp* client; here I explain how to enable the server side of things.

Setting Up Interactive ListProcessor

When Listproc has been compiled to "go interactive," *serverd* spawns an interactive version of itself when Listproc is started. The interactive *serverd* listens for Internet connections by the Interactive ListProcessor client, *ilp*, and forks another copy of itself to handle each interactive connection (up to MAX_CONNECTIONS, as defined in *src/Makefile*).

Here's a checklist for setting up Interactive ListProcessor:

1. Decide if you want to run the interactive server daemon as *root*. If you run *serverd* as *root*, it can use the assigned Listproc port number for interactive connections, and other interactive Listprocs on the Net can contact yours. *serverd* gives up its root privileges once it controls the Listproc port. Nonetheless, running any complex software as *root* increases the possibility that someone could exploit the software to damage your system.

    If you choose not to run *serverd* setuid *root*, add -DILP_PORT=*port* to your compilation flags in *src/Makefile* and choose a port number above 1024. If you've been compiling with -DDONT_GO_INTERACTIVE, remove that definition. You may also wish to adjust MAX_CONNECTIONS, the maximum number of simultaneous connections, which defaults to 5. Recompile Listproc by running *setup*.

2. Add a line to */etc/services*, assigning a port number for the Listproc server. If you are running *serverd* setuid *root*, you can use the official Listproc port

number, 372. If you aren't running setuid *root*, use the port you assigned when you compiled with -DILP_PORT=*port*. The line should look like:

```
ulistproc        372/tcp
```

3. Edit the files *unwanted.hosts* or *priv.hosts*; which file you should use depends on your security policy. If you want to allow most hosts to access your Interactive ListProcessor, edit *unwanted.hosts* and list any hostnames or IP addresses that you want to disallow from connecting. If you want to disallow most hosts, create *priv.hosts* and add hostnames or IP addresses that you want to allow to connect. When *priv.hosts* exists, *unwanted.hosts* is ignored.

4. Edit the file *welcome.live* if you want to change the welcome message that users see when they connect interactively. Edit the file *help/live* if you want to change the server's response to a help live request. By default, *help/live* is a shell script that figures out your system's hostname and returns detailed instructions for getting the *ilp* client source code from your *ilp* archive and using it to connect interactively.

5. Edit your *config* file and be sure that *serverd* is started interactively by adding the -i *seconds* switch to the serverd directive. *seconds* is the number of seconds that an *ilp* session can last; the server disconnects users after this amount of time, to prevent a forgetful user from tying up the server indefinitely. 300 (5 minutes) is usually a reasonable value for *seconds*.

6. Restart your server by running *start*. Watch the logs to be sure it starts up correctly.

7. Test the server by using the *ilp* program to connect to your server. The syntax for using *ilp* is:

```
ilp hostname [port]
```

Your subscribers won't have *ilp* initially, but they can download its source code from the *ilp* archive that comes with Listproc.

Daily Maintenance and Troubleshooting

As you continue to run Listproc, you may face a number of problems. The key to solving most Listproc problems is keeping an eye on the log files. If you configured Listproc to use *syslog* for logging, you should know where to find records of Listproc's operations. If you didn't, check out the files that begin with *.report*, the *.warning* file, and *lists/LISTNAME/.report.list* in each list directory.

Is Listproc Still Running?

The Listproc server daemon, *serverd*, is supposed to run continuously as a back-ground process. If *serverd* crashes, mail to lists is not distributed, and requests aren't answered; the messages and requests are held until *serverd* is restarted.

If mail isn't being delivered, check to see if *serverd* is running by logging into the *server* account and issuing a `ps` command:

```
% ps -gx          On BSD systems; Use ps -ef on SysV systems
  PID TT STAT   TIME COMMAND
 6392 ?  IW    14:07 /home/server/serverd -l 3 -e
24500 p1 S      0:00 -u (tcsh)
24506 p1 R      0:00 ps -gx
```

If a *serverd* process isn't present in the list, restart the server.

Files to Trim

Listproc saves copies of all requests to *mbox*. This file should be trimmed regu-larly. Messages sent to list addresses are saved in *lists/LISTNAME/mbox*; copies of those actually distributed to the list also appear in *lists/LISTNAME/archive*. These files can easily grow quite large and should be trimmed or archived regularly. The *archive* file can be replaced with a link to */dev/null* if you are archiving the list automatically or if it is otherwise unnecessary.

If you're not using *syslog*, old report files accumulate in files ending in *.acc*, in both the server home directory and each list directory. These should be periodi-cally reviewed and trimmed or archived.

Forcing Requests to Be Processed

If you're trying to find a problem by sending requests to *listproc* yourself, you may not want to wait for *serverd* to spawn *listproc* to handle requests. To force *listproc* to process requests immediately, simply run *listproc* with the −1 switch:

```
% listproc -1
```

You can similarly force a list's mail to be processed by running *list* with the −1 switch:

```
% list -1 -L LISTNAME switches
```

Note that you must include all of the switches you define for the list in its `list` directive in the *config* file to cause it to process mail as it usually would.

The Mail Queue

When Listproc can't deliver a message due to a problem with the system, it leaves a copy of the message in a numbered file in its *mqueue* directory.* In normal operation, the *mqueue* directory is empty, but if you notice messages in it, you can run the *queued* daemon, which periodically attempts to redeliver the queued messages.

If you want to be able to run *queued* remotely, include the following alias in your MTA's *aliases* file:

```
proc-queue: "|/usr/server/queued 60 & > /dev/null"
```

Common Error Messages

If you're the server manager, you'll receive email when something goes wrong with a Listproc program. Some common messages and their causes, include:

`Could not open file`
> An essential file could not be found or opened. Check to be sure that the file and its directory exists and that the server user has permission to read the file. This error can also occur if HOMEDIR was not set correctly in *src/Makefile*; in that case you have to reset it and run *setup* again to rebuild the system.

`Could not lock file`
> Listproc needs to lock files in order to prevent two processes from opening the same file at the same time. In particular, the files *.lock.serverd*, *.lock.pqueue*, *requests*, *batch*, and the *mail* and *moderated* files in each list subdirectory are locked at times. This message means that either Listproc couldn't find or access the file (see the suggestions above), or that another program has locked the file. The *tlock* program displays all locked files. If you need to remove the locks on *.lock.serverd* and *.lock.pqueue*, you can use the *ulock* script.

`Command line option error`
> One of the `list`, `server`, or `serverd` directives in the *config* file is using a bad option. Fix the *config* file and restart the system.

`Syntax error in file`
> Some error was made in the *config* or *owners* file. The log files should show in which file and at what line the error occurred.

---

* Not to be confused with *sendmail*'s */usr/spool/mqueue* directory.

Could not spawn

> This error message indicates that Listproc was unable to fork a child process at some point, usually due to process table limitations or possibly memory constraints. This message should rarely occur, and the solution may require rebuilding your system's kernel to allow more processes per user, which is beyond the scope of this book.*

Received system signal

> This message is sent whenever a Listproc program is terminated by a signal caused by either the *kill* command or by a segmentation violation or other serious error. Debugging the latter is beyond the scope of this book.

Peer Lists and News Connections

Listproc lists can easily be connected to each other as peer lists or to Usenet newsgroups. The *peer* and *news* programs establish peer list and newsgroup connections. To use either of these programs, you must log in as the server user; they are run from the Unix shell.

peer *LISTNAME* peer-list peer-list-address peer-server-address

> The *peer* program causes *LISTNAME* to send messages and recipients requests on to peer-list. Messages are delivered to peer-list-address and requests to peer-server-address. In the typical peer setup, each peer's server administrator runs the *peer* program to cause Listproc to recognize the other peers. For example, if *biglist@peer1.com*, *biglist@peer2.com*, and *the-biglist@peer3.com* are to be peers of one another, the server administrator at *peer1.com* would type:

```
% peer BIGLIST biglist biglist@peer2.com listproc@peer2.com
% peer BIGLIST the-biglist the-biglist@peer3.com listproc@peer3.com
```

Similarly, the server administrator at *peer2.com* would type:

```
% peer BIGLIST biglist biglist@peer1.com listproc@peer1.com
% peer BIGLIST the-biglist the-biglist@peer3.com listproc@peer3.com
```

Finally, the server administrator at *peer3.com* would type:

```
% peer THE-BIGLIST biglist biglist@peer1.com listproc@peer1.com
% peer THE-BIGLIST biglist biglist@peer2.com listproc@peer2.com
```

Information about list peers is stored in *lists/LISTNAME/.peers*.

---

* A good reference for kernel rebuilding is O'Reilly & Associates' *System Performance Tuning*, by Mike Loukides.

```
news LISTNAME newsgroup news-source-address
[receive|send_receive]
```

The *news* program instructs **LISTNAME** to receive, or send and receive, messages from **newsgroup**. The news administrator must configure her news software to email postings to the list and should inform the server administrator of the SMTP From header the news software uses when it emails postings. The address in this header (often *news@news-server-host*) is the *news-source-address* expected by the *news* program. If the `send_receive` method is used, list messages are also posted to the newsgroup using *inews* or sent by email to a news gateway, depending on whether the `post_mail` or `gate_mail` option is set in the *config* file. For example, to configure the list *managing-lists@host.com* to send and receive messages from the newsgroup *alt.managing.lists*, the server administrator at *host.com* types:

```
% news MANAGING-LISTS alt.managing.lists news@news.host.com send_receive
```

Mail sent to *managing-lists@hosts.com* is now posted to *alt.managing.lists*. To complete the connection in the other direction, the news adminstrator responsible for *news.host.com* must configure her news software to distribute messages from the *alt.managing.lists* newsgroup to the *managing-lists@host.com* address.

Information about newsgroups is stored in *lists/LISTNAME/.news*.

Local Modifications

The Listproc 6.0c license agreement prohibits any Listproc user from altering certain functions and from distributing local modifications. Accordingly, this section provides only ideas for changes that might be useful, and suggestions for how to implement them.

Welcome and Error Messages

Some Listproc administrators don't like the information message Listproc includes before the list's *.welcome* file. This initial message, which includes information about subscriber passwords for using the Interactive ListProcessor and changing subscription addresses, can be found starting at line 2078 of *src/listproc.c*, should you wish to change it.

Many administrators find that the error messages Listproc sends to users when it rejects their mailings are arcane and confusing. Here are three common examples:

- Listproc rejects messages whose subject lines match the regular expression SUSP_SUBJECT in *src/defs.h*. The goal is to prevent messages that are recognized as bounces or auto-reply messages from being posted to lists. The list of matching expressions, however, includes such things as "unsubscribe," "remove me," "add me," and other possibly common subjects from new users. Worse yet, the error message that's returned simply says that the message was rejected because of a suspicious subject (which is easily misinterpreted by a new user!) `SUSP_SUBJECT` can be edited in *src/defs.h*, and the error message can be expanded. It's at line 937 in *src/listproc.c* and line 1470 in *src/list.c*.

- Similarly, mail from mailer daemons is recognized by matching `MAILER_DAEMON` in *src/defs.h*, and rejected messages are identified only as coming from a "suspicious address." This can be confusing to list owners who receive these errors. A better explanation could be added at line 936 in *src/listproc.c* and line 1469 in *src/list.c*.

- Finally, administrative requests sent to mailing lists are rejected with a curt "request sensed" error. A better explanation could be provided at line 1471 in *src/list.c*

PGP Signatures

Listproc tries hard to prevent mail loops. One of its tactics is to refuse to distribute messages that have an X-ListProcessor-Version, X-Listserver-Version, or Version header anywhere in the message body. Earlier versions of Listproc used Version to indicate the Listproc version that distributed the message.

Unfortunately, messages signed with PGP contain a line that gives the PGP version number, and begins with Version, which causes Listproc to bounce all PGP-signed messages.

The fix is to edit the `LISTPROC_ID` regular expression defined in *src/defs.h* to remove the checking for a plain Version header. A better definition of `LIST-PROC_ID` might be:

```
#define LISTPROC_ID "^X-ListProcessor-Version:[ \t]|\
X-Listserve?r?-Version:[ \t]"
```

Fixing Multiline Headers

Multiline headers are becoming more and more common as more people send mail with MIME attachments. Unfortunately, Listproc 6.0c doesn't always deal well with multiline headers.

The easiest solution lies outside of Listproc. You can concatenate multiline headers into a single long line by putting a utility program into the pipe to *catmail* in your *aliases* file. For example, if your system has *procmail* installed, its *formail* utility can concatenate multiline headers. Here's what a *sendmail* alias might look like:

```
mylist: "|/usr/local/bin/formail -c | /usr/server/catmail -L MYLIST -f"
```

If you don't have *formail*, try this Perl script:

```
#!/usr/bin/perl
#
# hconcat - read a mail message from stdin, concatenate long headers,
#           and output on stdout.
#
# Usage with Listproc in /etc/aliases:
#   mylist: "|/usr/local/bin/hconcat | /usr/server/catmail -L MYLIST -f"
#
while (<STDIN>) {
  chop;
  if (/^\s/) {
    # This line is a continuation
    $line .= $_;
  } else {
    # This is a new line. Print the line we've finished.
    print $line,"\n" if $line;
    $line = $_;
  }
  last if /^$/;
}
print "\n";
print <STDIN>;
```

Bounce Handling

The file *src/list.h* defines three important lists of regular expressions that are checked when ERROR_MAIL_ANALYSIS has been defined in *src/Makefile*, and Listproc receives a bounce message:

warnings

The list of warnings beginning at line 356 indicates soft bounces, transient conditions that prevent mail delivery. Messages that match one of these warnings and have fatal subjects (see below) cause Listproc to set the mail mode of their subscribers to POSTPONE.

errors

The list of errors at line 383 indicates hard bounces, permanent conditions that cause delivery to fail. Typically, this means either the host or the user doesn't exist. Listproc searches messages that match this list for users to remove from the list's subscriber file.

fatal_subjects

The fatal_subjects list at line 393 are subject lines of the form "Can't send mail for *some period of time.*"

New error messages that Listproc doesn't recognize are stored in each list's *.errors* file. You can improve Listproc's automatic bounce-handling capability by adding some of these to the **warnings** or **errors** pattern lists.

The To Header

When you've defined a list with both the **-m** and **-P** options in the *config* file's **list** directive, messages to the list have a To header that looks like this:

```
To: Multiple Recipients of List <listname@yourhost>
```

If you find that header too long, it can be changed at line 2267 of *src/list.c*. I prefer shortening it to **List** *<listname@yourhost>*.

Better Handling of catmail Failure

If *catmail* can't deposit an incoming message or request into the list's *mail* file or the *requests* file, it logs an error message and returns exit code 3, which causes *sendmail* to bounce the message back to the sender. The patch below changes the exit code to 75, which causes *sendmail* to queue the message and try to redeliver it later, and to notify the postmaster of the Listproc site, who is also likely to be the Listproc administrator.

```
*** catmail.c.old     Thu May  2 20:44:03 1996
--- catmail.c  Thu May  2 20:47:20 1996
***************
*** 103,108 ****
--- 103,109 ----
  int     get_tag_id (void);
  void    usage (void);
  int     gexit (int);
+ int     exit_and_queue (int);

  void main (int argc, char **argv, char **envp)
  {
***************
*** 143,149 ****
      mask = "066",
      umask (S_IRWXG|S_IRWXO); /* 600 */

!   signal (SIGALRM, (void (*)()) gexit);
    alarm (120);       /* Timeout after 2 mins */
  #ifdef SYSLOG
    openlog ("ListProcessor: catmail", LOG_NDELAY
--- 144,150 ----
      mask = "066",
      umask (S_IRWXG|S_IRWXO); /* 600 */

!   signal (SIGALRM, (void (*)()) exit_and_queue);
    alarm (120);       /* Timeout after 2 mins */
```

```
   #ifdef SYSLOG
     openlog ("ListProcessor: catmail", LOG_NDELAY
***************
*** 189,201 ****
     setup_string (list_mail_f, list_alias, LIST_MAIL_FILE);
   }
 #ifndef NO_LOCKS
!  signal (SIGINT, (void (*)()) gexit);
   if ((lfd = lock_file (file, O_RDWR | O_CREAT, 0640, TRUE)) < 0)
     switch (lfd) {
     case CANT_OPEN:
       report_progress (report, tsprintf ("\nCould not stat file %s",
                        file), TRUE);
!       exit (1);
     case CANT_LOCK:
       if (requests)
       strcpy (file, LOST_REQUESTS);
--- 190,202 ----
     setup_string (list_mail_f, list_alias, LIST_MAIL_FILE);
   }
 #ifndef NO_LOCKS
!  signal (SIGINT, (void (*)()) exit_and_queue);
   if ((lfd = lock_file (file, O_RDWR | O_CREAT, 0640, TRUE)) < 0)
     switch (lfd) {
     case CANT_OPEN:
       report_progress (report, tsprintf ("\nCould not stat file %s",
                        file), TRUE);
!       exit_and_queue (1);
     case CANT_LOCK:
       if (requests)
       strcpy (file, LOST_REQUESTS);
***************
*** 210,216 ****
       case CANT_OPEN:
         report_progress (report, tsprintf ("\nCould not stat file %s",
                          SERVER_MAIL_FILE), TRUE);
!         gexit (1);
       case CANT_LOCK:
         report_progress (report,
             tsprintf ("\nCANNOT LOCK FILE %s: TAKING MY CHANCES",
--- 211,217 ----
       case CANT_OPEN:
         report_progress (report, tsprintf ("\nCould not stat file %s",
                          SERVER_MAIL_FILE), TRUE);
!         exit_and_queue (1);
       case CANT_LOCK:
         report_progress (report,
             tsprintf ("\nCANNOT LOCK FILE %s: TAKING MY CHANCES",
***************
*** 221,227 ****
       case CANT_OPEN:
         report_progress (report, tsprintf ("\nCould not stat file %s",
                          list_mail_f), TRUE);
!         gexit (1);
```

```
        case CANT_LOCK:
          report_progress (report,
              tsprintf ("\nCANNOT LOCK FILE %s: TAKING MY CHANCES",
--- 222,228 ----
        case CANT_OPEN:
          report_progress (report, tsprintf ("\nCould not stat file %s",
                          list_mail_f), TRUE);
!         exit_and_queue (1);
        case CANT_LOCK:
          report_progress (report,
              tsprintf ("\nCANNOT LOCK FILE %s: TAKING MY CHANCES",
***************
*** 356,359 ****
--- 357,374 ----
    unlock_file (lfd3);
  #endif
    exit (exitcode);
+ }
+
+
+ /* Graceful exit but give exit code 75 so sendmail will requeue
+  * mail and try to deliver later.
+  */
+ int exit_and_queue (int exitcode)
+ {
+ #ifndef NO_LOCKS
+   unlock_file (lfd);
+   unlock_file (lfd2);
+   unlock_file (lfd3);
+ #endif
+   exit (75);
  }
```

Easier List Creation with add_list.sh

The *add_list.sh* script simplifies creating new lists. When the server administrator runs *add_list.sh*, it prompts for the name of the list, its owner's address, and other important information. It creates *config* and *owners* entries for the list and suggests the *aliases* entry for the list. *add_list.sh* can be downloaded at *ftp://ftp.oreilly.com/pub/examples/nutshell/mailing_lists*.

10

Administering Majordomo

The Majordomo MLM, originally written by Brent Chapman and currently maintained by Chan Wilson, is very popular for mailing list management. Majordomo doesn't attempt to do everything, though it's capable of most sophisticated list server features. It offers exceptional remote owner administration capabilities; remote list owners have nearly total control over the configuration of their lists, far more than Listproc or SmartList offers.

This chapter covers how to install, configure, and use Majordomo 1.94.4, the latest released version at the time of this writing. If you're using an earlier version of Majordomo, upgrading to 1.94.4 is a good idea; in particular, versions before 1.92 have serious security problems that can compromise your computer's security.*

Overview of Operations

Majordomo is a suite of Perl scripts (and a few C programs) that are run in response to email to the list server address or a mailing list address. Mail to any Majordomo-managed address is piped to the *wrapper* program, a setuid wrapper that sets the effective user ID and group ID to that of the Majordomo user and group and then runs one of the Perl scripts. To implement this security system, all Majordomo files and directories must be owned by a special Majordomo group, and they must be writable by both owner and group (mode 664 or 660 for files and 775 or 770 for directories).

---

* This chapter owes much to Jerry Peek's Chapter 24, "Automating Mailing Lists with Majordomo," of O'Reilly & Associates' *Managing Internet Information Services.*

Majordomo typically expects users to communicate with the list server at the *majordomo@host* address; it includes a script to respond to mail sent to `list-name-request@host` by informing the user to email *majordomo* instead. It's also possible to have Majordomo directly process mail sent to -*request* addresses, if you prefer.

Mail sent to a list address is piped through *wrapper* to the *resend* program. *resend* formats the message for distribution to the subscribers or moderator and then remails it to the list's outgoing address, which is an `:include:` *sendmail* alias. Subscribers are generally not told the outgoing address, to prevent them from circumventing *resend*.

By including other programs in the list address alias, Majordomo can archive messages or create message digests.

Preparing to Install Majordomo

Majordomo is written primarily in Perl, so be sure you have Perl available on your system. Majordomo expects either Perl 4.036 or a Perl version later than 5.002; using Perl 5 is recommended. You can get Perl at *http://www.perl.com/CPAN/src/*.

Setting Up the Majordomo User and Group

Majordomo must be installed in the account of a special user. You must create a new user and group for Majordomo and install the files in that user's home directory. Pick any name for the user; *majordom* is the most common choice (*majordomo* is longer than eight characters and causes problems on some systems).

You must also choose what group ID Majordomo runs under. By default, this is *daemon*, but you can change it to something different (like *majordom*).

This chapter assumes that you've chosen to create user *majordom* and group *majordom*, and that *majordom*'s home directory is */home/majordomo*. The mode of the home directory should be 775.

The server administrator can manage Majordomo by using *su* to become *majordom*. Alternatively, you can add the server administrator to the *majordom* group. Most of the rest of this installation should be performed as the *majordom* user.

Getting Majordomo

The source code for Majordomo is available by anonymous FTP from *ftp.greatcircle.com* in */pub/majordomo*. You should download *majordomo-1.94.4.tar.gz* into */home/majordomo* and unpack it. The *tar* file creates a directory called *majordomo-1.94.4*, into which you should *cd* after unpacking:

```
% gzcat majordomo-1.94.4.tar.gz | tar xvf -     Use tar xovf on System V systems
% cd majordomo-1.94.4
```

Compiling and Installing

Now you're ready to actually compile the Majordomo *wrapper* program and install the system.

Building the Wrapper

Majordomo uses a setuid program called *wrapper* to ensure that its scripts are run as a trusted user in the Majordomo group when they are called from the *sendmail aliases* file. To build the wrapper program, you first edit its *Makefile* and then run *make wrapper*.

Some of the important macros in the *Makefile* include:

PERL

> The full pathname to Perl.

W_HOME

> The directory where the Majordomo programs are kept. *wrapper* only runs programs in this directory. The default installation uses the *majordom* user's home directory. Because a number of files and subdirectories are created, I've found it's often tidier to create a subdirectory and set W_HOME to that instead. This chapter assumes you've created the subdirectory */home/majordomo/runtime* and set W_HOME to point there.

W_USER and W_GROUP

> W_USER and W_GROUP are the user ID and group ID for Majordomo. You must use user ID and group ID numbers, not names, for these macros.

FILE_MODE, EXEC_MODE, and HOME_MODE

> These macros set the permissions for installed files, executables, and the W_HOME directory. The defaults allow read access by anyone; if this is too permissive, you might try a FILE_MODE of 640 and an EXEC_MODE of 750.

WRAPPER_* and POSIX

> The three WRAPPER_ macros and the POSIX macro work together to insure that Majordomo handles permissions correctly. Follow the *Makefile* instructions about which set of macros to use.

MAIL_GID

> Some MTAs, including early versions of *sendmail*, did not allow mail programs to set the SMTP From header. Majordomo tries to set the SMTP From header so that messages appear to be from the mailing list's *-request* address, rather

than from the *majordom* user. If this fails on your system, you may have to set
MAIL_GID to the group ID number of the MTA's group.

W_PATH, W_SHELL, and W_MAJORDOMO_CF
These macros become environment variables when *wrapper* runs a Perl script.
The defaults are usually fine.

After you modify the *Makefile*, use *make wrapper* to build the wrapper program.

Installing the System

Use *make install* to install the other Majordomo scripts into */home/majordomo/
runtime*. The installation creates three subdirectories (*Tools*, *bin*, and *man*) and
uses the provided *sample.cf* file to create a starting *majordomo.cf* file.

Add the directory */home/majordomo/runtime/bin* to the search path of the Majordomo user and of any local user in the *majordom* group who is going to be
administering the server.

If you plan to archive your mailing lists, you need to install an archive script for
creating archives. Three such scripts are provided: *archive.pl* creates LISTSERV-
style archives, *archive2.pl* creates more flexible date-based archives, and
archive_mh.pl uses the *rcvstore* program from the *mh* mail system to manage the
archive. You can install one of these scripts with *make install-archive*, *make
install-archive2*, or *make install-archive_mh*, respectively. This chapter assumes
you're using *archive2.pl*.

Installing and Testing the Wrapper

As *root*, run *make install-wrapper* to install *wrapper* as a setuid program.

Then, as another user—not *root* or the Majordomo user—go to the *runtime* directory and run *./wrapper config-test*. This command tests the system configuration
and lets you know about any problems with the installation that should be cor-
rected. Example 10-1 shows an example of the output from this command.

Example 10-1: Testing the Majordomo System Configuration

```
% cd /home/majordomo/runtime
% ./wrapper config-test
-------------------- Obvious things: --------------------
------------------ environment variables -----------------
    HOME=/home/majordomo/runtime
    LOGNAME=alansz
    MAJORDOMO_CF=/home/majordomo/runtime/majordomo.cf
    PATH=/bin:/usr/bin:/usr/ucb
    SHELL=/bin/csh
    USER=alansz
```

Example 10-1: Testing the Majordomo System Configuration (continued)

```
-------------------- euid/egid checks --------------------
   effective user  = majordomo (uid 136)
   effective group = majordomo (gid 310)
-------------------- uid/gid checks --------------------
   real      user  = majordomo (uid 136)
   real      group = majordomo (gid 310 )
-------------------------- --------------------------


     Non obvious things that cause headaches:


-------------------------- --------------------------
Good: "require"d /home/majordomo/runtime/majordomo.cf okay.
Good: found ctime.pl okay.
Good: found majordomo_version.pl okay.
Good: found majordomo.pl okay.
Good: found shlock.pl okay.
Good: found config_parse.pl okay.

You're running Majordomo Version 1.94.4.

--==> Majordomo home directory is /home/majordomo/runtime.
------------------ Include directories ------------------
      /home/majordomo/runtime
      /usr/local/lib/perl5/sun4-sunos/5.003
      /usr/local/lib/perl5
      /usr/local/lib/perl5/site_perl/sun4-sunos
      /usr/local/lib/perl5/site_perl
      /usr/local/lib/perl5/sun4-sunos
            .
-------------------------- Home --------------------------
Good: changedir to /home/majordomo/runtime succeeded.
Good: Created a mock lock file.
-------------------- temp directory --------------------
Good: Created a temp file in $TMPDIR (/usr/tmp).
-------------------- list directory --------------------
Good: list directory /home/majordomo/runtime/lists has good permissions.
-------------------------- log --------------------------
Good: logfile /home/majordomo/runtime/Log exists and is writeable.
----------------------- Mailers -----------------------
You have defined a mailer for delivery.
Attempting to verify that this is a valid mailer...looks okay.
You have defined a mailer for delivering administrative messages.
Attempting to verify that this is a valid mailer...looks okay.
----------------- Checking majordomo.cf -----------------
Checking to see if there are new variables that should be in
your majordomo.cf file...Nope, none that I see.
---------------------- end of tests ----------------------

Nothing bad found!  Majordomo _should_ work correctly.
```

Setting Up the Directory Structure

You can put the Majordomo list, archive, and digest work directories anywhere you like. The *majordomo.cf* file tells Majordomo where to find them (see the section on configuring the server below). You need to create these directories, however. One convenient structure is to create three subdirectories under */home/majordomo*:

lists

Holds the files for lists. Each list has a configuration file, a subscriber file, a password file, and possibly others.

archives

Contains the archived files for all the lists.

digests

Acts as the work area for the *digest* program.

Here's how to set up this structure:

```
% cd /home/majordomo
% mkdir lists archives digests
% chmod 775 lists archives digests
% ls -lgdF lists archives digests
drwxrwxr-x  3 majordom majordom      512 Apr  1 14:26 archives/
drwxrwxr-x  3 majordom majordom      512 Apr  1 14:26 digests/
drwxrwxr-x  3 majordom majordom      512 Apr  1 14:26 lists/
```

Another possibility is to store list archives as subdirectories of the *lists* directory with names ending in *.archive* or *.files*. For example, the archives for the *zodiac* mailing list could be kept in */home/majordomo/lists/zodiac.archive*. In this case, you don't have to create a separate *archives* directory.

Figure 10-1 shows the subdirectories in */home/majordomo* that you should have at the end of the installation.

The *runtime* directory (or, more generally, the W_HOME directory), contains the Majordomo programs themselves, the server configuration file, and supporting scripts (which end in *.pl*). Here's a quick rundown of the Majordomo programs that you'll use frequently:

bounce-remind

Part of Majordomo's system for managing subscribers to whom email bounces.

digest

Adds mail messages to a list digest. It's called from the *sendmail* alias for the digested list.

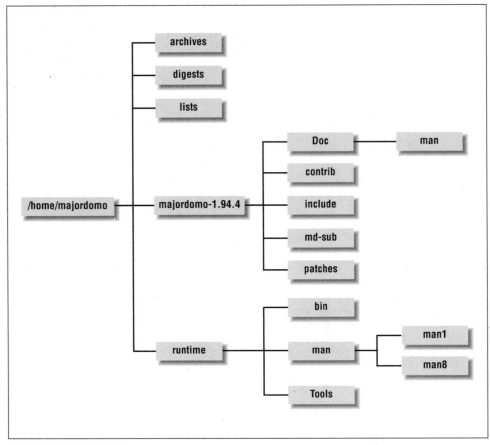

Figure 10-1: The Majordomo directory structure

majordomo

Majordomo's administrative request server; it answers mail sent to the *major-domo* address (and to the *-request* addresses of lists if you want) and processes commands in the message.

new-list

Simply returns a message saying that a mailing list is new and not yet ready for messages. It's used in the *sendmail aliases* file to respond to the list address when a list is new and still acquiring subscribers.

request-answer

Returns a message explaining that administrative commands should be sent to *majordomo@host*, not `listname-request@host`.

resend
> Actually processes and distributes list mail, optionally adding or removing special headers, filtering out administrative requests, and enforcing a maximum message length.

The *runtime* directory also contains three subdirectories: *bin*, *man*, and *Tools*. The *bin* directory contains two Perl scripts that are useful for list owners (*approve* and *bounce*) and one for the server administrator (*medit*). Owners of moderated lists can pipe messages to *approve* in order to approve them for posting to the list. The *bounce* script makes it easy for list owners to unsubscribe users whose email is bouncing. *medit* is used to edit Majordomo files; it locks the files to prevent them from being used by Majordomo while they are in an inconsistent state, runs your editor, and then unlocks the files.

The *man* directory contains two manual pages (formatted with *nroff*) that you might want to install in your system's manual page directories or distribute to list owners. The file *man/man1/approve.1* is the manual page for the *approve* script; *man/man8/majordomo.1* is an old manual page for Majordomo itself.

The *Tools* directory contains tools that Majordomo uses for archiving, indexing, and digesting lists.

Setting Up the Majordomo Aliases

As *root*, edit your *sendmail aliases* file and add the following aliases:

```
majordomo: "|/home/majordomo/runtime/wrapper majordomo"
owner-majordomo: alan,nobody
majordom: owner-majordomo
Majordomo-Owner: owner-majordomo
nobody: /dev/null
```

The *majordomo* alias is the heart of the system; it runs the *wrapper* program, and *wrapper* runs *W_HOME/majordomo*, the administrative request server. The *owner-majordomo* alias is used as the SMTP From header of outgoing messages; it's where delivery problems are sent.

The *Majordomo-Owner* alias is used by some sites instead of *owner-majordomo*, so you may want to define it in case someone expects it and sends email there.

The *nobody* alias simply discards mail by saving it to */dev/null*, the Unix null device. As you'll see later in this chapter, this alias is added to the recipient list of other aliases to finesse *sendmail* into believing that it's delivering a message to multiple recipients. If you can't use the alias *nobody*, pick a different name and use that wherever *nobody* is mentioned.

Remember to run *newaliases* after adding the aliases.

Configuring the Server

While each Majordomo list has its own configuration file, the Majordomo system also has a master configuration file, *majordomo.cf,* that controls global properties of the system. You need to edit *majordomo.cf* (which can be found in the W_HOME directory) to set the locations of the Majordomo directories and files. *major-domo.cf* is written in Perl, so every line (except comment lines) must end with a semicolon (`;`), and the last line must be `1;`.

majordomo.cf is well-commented and self-explanatory. Here's a piece of it:

```
# If you are using majordomo at the -request address, set the
# following variable to 1. This affects the welcome message that is
# sent to a new subscriber as well as the help text that is generated.
#
$majordomo_request = 0;

# If you have lists that have who turned off, but still allow which
# requests to work for subscribed members, and you don't want to have
# "which @" to act like a who, the variable $max_which_hits sets the
# number of hits that are allowed using which before an error is
# returned. Arguably this should be a per list settable number.
#
$max_which_hits = 5;
```

`$majordomo_request` should be set to 1 if you plan to have each list's *-request* alias pipe its messages to *majordomo* for processing instead of passing them to the *request-answer* script. `$max_which_hits` prevents users from circumventing restrictions on the **who** command by asking which users have an at sign (@) or a dot (`.`) in their email addresses.

It's a good idea to run *./wrapper config-test* whenever you modify your *major-domo.cf* file, to ensure that you haven't made any mistakes.

Adding Lists

The steps to add a simple Majordomo mailing list are:

1. Create a subscriber file and a password file in the *lists* directory. The subscriber filename should be the same as the name of the list; the file should initially be empty and have file mode 664. The password file is named `listname.passwd`. It should contain only the list's administrative password and should have file mode 660. Both files should be owned by the Majordomo user and group. Here's how we might set up these files for the *haberdashers* list from Chapter 4, *Maintaining Lists with Majordomo*:

```
% su - majordom
% cd lists
% touch haberdashers
% chmod 644 haberdashers
% echo "fez" > haberdashers.passwd
% chmod 600 haberdashers.passwd
```

Doublecheck that the owner, group, and permissions are correct for these files.

2. Create a file that contains the command-line arguments for *resend*. By placing the *resend* arguments in a file, you make it more difficult for subscribers to discover the name of the list's outgoing alias.* This file can be given any name, but *listname.resend* makes sense; its file mode should be set to 644:

```
% echo "-l haberdashers -h hats.com haberdashers-doit,nobody"
  > haberdashers.resend
% chmod 644 haberdashers.resend
```

The -l argument gives the name of the list, while the -h argument gives the name of the host serving the list. The final argument is the alias or aliases (separated by commas) to which the list is distributed. Including the *nobody* alias prevents *sendmail* from adding a Received header that lists *haberdashers-doit* to the outgoing messages.

3. Add aliases for the list to the *sendmail aliases* file. Here's the set of aliases for *haberdashers@hats.com*:

```
owner-haberdashers: sombrero@casa.mx,nobody
haberdashers:
  "|/home/majordomo/runtime/wrapper resend
   @/home/majordomo/lists/haberdashers.resend"
haberdashers-approval: owner-haberdashers
haberdashers-doit: :include:/home/majordomo/lists/haberdashers
owner-haberdashers-doit: owner-haberdashers
haberdashers-request:
  "/home/majordomo/runtime/wrapper request-answer haberdashers"
owner-haberdashers-request: owner-haberdashers
```

The aliases are:

owner-haberdashers

The list owner: the address to which *sendmail* sends error messages and the address that is used in the SMTP From header of messages sent to the list. Including *nobody* in this alias prevents *sendmail* version 8 from putting *sombrero@casa.mx* into the SMTP From instead of *owner-haberdashers@hats.com*. Many of the other aliases point to this one; in

---

* A subscriber might try to discover the list's outgoing alias by telnetting to the host's SMTP port and issuing an EXPN *listname* request. Seeing that the list's alias expands to a call to *resend* with arguments taken from a file doesn't show the subscriber what the arguments actually are.

particular, each alias that generates mail has an *owner-* alias that points to *owner-haberdashers.*

haberdashers

Pipes incoming list messages to the *wrapper* program, which sets the correct user and group IDs and then runs *resend* to process the message. `@/home/majordomo/lists/haberdashers.resend` directs *resend* to take its command-line arguments from the file */home/majordomo/lists/ haberdashers.resend* discussed above.

haberdashers-approval

Points to the person (or people) who approves subscriptions to closed lists, third-party subscriptions, and messages to moderated lists. This is usually the list owner, *owner-haberdashers* in our example.

haberdashers-doit

The actual list of subscribers. This is the alias to which *resend* mails messages for the list. More traditional names for this alias would be *haberdashers-outgoing* or *haberdashers-dist*, but most list owners prefer that their subscribers (and others) not be able to determine this alias and thus avoid *resend.*

haberdashers-request

By convention, many Internet mailing lists (especially those maintained by hand) use `listname-request` as the request address. Majordomo offers two ways to handle mail to `listname-request`. The method used above instructs *wrapper* to run the *request-answer* script, which returns a message telling the sender to send requests to *majordomo@hats.com* instead. You can also instruct Majordomo to accept requests at the *haberdashers-request* address by using this alias instead:

```
haberdashers-request:
 "|/home/majordomo/runtime/wrapper majordomo -l haberdashers"
```

The `-l` option gives the list name. If you choose to answer *-request* addresses like this, you must set the `$majordomo_request` variable in *majordomo.cf* to 1. As a consequence, all of your lists need to use *majordomo* for their *-request* addresses. In other words, you can't mix the two techniques; when `$majordomo_request` is set, help files and other automated responses direct users to send requests to the *-request* addresses.

4. Instruct the list owner to use the `config`, `newintro`, and `newinfo` commands to set up the list's initial configuration, welcome, and info files. For our *haberdashers* list, *sombrero@casa.mxs* would send email to *majordomo@hats.com* with the following commands:

```
config haberdashers password
newintro haberdashers password
```

Welcome file contents here
EOF

```
newinfo haberdashers password
```

Info file contents here
EOF

The `config` command creates a default configuration file for the list and emails it to the list owner, who can modify it and reinstall it with the **new-config** command. See Chapter 4 for details. The `newintro` and `newinfo` commands create the *listname.intro* and *listname.info* files with the given contents. Each file must end with a line that begins with the three uppercase letters `EOF`.

At this point the list has been created, and the list owner has a copy of its configuration file. No additional steps are necessary for a moderated list; the list owner can control the moderation status of the list through the configuration file. It's probably a good idea to send the list owner a copy of *Doc/list-owner-info*, which contains a lot of useful information for new list owners.

Digested Lists

Majordomo can produce a separate digested version of a list. In order to illustrate the steps in creating a digested list, let's assume that we want to create the *haberdashers* and *haberdashers-digest* mailing lists. Here are the steps:

1. Make sure the *digest* program has been installed in the directory containing *majordomo.cf*. By default, *digest* is in the *Tools/* subdirectory, so use the following command:

   ```
   % cd /home/majordomo/runtime
   % ln Tools/digest digest
   ```

2. Create the undigested list and digested list as described in the section on adding lists above.

3. Modify the outgoing alias for the undigested list to include a call to *digest*. Make the list alias for the digested list point to the undigested list. Here are a complete set of aliases:

   ```
   haberdashers-doit: :include:/home/majordomo/lists/haberdashers,
     "|/home/majordomo/runtime/wrapper digest -r -C
      -l haberdashers-digest haberdashers-digest-outgoing"
   haberdashers:
     "|/home/majordomo/runtime/wrapper resend
   ```

```
         @/home/majordomo/lists/haberdashers.resend"
owner-haberdashers: sombrero@casa.mx,nobody
haberdashers-approval: owner-haberdashers
owner-haberdashers-doit: owner-haberdashers
haberdashers-request:
  "/home/majordomo/runtime/wrapper request-answer haberdashers"
owner-haberdashers-request: owner-haberdashers

haberdashers-digest: haberdashers
haberdashers-digest-doit:
  :include:/home/majordomo/lists/haberdashers-digest
owner-haberdashers-digest: owner-haberdashers
haberdashers-digest-approval: owner-haberdashers
owner-haberdashers-digest-doit: owner-haberdashers
haberdashers-digest-request:
  "/home/majordomo/runtime/wrapper
   request-answer haberdashers-digest"
owner-haberdashers-digest-request: owner-haberdashers
```

Note that aliases should not be split across lines in the */etc/aliases* file; they're only split here for cosmetic reasons.

4. Add a work directory for the digest in `$digest_work_dir`:

   ```
   % cd /home/majordomo
   % mkdir digests/haberdashers-digest
   % chmod 770 digests/haberdashers-digest
   % chgrp majordomo digests/haberdashers-digest
   ```

5. If you want to archive list digests, create an archive directory, `$filedir/`*haberdashers-digest*`$filedir_suffix`, for the digests:*

   ```
   % cd /home/majordomo
   % mkdir archives/haberdashers-digest
   % chmod 770 archives/haberdashers-digest
   % chgrp majordomo archives/haberdashers-digest
   ```

   If you don't want to archive list digests, you can use a *cron* job to remove the archives periodically:

   ```
   cd /home/majordomo/archives &&
       find *-digest/. -type f -mtime +1 -exec rm {} \;
   ```

6. Create the *config* file for the digested list by copying the file from the undigested list. Then modify the *config* file for the digested list and make the following changes:

   • Change `digest_name` from *haberdashers* to *haberdashers-digest*.

---

* If you use Majordomo 1.93, you must create this directory even if you don't intend to archive list digests. Even better, upgrade to 1.94.4.

- Set `maxlength` to the maximum length (in bytes) you want digests to grow before being sent automatically.

- Set `reply-to` to *haberdashers*, not *haberdashers-digest*, so that replies are directed to the undigested list.

- Change `sender` from *owner-haberdashers* to *owner-haberdashers-digest*.

- Check `message_headers`, `message_fronter`, and `message_footer`. These behave differently for digested lists.

A digest is sent to digest subscribers whenever it becomes longer than `maxlength` bytes or `digest_maxlines` lines or is older than `digest_maxdays` days. The list owner can also force a digest to be sent by sending a `mkdigest` *listname password* command to *majordomo*.

Alternatively, if you only want to send a digest at fixed times (such as once a day), you can replace the `-r` in the digest alias with `-R`, which causes messages to be added to the digest, but doesn't automatically send the digest:

```
haberdashers-doit: :include:/home/majordomo/lists/haberdashers,
  "|/home/majordomo/runtime/wrapper digest -R -C
  -l haberdashers-digest haberdashers-digest-outgoing"
```

Then, establish a *cron* job to send the digest regularly, if there is a digest to send, by calling *digest* with the `-p` switch. Here's an example of distributing a digest weekly:

```
0  8  *  *  1 /home/majordomo/runtime/wrapper digest -p -C -l listname
```

The `-p` flag causes *digest* to distribute a digest if possible. `-C` indicates that configuration information should be read from the list's *config* file, and `-l` *listname* specifies the list.

Archives

Majordomo can archive text files and list messages. While it doesn't offer password protection for archives, you can restrict use of the `get` and `index` commands to list subscribers.

Majordomo offers a lot of flexibility about where to locate archives. The `$filedir` and `$filedir_suffix` variables in *runtime/majordomo.cf* control the location of archives. A list's archive is in `$filedir/`*listname*`$filedir_suffix`. Here are three places you could locate archives:

Subdirectories of lists

To put archives in subdirectories of the *lists* directory that contains list information, use these lines in *runtime/majordomo.cf:*

```
$filedir = "$listdir";
$filedir_suffix = ".archive";
```

Archives are kept in the directories *lists/listname.archive*.

Only a Digested List

Digested lists are most commonly used as companions to undigested lists. But what if you want to create a Majordomo list that's only available as a digest, and you don't want to moderate the list and create the digest yourself? Here's how. Again, we'll use the example of setting up a *haberdashers-digest* list, but this time, without a *haberdashers* list.

Follow the instructions for setting up a digested companion list with Majordomo, but keep the `reply-to` in *haberdashers-digest.config* set to *haberdashers-digest* and `sender` set to *owner-haberdashers-digest*. Don't use `message_fronter` or `message_footer` as they'll be applied to each message in the digest as well as to the digest itself. Create the file *haberdashers-digest.resend* in the *lists* directory, containing:

```
-l haberdashers -digest -h hats.com haberdashers-to-digest
```

Finally, add these aliases to the MTA's aliases file:

```
haberdashers-digest:
 "|/home/majordomo/runtime/wrapper resend @haberdashers-digest.resend"
haberdashers-to-digest:
 "|/home/majordomo/runtime/wrapper digest -r -C
  -l haberdashers-digest haberdashers-digest-outgoing"
haberdashers-digest-outgoing:
 :include:/home/majordomo/lists/haberdashers-digest
haberdashers-digest-request:
 "|/home/majordomo/runtime/wrapper request-answer haberdashers-digest"
owner-haberdashers-digest: sombrero@casa.mx
haberdashers-digest-owner: owner-haberdashers-digest
haberdashers-digest-approval: owner-haberdashers-digest
```

The alias for the actual subscriber list must be called *haberdashers-digest-outgoing* in order for the `mkdigest` command to function correctly.

Creating digest-only lists is easier in SmartList; it's impossible in Listproc or LISTSERV Lite without moderation or turning off the `set` command.

In an archives directory

To put archives in subdirectories of a directory called *archives*, create the directory */home/majordomo/archives* and use these lines in *runtime/majordomo.cf*:

```
$filedir = "/home/majordomo/archives";
$filedir_suffix = "";
```

Archives are kept in the directories *archives/listname*.

In an anonymous FTP directory

If the Majordomo user can write to a directory in your anonymous FTP area, you can keep your archives there. If your anonymous FTP directory for archives is */home/ftp/pub/list-archives*, use these lines in *runtime/majordomo.cf*:

```
$filedir = "/home/ftp/pub/list-archives";
$filedir_suffix = "";
```

Archives are kept in the directories */home/ftp/pub/list-archives/listname*.

Another relevant variable in *runtime/majordomo.cf* is $index_command, the command used to list an archive directory. By default, $index_command is set to */bin/ls -lRL*, which uses the *ls* command to produce a long-format listing of the archive directory and its subdirectories. If you want an alternative format, you can set $index_command to some other program that can produce an index.

Automatically Archiving Lists

If a list is digested, its digests are automatically placed in the list's archive directory, named by volume and issue number. Majordomo can also automatically archive individual list messages into a single archive file or into yearly, monthly, or daily files of messages. The *archive* program appends outgoing list messages to archives. It can also process a mailbox file and archive each message in the file.

archive is not installed with Majordomo; you can find it as *runtime/ Tools/archive2.pl*. If you plan to use it, you should probably copy it to the *runtime* directory:

```
% cd runtime
% cp Tools/archive2.pl archive
% chown majordom.majordom archive
% chmod 755 archive
```

archive's syntax is:

```
archive -f basename input-option [date-option] [file(s)]
```

The messages to be archived may be given as files on the command line or as standard input. If *input-option* is -u, the input is assumed to be one or more messages in Unix mailbox format. If the *input-option* is -a, the input is assumed to be a single mail message. The base filename for the archive is *basename*; the actual names of the archives depend on which *date-option*, if any, is used:

-d Create daily archives named *basename*. *YYMMDD*

-m Create monthly archives named *basename*. *YYMM*

-y Create yearly archives named *basename*. *YY*

no *date-option*
    Create a single archive file named *basename*

To create an archived list, modify the list's entry in your MTA's *aliases* file to include a call to the *archive* program. Here's how you'd set up aliases to archive the *plushdolls@stuffed.org* mailing list into monthly files with names like *plushdolls.9601*.

```
plushdolls: \
 "|/home/majordomo/runtime/wrapper resend -l
  plushdolls plushdolls-outgoing"
plushdolls-outgoing: \
  :include:/home/majordomo/lists/plushdolls,plushdolls-archive
plushdolls-request: \
 "|/home/majordomo/runtime/wrapper request-answer plushdolls"
owner-plushdolls: teddy
plushdolls-owner: owner-plushdolls
plushdolls-approval: owner-plushdolls
plushdolls-archive: "|/home/majordomo/runtime/wrapper archive
        -f /home/majordomo/lists/plushdolls-archive/plushdolls
        -m -a"
```

The *archive* program can also be used to add email messages or mailboxes to an archive, by using the -u *input-option*.

Archiving Other Files

You can put any text file into a Majordomo archive directory by simply copying it to the directory and making sure it's owned and readable by the Majordomo user and group.

Majordomo can't send binary files in response to archive requests. If you want to make binary files available, you can *uuencode* them and archive the encoded file or you can use *ftpmail*.

If your archives are located in your system's anonymous FTP area, users can retrieve them by FTP. *ftpmail* servers allow people to retrieve files from anonymous FTP sites by email. Majordomo has built-in support for *ftpmail*; it can forward archive retrieval commands to an *ftpmail* server, which returns the file (suitably encoded) to the user.

To use *ftpmail* instead of Majordomo's built-in archive retrieval, make sure your archives are accessible by anonymous FTP and uncomment these lines in *runtime/majordomo.cf*:

```
$ftpmail_address = "ftpmail@decwrl.dec.com";
$ftpmail_location = "FTP.$whereami";
```

Choose an `$ftpmail_address` for a site that's close to you. A list of all *ftpmail* servers can be found on the Web at *http://src.doc.ic.ac.uk/ftpmail-servers.html.*

Daily Maintenance and Troubleshooting

Majordomo requires little management by the server administrator; most of the work is distributed among the list owners. But there are a few tips that server administrators should know.

Bounces List

Majordomo is unique in its handling of bounced email messages. It doesn't automatically remove users whose addresses bounce. Instead, when a list owner removes a bouncing address, it can be placed on a special *bounces* mailing list. The *bounce-remind* program, typically run nightly, attempts to contact removed users and tell them how to resubscribe to the list.

In order to provide this kind of bounce handling, a *bounces* list must be created. To set up the *bounces* list:

1. Create a list called *bounces* just as you would any mailing list.

2. In *bounces.config*:

   - Set `precedence` to `bulk` to prevent returned mail from this list.

   - Set `reply_to` and `sender` to *nobody* so that any replies are quietly ignored.

   - Set `strip` to `no`; the comments in the subscriber list are used by *bounce-remind* to track the list from which the subscriber was removed.

   - Set `noadvertise` to `/./` (slash dot slash); that regular expression matches all addresses, so the list won't appear in response to any user's *lists* request.

3. Check the *bounce-remind* script to be sure that the path to Perl on the first line is correct.

4. Create a *crontab* entry that runs *bounce-remind* nightly. *bounce-remind* expects to find the location of your *majordomo.cf* file in the the environment variable `MAJORDOMO_CF`; if *cron* doesn't set that environment variable, use an entry like this:

```
30 3 * * * MAJORDOMO_CF=/home/majordomo/runtime/majordomo.cf
            /home/majordomo/runtime/wrapper bounce-remind
```

5. Send all list owners a copy of the *bounce* script and the *bounces* list password to include in their *.majordomo* files. The *bounce* script and *.majordomo* file are discussed in Chapter 4.

When *bounce-remind* runs, it sends a message like this to each address on the *bounces* list:

```
To: Bounces@hats.com
From: nobody@hats.com
Subject: Bouncing email from mailing lists at hats.com
Reply-To: nobody@hats.com

Your address has been moved to Bounces@hats.com
from some other mailing list at hats.com
because email to you was bouncing.

Here are the addresses currently on Bounces@hats.com
so that you can see which of your addresses is among them.
The comment for each address shows the date it was moved,
and the first list it was removed from.  If you were on
multiple lists here, you may have been removed from them
as well, but only the first list you were removed from
will show up in the comment below.

        user@whoknows.edu (960610 haberdashers)
        . . .

If the problem has been fixed, you can get off of
Bounces and back on to the other list by sending the
following to majordomo@hats.com:

    subscribe your_list
    unsubscribe bounces

To subscribe or unsubscribe an address other than where you're
sending the command from, append the other address to the end
of the "subscribe" or "unsubscribe" command (for example,
"subscribe your_list foo@bar.com").

You'll need to access the mailing list archives if you want to catch
up on whatever you missed while you were off the main list.

If you don't want to keep getting these reminders every day, but
don't want to resubscribe to the list, send just the "unsubscribe"
command shown above.

If you need to contact a human being regarding this, send a message
to owner-majordomo@hats.com
```

If the mail gets through to a subscriber, the subscriber will find out what has happened and how to fix it. You or the list owners should periodically check the *bounces* subscribers file (send a **who bounces** request) and remove subscribers who have been on the *bounces* list for over a month or so.

Temporarily Disabling Majordomo

Majordomo's programs are called whenever incoming mail arrives for a Majordomo-managed address. This complicates maintenance of the Majordomo files. If you make a mistake, incoming mail can be returned as undeliverable. You can avoid many problems by using the *medit* script to edit Majordomo files. Sometimes, however, it's useful to be able to temporarily disable Majordomo. Here's how:

1. Create a shell script called *majordomo.hold* in your *runtime* directory:

```
#!/bin/sh
exit 75
```

2. Make the script executable:

```
% chmod 755 majordomo.hold
```

3. When you're ready to disable Majordomo, quickly swap the *majordomo* script for *majordomo.hold*:

```
% cp majordomo majordomo.tmp && cp majordomo.hold majordomo
```

(The shell's && operator lets you type both commands before executing either of them; it does the second *cp* command only if the first *cp* succeeds.) Now when mail for *majordomo* comes in, your little script runs and returns an exit status of 75, which causes *sendmail* to defer (queue) the incoming message and try to deliver it again later. (Special exit status codes like 75 are listed in the file */usr/include/sysexits.h*.)

4. When you're done with your maintenance, you can return to normal operation by restoring the real *majordomo* script:

```
% cp majordomo.tmp majordomo
```

You can also swap *resend* with *majordomo.hold* to disable all list addresses.

Note that your *sendmail* may convert pathnames of commands run by deferred messages to all lowercase letters. For example, if your *archive* alias looks like this:

```
haberdashers-archive: "|/usr/local/majordomo/wrapper archive
  -f /usr/local/majordomo/Archives/haberdashers/haberdashers -m -a"
```

The A in the pathname may be changed to a lowercase a when the message is deferred, and the *archive* script won't be able to find the archive directory. The fix for this problem is to either change your *sendmail.cf* file (so it doesn't change case), add a symbolic link to the directory using the lowercase name (e.g., link *archives* to *Archives*), or use only lowercase letters in your file and directory names.

11

Administering SmartList

SmartList is an MLM that is both admirably simple to use and reasonably powerful and flexible. It is suitable for lists of any size and medium traffic. This chapter details the installation, configuration, and operation of SmartList 3.10.*

Overview of Operations

The SmartList server administrator sets up two mail aliases for each mailing list: the list alias and the list-request alias. When mail is sent to a list or list-request address, it is piped to the *flist* program, a setuid wrapper that invokes *procmail* as the SmartList user from the list's directory. The list operations are managed by a set of *procmail rc* files that analyze and respond to administrative requests, distribute messages to the list, and pass on anything unrecognized to the list owner.

You need the *procmail* source code in order to compile SmartList; SmartList requires that *procmail* be installed on your system in order to operate. While this chapter centers on SmartList, *procmail* itself is a powerful and useful utility that is worth having available.

Preparing to Install SmartList

SmartList isn't difficult to install, though like any MLM, the installation process has many steps.

---

* At the time of this writing, SmartList 3.11 was under development, and alpha versions were available. Some bugs that are fixed in v3.11 are noted in this chapter.

Setting Up the List User and Group

SmartList works best when installed with its own account. The SmartList installation guide recommends creating a user called *list* and a *list* group, but you can use any names you like. The user's home directory should be owned by the user and group you create.

It's also possible to install SmartList into a subdirectory of an existing user's account and have SmartList run as that user. Unless you have a really good reason, however, creating a new account is usually a much better solution.

This chapter assumes that you've created a user called *smart*, with home directory */home/smart*, and a *smart* group. Here's what */home/smart* looks like:

```
drwxr-xr-x  7 smart    smart        512 Mar  3 12:17 /home/smart/
```

Making the SmartList User Trusted

Because SmartList uses *sendmail*'s `-f` option to set the SMTP From header, the SmartList user must be a *sendmail* "trusted user." To add *smart* to the set of trusted users, edit *sendmail*'s configuration file, usually */etc/sendmail.cf* or */usr/lib/sendmail.cf*, and search for the lines that begin with uppercase T's. Add a line like this:

```
Tsmart
```

If your version of *sendmail* uses "frozen" configuration files (*sendmail.fc*), run *sendmail -bz* to create a new *sendmail.fc* from your *sendmail.cf*.

Getting SmartList

The source code for SmartList and *procmail* is available by anonymous FTP from *ftp.informatik.rwth-aachen.de* in */pub/packages/procmail*. You should download *procmail.tar.gz* and *SmartList.tar.gz*. Uncompress and untar each file in the same directory. This need not be */home/smart*; you can put the source code wherever you keep source code on your system, but the SmartList user must be able to read and access the code.

Compiling and Installing

Compiling SmartList is a two-step process. First, you must build and install *procmail*. Then you can build SmartList itself.

Building procmail

Here are the steps required to build *procmail* in order to use SmartList:

1. Change to the *procmail-3.10* directory.

2. Edit *Makefile* and set `BASENAME` to be the name of the directory that contains the *bin* and *man* subdirectories into which you want *procmail* installed. The default is */usr/local*.

3. Edit *config.h* to control *procmail*'s behavior. Follow the instructions in the file. In particular, you may want to be sure that `TRUSTED_IDS` matches the list of trusted users in your *sendmail.cf* file and includes the SmartList user.

4. Type *make* to configure *procmail*'s *Makefiles* and compile *procmail*. During the configuration process, you'll be asked a question about directories to use for file-locking tests. Follow the instructions or accept the defaults.

5. As *root*, use *make install-suid* to install *procmail* in its recommended setuid root configuration. *procmail* is designed to be run setuid root and takes extensive security precautions (see the *examples/advanced* file for details), but if you're squeamish, you could also try simply *make install*.

6. As *root*:

```
# (cd /usr/local/bin; chmod a+rx procmail formail mailstat)
# cd /usr/local/man
# (cd man1; chmod a+r procmail.1 formail.1 lockfile.1)
# (cd man5; chmod a+r procmailrc.1 procmailex.1 procmailsc.1)
```

Building SmartList

Once *procmail* has been built, the next steps to install SmartList are:

1. Change directory to *procmail-3.10/SmartList*.

2. Make sure that *root*'s path includes */usr/local/bin* or wherever *procmail* was installed. If your *root* shell isn't */bin/sh*, you may have to use *rehash* in order for the shell to find *procmail*.

3. As *root*, use *sh install.sh /home/smart*. Replace */home/smart* with the SmartList user's home directory, if it's different.*

4. Log in as the SmartList user and make sure that your path includes */home/smart/.bin*.

---

* On at least one older operating system (Ultrix 4.2), */bin/sh* doesn't correctly execute the *install.sh* shell script and claims it can't extract the value of `SENDMAIL` from *procmail*. Try using the GNU *bash* shell, or edit line 65 and remove the characters | [! /] *. This has been fixed in SmartList 3.11.

5. Edit */home/smart/.etc/rc.init* and set the values of PATH, domain, and list-master. PATH should include the path to *procmail* and *formail* (usually */usr/local/bin*) as well as the *metamail* package, if you want SmartList to be able to send MIME messages. domain should be set to the fully qualified domain name of your host. listmaster can either be set to the email address of another user who is responsible for the system or to "" if the SmartList user itself should manage the system.

6. As the SmartList user, create the file *.forward* in */home/smart*. The file should contain this line:

```
|"IFS=' '; exec /usr/local/bin/procmail #smart"
```

Make the file world-readable with *chmod a+r .forward*.

7. If you plan to have digested mailing lists, create a *cron* entry for the SmartList user that runs */home/smart/.bin/cronlist*. The *cronlist* script insures that digests are generated regularly.

Figure 11-1 shows what the directory structure should look like after you install SmartList.

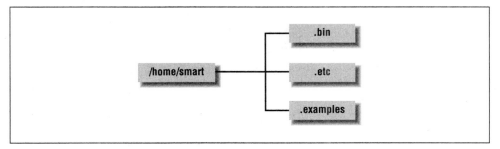

Figure 11-1: The SmartList directory structure

The SmartList user's home directory need contain only two files: *.forward* and *.procmailrc*.* SmartList uses *procmail* to scan incoming mail messages for administrative requests and act on them. The *.forward* file that we created during the installation forwards incoming mail to *procmail*. The *.procmailrc* file controls the operation of *procmail*.

---

* In fact, if *procmail* is used as the local mail delivery agent on your system, even *.forward* is unnecessary. But it doesn't hurt to have it anyway.

The *.bin* subdirectory contains the SmartList programs themselves. Five of these files, *choplist, flist, idhash, multigram,* and *senddigest,* are links to the same setuid root program, which behaves differently depending on its name when run.* Other files are Bourne shell scripts that add and delete lists (*createlist* and *removelist*), manage list files (*delink, showlink, led,* and *donatelist*), distribute messages (*mimesend*), handle requests (*subscribe, unsubscribe,* and *x_command*), and manage archives and digests (*arch_retrieve, arch_trunc, cronlist, digest,* and *flush_digests*).

led deserves special mention. It's dangerous to edit SmartList's scripts and configuration files while SmartList is active; your editor might save a file in an unfinished state while you're working on it and cause errors when list mail is received. The *led* script allows you to use your editor safely. It creates lockfiles that prevent SmartList from processing mail until your editing is complete and ensures that your editor hasn't modified the file permissions on the files. *led* uses the editor specified by your **VISUAL** environment variable or *vi* if **VISUAL** isn't set.

Most of the files in the *.etc* subdirectory are master copies of the *procmail* scripts that control the operation of lists. When a new list is created, its directory initially includes links to these master files. By delinking and modifying these files, you can change the default behavior for newly created lists.

The *.etc* subdirectory also contains the help files for list subscribers. You may want to edit these files to suit the policies of your site. The *help.txt* file is sent in response to a **help** request. It explains how to subscribe and unsubscribe from a list. The *archive.txt* file is sent in response to an **archive help** request and explains the archive commands. The *subscribe.txt* and *unsubscribe.txt* files are sent as part of the message a user receives when she subscribes or unsubscribes from a SmartList mailing list.

The most important files in *.etc* are the *rc* scripts. The filenames that begin with *rc.* are the *procmail* scripts that constitute SmartList itself. They're organized like this:

rc.init

> Initializes all of the variables that are used in the other scripts. It also calls *rc.custom*, which initializes per-list variables.

rc.post

> Saves a copy of a message to the file *.etc/request* and sends a copy to the SmartList listmaster, if one has been defined.

rc.request

> Processes mail sent to a list-request address. It recognizes administrative requests and calls the programs to handle them. Unrecognized requests are

---

* The source code for this program is *multigram.c* in the *procmail src* directory.

stored in the list's *request* file, forwarded to the list owner, and passed to *rc.post*.

rc.submit

Processes mail sent to a SmartList mailing list address. It identifies administrative requests sent to the list address and redirects them to *rc.request*, and distributes legitimate messages to the mailing list, digest, and archive.

rc.archive

Processes mail sent to an archive server. It calls *arch_retrieve* to handle archive requests. Unrecognized requests are stored in the archive's *request* file, forwarded to the archive owner, and passed to *rc.post*.

rc.main

A link to */home/smart/.procmailrc*, the script that handles mail sent to the SmartList user. It uses *rc.init* to initialize its variables and then runs *rc.post*.

The file *rc.lock* doesn't appear in the *.etc* directory by default, but if you create it, SmartList postpones processing incoming mail for up to 17 minutes from its last-access date. You can use this if you need to modify important files, such as *rc.init* on an active SmartList account. If you need more than 17 minutes, *touch* the *rc.lock* file every 15 minutes or so. Remove the file to resume normal operation. Figure 11-2 shows the relationship between the *rc* scripts.

The *.examples* directory contains examples of files and scripts that may be useful in working with SmartList.

Adding Lists

Adding a list to a SmartList server involves first creating the list's files and directories, and then configuring the list by delinking and editing files.

Creating the List

Creating a mailing list is simple. The *createlist* command creates a directory for the list, copies or links important files into the directory, and tells you which aliases to add to your *sendmail aliases* file.* The syntax for creating a mailing list is:

```
createlist listname [list-owner]
```

Unrecognized administrative requests for the list are forwarded to the list owner. If no `list-owner` is given, these requests are stored in the list's *request* file.

---

* *createlist* assumes your *aliases* file is */usr/lib/aliases* and suggests adding aliases there. You can easily edit the *createlist* script (it's in the *.bin/* subdirectory) and change this to */etc/aliases*, or wherever your *aliases* file is located, to avoid confusion.

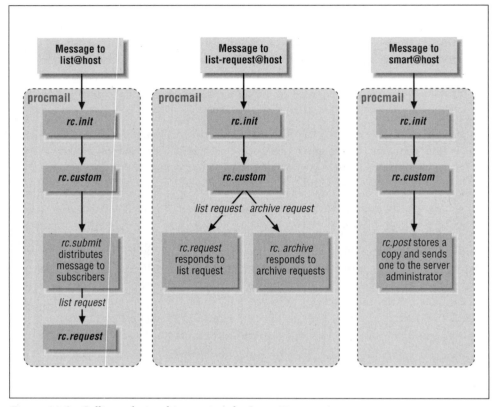

Figure 11-2: Calling relationships among the SmartList rc scripts

To illustrate the use of *createlist*, here's how to create the *lightbulb-jokes* list* from Chapter 5, *Maintaining Lists with SmartList*. This list is owned by *sally@happy.fun.org*:

```
% createlist lightbulb-jokes sally@happy.fun.org

Installed the following files (many hardlinked):

drwxrws--x  3 smart    512 Mar 10 15:20 lightbulb-jokes
-rw-rw-r--  2 smart     62 Mar 10 15:20 lightbulb-jokes/accept
drwxrwx---  3 smart    512 Mar 10 15:20 lightbulb-jokes/archive
-rw-r--r--  2 smart    629 Mar  3 17:47 lightbulb-jokes/archive.txt
drwxrwx---  2 smart    512 Mar 10 15:20 lightbulb-jokes/archive/latest
-rw-rw-r--  2 smart     62 Mar 10 15:20 lightbulb-jokes/dist
```

---

* How many list owners does it take to screw in a lightbulb? Four: one to screw in the lightbulb and three to remind subscribers that lightbulb requests should be sent to the request address, not the list address.

```
-rw-r--r--  2 smart   2189 Mar  3 17:47 lightbulb-jokes/help.txt
-rw-rw----  1 smart   4090 Mar 10 15:20 lightbulb-jokes/rc.custom
-rw-r-----  2 smart  10044 Mar  3 18:03 lightbulb-jokes/rc.init
-rw-r--r--  2 smart   8060 Mar  3 17:47 lightbulb-jokes/rc.request
-rw-r--r--  2 smart   6351 Mar  3 17:47 lightbulb-jokes/rc.submit
-rw-rw----  2 smart      0 Mar 10 15:20 lightbulb-jokes/reject
-rw-r--r--  2 smart    351 Mar  3 17:47 lightbulb-jokes/subscribe.txt
-rw-r--r--  2 smart    258 Mar  3 17:47 lightbulb-jokes/unsubscribe.txt
```

```
Now make the following entries in your /usr/lib/aliases file:
######################################################################
lightbulb-jokes: "|exec /home/rt/.bin/flist lightbulb-jokes"
lightbulb-jokes-request: "|exec /home/smart/.bin/flistlightbulb-jokes-
request"
lightbulb-jokes-dist: :include:/home/smart/lightbulb-jokes/dist
######################################################################
And make sure to run newaliases afterwards.
```

By default, SmartList uses its *choplist* program to preprocess subscriber addresses, chopping them into subsets that it passes on to *sendmail* for delivery. Using *choplist* can make message distribution faster, and it doesn't require the *-dist* address in your *aliases* file. In fact, it's better not to include it, to prevent nonsubscribers from sending mail directly to the *-dist* address.*

The command *removelist* `listname` removes a mailing list, should you need to.

Configuring the List

Each list has its own directory beneath the SmartList user's home directory. A list is configured by editing files in the list directory. There are two important things to remember about editing list configuration files: check for links and use *led*.

When a new list is created, most of its configuration files are linked to the master configuration files in *.etc* (*rc.custom* is a notable exception to this rule). You can identify linked files in a long-format directory listing (of the sort produced by *ls -l*) by checking the number that appears just after the permissions information that begins the listing. A number greater than 1 indicates that the file is linked to others. For *rc* files, you can also use the *showlink* command (e.g., *showlink rc.init*).

If you edit a linked file, you'll change the configuration of every list that is linked to that file. Usually, you want to use the *delink* program to remove the link and create a wholly separate copy of the file before you edit it (e.g., *delink rc.init*).

It's important to use the *led* utility to edit list configuration files. *led* ensures that mail is not delivered to the mailing list while you are configuring it, and that your

---

* If for some reason you don't want to use *choplist*, edit *rc.init* and uncomment the line that says `alt_sendmail`. SmartList then uses *sendmail* with no preprocessing; in this case, the *-dist* alias is necessary.

editor doesn't break links or change the permissions of the files. To use *led*, make sure your VISUAL environment variable contains the name of your editor and then use *led* in its place:

```
% setenv VISUAL emacs          If you use csh
$ VISUAL=emacs; export VISUAL  If you use sh

% led rc.init
```

As an alternative to *led*, you can create the file *rc.lock* in the list's directory, which causes incoming mail processing to be postponed for up to 17 minutes from the file's access date.

Basic configuration: rc.custom

The place to begin list configuration is the *rc.custom* file. This file contains directives you can use to customize the list's behavior. A separate copy is made for each list, so delinking it is not necessary.

Like the other *rc* files, *rc.custom* is a *procmail* script. Its format, however, is extremely simple. It sets a number of variables using a shell-like syntax, where *variable=value* sets a variable, and *variable* alone clears a variable. Lines beginning with a pound sign (#) are comments, and variables that aren't set receive default values from *rc.init*. Here are the most important variables you'll need to set in *rc.custom*:

maintainer

> Must be set to the complete email address of the list owner. If you leave maintainer blank, list requests are stored in the list's *request* file, rather than being sent to the list owner. For *lightbulb-jokes*, the maintainer is *sally@happy.fun.org*:
>
>   maintainer=sally@happy.fun.org

auto_subscribe, auto_unsubscribe

> If this variable is set to **yes** (the default), people may subscribe themselves without the aid of the list owner. If undefined, the list owner must process all subscriptions. Similarly, **auto_unsubscribe** controls whether subscribers may unsubscribe themselves without approval. For *lightbulb-jokes*, automatic subscription and unsubscription are appropriate:
>
>   auto_subscribe=yes
>   auto_unsubscribe=yes

pass_diverts

> SmartList tries to filter out administrative requests that are sent to the list address. By default, such requests are handled as if they were sent to the list-request address. If **pass_diverts** is set to **yes**, however, the requests are

sent to the list owner unprocessed instead.* For *lightbulb-jokes*, SmartList should filter out requests and treat them as if they were sent to the request address, so **pass_diverts** should be undefined:

```
pass_diverts
```

reply_to

By default, SmartList doesn't include a Reply-To header in outgoing list mail. If you'd like one, set **reply_to** to the header you'd like added. The variable **$listaddr** contains the address of the list, so to force replies to be sent to the list, you can use:

```
reply_to = "Reply-To: $listaddr"
```

X_COMMAND, X_COMMAND_PASSWORD

Remote list owners can subscribe and unsubscribe users and perform other administrative functions by sending email to their list's request address with a special header field. By default, the header field is X-Command followed by the owner's email address, the list password, and the command to execute. The **X_COMMAND** variable changes the name of the header from X-Command to something else. The **X_COMMAND_PASSWORD** header sets the list password; it defaults to **password**. It's a good idea to change both of these to prevent other users from executing list owner commands.

Text files

There are six text files that SmartList sends to users. Customizing (or in some cases, creating) these files is essential to personalizing a list. The files are:

help.txt and *info.txt*

SmartList sends the *help.txt* and *info.txt* files in response to a **help** request (or an invalid request if **auto_help** is set in *rc.custom*). *help.txt* contains the standard SmartList help message. *info.txt* must be created and is meant for custom list information. It appears after *help.txt* in SmartList's help mailings.

archive.txt

SmartList sends *archive.txt* when subscribers request help for the archive server.

subscribe.txt and *unsubscribe.txt*

SmartList sends *subscribe.txt* to new subscribers and *unsubscribe.txt* in response to unsubscription requests. In either case, the text file is followed by a quoted copy of the user's request mail. You can customize *subscribe.txt* to

---

* SmartList 3.11 adds another *rc.custom* variable, **divertcheck**, that controls whether SmartList filters out administrative requests at all.

be the list's welcome message; the list maintainer will probably tell you what she'd like it to contain.

You can also create a file called *subscribe.files*, containing archive commands to be run on behalf of the new user, if you want to place your welcome messages in your archive.* For example, *subscribe.files* might contain:

```
get welcome.msg
get list-faq
```

accept.txt

SmartList sends *accept.txt* to people who try, but aren't allowed, to send messages to the list. *accept.txt* isn't created by default, but you should create one. If you don't, SmartList bounces their message back with only an X-Diagnostic header to indicate why.

Controlling subscriptions

The *dist* file contains the list of subscribers to the mailing list. A brand new *dist* file contains only the single line:

```
(Only addresses below this line can be automatically removed)
```

New subscribers are added below the line. If, when you create the list, you know that there are some subscribers that should never be unsubscribed (the list owner, for example), add their email addresses above the line in this format:

```
email-address (optional-parenthesized-comment)
```

If you remove the "Only addresses below" line, SmartList never automatically unsubscribes subscribers.

SmartList offers considerable flexibility in restricting who may subscribe to a list. Like most MLMs, SmartList can automatically process subscription requests or send them on to the list owner. Automatic processing can be customized by creating a *reject* file, a *subscreen* program, or both.

If you create the file *reject* in a list's directory, would-be subscribers whose email addresses match those in the file are rejected. The file should contain one address per line.

For even finer control, you can create an executable shell script or program called *subscreen*. SmartList calls *subscreen* with the would-be subscriber's email address as its first argument. *subscreen* should return an exit code of 0 if the address should be allowed to subscribe to the list, or 1 if the subscription should be

---

* In SmartList 3.10, *subscribe.files* is ignored when a subscriber is added by a third party; SmartList 3.11 corrects this bug.

rejected. Example 11-1 gives an example of using a *subscreen* Perl script to reject subscription requests that come from outside of the local domain.

Example 11-1: The subscreen Script

```
#!/usr/bin/perl
#
# subscreen - perl script called by SmartList to determine if an
#             email address should be allowed to subscribe.
#             This version allows those from our local domain.
#
# Usage: (by SmartList)
#    subscreen email-address
# Returns exit code 0 if the address is ok, 1 if not.
#

$address = $ARGV[0];
exit 1 unless $address;

# Set $nameprog to the full path to your "hostname" program.
# If you don't have one, read on.
$nameprog='/bin/hostname';

# What's my local domain? If the "hostname" command on your system
# doesn't return your fully-qualified host name, uncomment the line
# below and set it to your local domain name.
#$domain='berkeley.edu';

unless ($domain) {
  $domain = `$nameprog`;
  $domain =~ s/^.*([^\.]+\.[^\.]+)$/$1/;
}

exit ($address !~ /$domain$/ ? 1 : 0);
```

Controlling submissions

By default, anyone may send messages to a SmartList list. If the **foreign_submit** directive in *rc.custom* is undefined, only certain users may send messages to the list.

The *accept* file contains the list of people who are permitted to submit to the mailing list. This file is usually a link to *dist*, allowing all list subscribers to post to the list. If only a smaller group of people should be able to post to the list, delink *accept* and edit it. If a group of people in addition to the subscribers should be allowed to post, create a file called *accept2* and add their addresses there.

Here's how to implement some different submission policies:

Subscribers only
Keep *accept* linked to *dist* and don't create *accept2*.

A subset of subscribers

> Delink *accept* from *dist* and edit it, removing subscribers who should not be allowed to post.

Subscribers and others

> Create the *accept2* file and add the addresses of nonsubscribers who should be allowed to post to the list.

A subset of subscribers and others

> Combine the above two setups: delink and edit *accept* to include only subscribers who can post and add others to *accept2*.

When postings are rejected, the file *accept.txt* (which you must create) is sent back to the posting's author.

Even more control: rc.local files

If you're an experienced *procmail* user, you can customize SmartList's behavior at predefined points by writing local *procmail* recipes and uncommenting particular lines to tell SmartList when to run the local recipes.

Local recipes are customized on a per-list basis. For each recipe, a variable in *rc.custom* controls whether the recipe is run. Here is a list of the variables you can set and the recipes they run:

RC_LOCAL_SUMBIT_00

> If defined, *rc.local.s00* is called in *rc.submit* immediately after loading *rc.init* and *rc.custom* but before any other action.

RC_LOCAL_SUBMIT_10

> If defined, *rc.local.s10* is called in *rc.submit* after the incoming message has been accepted as not containing an administrative request and coming from a valid sender. This is a good place to filter the message for other criteria that might make it unsuitable for the list.

RC_LOCAL_SUBMIT_20

> If defined, *rc.local.s20* is called in *rc.submit* just before the message is distributed to the list subscribers. This is a good place to add or remove headers.

RC_LOCAL_REQUEST_00

> If defined, *rc.local.r00* is called in *rc.request* immediately after loading *rc.init* and *rc.custom* but before any other action.

RC_LOCAL_REQUEST_10

> If defined, *rc.local.r10* is called in *rc.request* before checking for requests in the message. This is a good place to add request recipes that override the standard requests.

RC_LOCAL_REQUEST_20

> If defined, *rc.local.r20* is called in *rc.request* just after checking for standard requests in the message. This is a good place to add new request recipes.

RC_LOCAL_REQUEST_30

> If defined, *rc.local.r30* is called in *rc.request* when no requests have matched, after the X-Diagnostic header has been set but before the failed message is sent on to the list maintainer. This could be used to automate responses to invalid requests.

Moderated Lists

Making a list moderated is simple, and SmartList excels in its support for multiple moderators.

To make a moderated list, create the file *moderators* in the list's directory and add the email addresses of the moderators, one per line, to the file. Use complete email addresses, including fully qualified domain names. Then simply define `moderated_flag` in *rc.custom* as `yes`.

Submissions to a moderated list are forwarded to all moderators. Any moderator can approve a message by sending it back to the list with an Approved header that contains his email address. SmartList won't send multiple copies of a message to the list, even if multiple moderators approve it. See Chapter 5 for a script to simplify approving messages.

The Approved header that the moderator adds appears on the message that's sent out to the list. Unfortunately, this means that any subscriber can learn a moderator's address from the Approved header and bypass the moderators by sending a message with an Approved header already added. You can prevent SmartList from including the Approved header in outgoing mail for the list by uncommenting the RC_LOCAL_SUBMIT_20 line in *listname/rc.custom* and creating the file *listname/rc.local.s20* containing the following:

```
# Remove Approved: headers before sending mail to the list
:0 fhw
| formail -I Approved:
```

Digested Lists

Each SmartList list sends either individual messages or digests; a user who subscribes to an ordinary list receives individual messages, while one who subscribes to a digested list receives digests. It's possible to offer the same mailing list in both digested and individual message formats by creating both lists and subscribing the digested list to the undigested list.

Digested lists are created by configuring variables in the list's *rc.custom* file. The relevant variables are:

digest_flag

> If set to **yes**, the list sends digests rather than individual messages.

digest_age

> The maximum number of seconds allowed between digests. A digest is sent if this many seconds have passed since the last digest.

digest_size

> The maximum number of bytes allowed in a single digest. A digest is sent if a message received causes the digest to exceed this many bytes.

undigested_list

> If you want to create digested and undigested versions of the same list, set this variable in the digested list's *rc.custom* to the email address of the *undigested* list. SmartList uses this address for the Reply-To header of the digested list, which causes replies to be returned to the undigested list (and from there to the digested list). If there's no corresponding undigested version of the list, set this to **$list@$domain**, which directs replies back to the digested list.

SmartList only checks to see if a digest should be sent out when the list receives mail. If the list receives no mail for a long period, a digest won't be sent, even if it's older than digest_age. To ensure that digests are sent as soon as they're ready, run the *.bin/cronlist* script daily from *cron. cronlist* runs *.bin/flush_digests*, which does the actual digest production. The SmartList administrator can force a digest to be sent by running *flush_digests* with the -c -f option from the list's directory:

```
% cd lightbulb-jokes-digest
% flush_digests -c -f
```

flush_digests doesn't work if there's only a single message in the digest.

Administrative notices can be added to the top of the next digest and/or every digest. To add an administrative notice to the next digest, place it in *list-name/archive/latest/digest.admin*. This file is deleted after each digest is created. To add an administrative notice to every digest, place it in *listname/digest.admin*.

List Administration

SmartList offers a limited set of remote list owner administration facilities and more comprehensive local list owner control. List administration by owners other than the SmartList user is probably SmartList's weakest point, perhaps because SmartList is designed to require little owner intervention once lists are created.

Remote Administration: X-Command

SmartList allows list owners to send administrative commands by email. Administrative commands are sent to the list's request address and appear in a special message header that defaults to X-Command. It looks like this:

```
X-Command: listowner@address password command
```

The remote list administration commands are covered in Chapter 5. List passwords default to **password**, so for security purposes you should change both the list password and the X-Command header itself. The list owner's address given in the header must be the same address used when the list was created with *createlist*.

The */home/smart/.examples* directory contains a script called *doxcommand* that you can distribute to list owners to simplify sending commands. However, the script requires the list owner to store the list's password in the script. If this makes you nervous, you may prefer to use my *newdoxcmd* script, which prompts for the list's password each time. You can get *newdoxcmd* at *ftp://ftp.oreilly.com/ pub/examples/nutshell/mailing_lists*.

Another possibility is to preprocess request mail to allow X-Command to appear as the first line of the message body, rather than in the headers. SmartList 3.11 includes an *rc.local.r00* that does just this. It should work with SmartList 3.10 as well. Here it is:

```
#
# This file contains several examples of how you can customize
# SmartList through the RC_LOCAL_REQUEST_00 hook.
#

#
# Allowing X-Command fields to be placed at the start of the body:
# (Glues the start of the body to the header, pull out the sed manual
# if you want to understand this one :-).
#

     :0 Bfw
     * $^^(^)*$X_COMMAND:
     | sed -e '/^$/,$ !b' -e '/./,$ !d'
```

Local Administration: donatelist

If one of the list owners has an account on the same system as the SmartList user, it's possible to give her complete control over her mailing list by using the *donatelist* command. *donatelist* changes the ownership of the list's directory and subdirectories to the local list owner, while keeping its group permissions set appropriately for SmartList.

You probably have to run *donatelist* as *root*. The syntax is:

```
donatelist local-owner-login-name listname
```

Check to be sure that each of the files in the list's directory are owned by the local owner and in the SmartList group. The local owner should use umask 007 when editing the files, to ensure that the group permissions, which are crucial to SmartList's operation in this situation, are not changed. You should be sure the local owner uses *led* when editing the files.

While *donatelist* allows you to give local list owners complete control over their lists, it also greatly complicates any centralized mailing-list management. In addition, machines devoted to running mailing lists often minimize the number of local users for security or performance reasons, which makes *donatelist* somewhat less useful than it first appears.

Archives

Every SmartList mailing list is also an archive server for its own messages and any other files you care to make available. You can also set up an archive server without an associated mailing list by giving the **-a** switch to *createlist*:

```
createlist -a joke-archive sally@happy.fun.org
```

Any file placed in the list's *archive* directory or subdirectories beneath *archive* can be retrieved. If SmartList's **PATH** includes the location of the *mimencode* and *split-mail* programs from the *metamail* package, binary files can be included in the archive and are sent MIME-encoded.

If the list is digested, its digests are archived by year in the list's *archive/volume***YY** subdirectory. Each digest is numbered consecutively.

Undigested lists are not archived permanently. When a new message is received, it is placed in the list's *archive/latest* subdirectory, consecutively numbered, and the *.bin/arch_trunc* script is run. *arch_trunc* removes all but the most recent messages in that subdirectory. The **archive_hist** variable in *rc.custom* controls the number of recent messages that are kept in the archive. The default is two.

If you want to permanently archive undigested list messages, you can make a copy of *.bin/arch_trunc* in the list's directory and modify it. Example 11-2 contains a version of *arch_trunc* that copies the messages into directories named *archive/***YYMM** before removing them.

Example 11-2: Permanently Archiving Messages with arch_trunc

```
#!/usr/bin/perl
#
# arch_trunc, a replacement for the distributed .bin/arch_trunc
# shell script in SmartList. To use it, put it in some list's directory.
```

Example 11-2: Permanently Archiving Messages with arch_trunc (continued)

```
#
# By Alan Schwartz
#
# This script is run whenever a submission is received and archived
# in archive/latest. It's responsible for cleaning up that directory.
# This version figures out the date of the each file in archive/latest
# that should be removed and appends it to the file archive/YYMM/DD
#
unless (chdir("archive/latest")) {
  print "Don't start this script directly, it is called by rc.request\n";
  exit 64;
}

# Only do the removing now and then to keep load down
if ($ENV{'ARCHIVE'} =~ /[248]$/) {
    opendir(DIR,".");
    @files = grep(/^\d+/,readdir(DIR));
    closedir(DIR);
    foreach (sort bytime @files) {
        $recent++;
        if ($recent > $ENV{'archive_hist'}) {
          # Archive these and delete them
          @time = localtime((stat($_))[9]);
          $newdir = sprintf("%02d%02d",$time[5],$time[4]+1);
          $newfile = sprintf("%02d",$time[3]);
          unless (-d "../$newdir") {
              mkdir("../$newdir",2770);
          }
          open(IN,$_);
          open(OUT,">>../$newdir/$newfile");
          print OUT <IN>;
          close(IN);
          close(OUT);
          unlink($_);
        }
    }
    unlink("_dummy_");
}

sub bytime {
  return -M $a <=> -M $b;
}
```

You can restrict access to the archives. If you define the `restrict_archive` variable in *rc.custom*, only users who appear in the list's *accept* or *accept2* file may access the archive.

Archiving Other Files

Archiving other files is as easy as putting them into the list's *archive* subdirectory (or any directory below it) and making them readable to the SmartList user or group. Many binary files can even be archived this way; if the *metamail* package is available, SmartList MIME encapsulates files before emailing them.

SmartList can recognize a number of file types by their extension or their contents and sets the outgoing message's MIME Content-Type header appropriately. If it can't recognize the file's type, SmartList uses a Content-Type of `application/octet-stream`, which is suitable for binary data.

Extending the Archive Server

The archive server is contained in *.bin/arch_retrieve*. It can be extended by creating the Bourne shell script *retrieve.local* either in *.bin* (for all lists) or in an individual list's directory. *retrieve.local* is sourced into *arch_retrieve* and therefore shouldn't use `exit` and should be careful about changing variables. Example 11-3 contains an example of a *retrieve.local* that adds an `index` command that behaves exactly like SmartList's `ls` command.

Example 11-3: Adding New Commands to the Archive Server

```
#!/bin/sh

# This script provides an example on how to extend the default archive
# server with your own custom commands (for more info, look in the
# .bin/arch_retrieve script).  For this to work, you should put this
# script in the .bin directory or the directory of a list itself.

# Since this script is sourced, and not executed, environment changes
# will be propagated back to the arch_retrieve script; also, you should
# not "exit" from this script, since that will exit arch_retrieve as well.

# $1 contains the command.
# $* contains the command + arguments (already expanded inside the archive
# directory).
# $line contains the original unexpanded command line.
# $maxfiles can be queried.
# $ILLEGAL can be set to first illegal filename encountered.
# $from contains the mail address of the sender.
# $tmpfrom is the name of the transaction logfile.
# $tmprequest is the name of the file containing the original mail.

# If a command has been found, you have to use "set" to clear $1
# afterward, so as to notify the arch_retrieve script.

# Here's an example of adding an "index" command that does the same
# thing as "ls". In fact, the "ls" entry is just copied from
# arch_retrieve here, and placed inside the case "$1" statement.
```

Example 11-3: Adding New Commands to the Archive Server (continued)

```
# Also, a "set" command is included at the end.

case "$1" in
      index|INDEX)
            shift
            # Prevent illegal pathnames
            case "$*" in
              *[/\ ]..[/\ ]*|..[/\ ]*|*[/\ ]..|..|[-/]*|*\ /*)
                  $echo "$from ILLEGAL ls $line" >>$tmpfrom
                  $test -z "$ILLEGAL" && ILLEGAL="$line";;
              *)
                  #
                  # Log the archive request
                  #
                  $touch tmp.lock
                  $echo "$from ls $line" >>$tmpfrom
                    ( $formail -rt -I"Subject: archive retrieval: ls $1" \
                      -i"From: $listreq" -A"X-Loop: $listaddr" \
 -i"Reply-To: Write.a.new.mail.instead.of.replying@FIRST.WORD.archive" \
                      -i"Content-ID: <$line%$listreq>" \
                      -I"Precedence: bulk" <$tmprequest
                  $test ! -z "$wrongaddress" && $echo "$wrongaddress"
                  cd $archivedir
                  #
                  # Anything echo'd to stdout gets mailed back.
                  #
                  $echo "ls -l $line"
                  $echo "BEGIN---------------cut here------------------"
                  $ls -lL "$@" 2>&1 | $sed -e $breakoff_ls'a\
Truncating after '$breakoff_ls' names...' -e ${breakoff_ls}q
                  $echo "END----------------cut here---------------"
                  ) | $SENDMAIL $sendmailOPT -t
                  $sleep $waitsleep ;;
            esac ;;
 set ;; # And clear the command line to notify arch_retrieve

esac
```

Peer Lists

True to its philosophy of "small and simple," SmartList supports peer lists in a straightforward manner. Peer lists are simply subscribed to one another by adding each list's address into the other's *dist* file. The *dist* file for *product-support@yoyos.com* would include this line:

Other subscribers
product-support-au@yoyos.co.au

The *dist* file for *product-support@yoyos.co.au* would include this line:

```
Other subscribers
product-support@yoyos.com
```

When a message is sent to *product-support@yoyos.com*, copies are distributed to the American subscribers to `product-support-au@yoyos.co.au`. SmartList adds an X-Loop header identifying the source of the message to each outgoing message:

```
X-Loop: product-support@yoyos.com
```

When the copy reaches *product-support-au*, it is distributed to the Australian subscribers, and a copy is sent back to *product-support@yoyos.com* with an additional X-Loop header added:

```
X-Loop: product-support@yoyos.com
X-Loop: product-support-au@yoyos.co.au
```

When `product-support` receives the message, it notes this is a message that it has already distributed (because it contains an `X-Loop: product-support@yoyos.com` header), and ignores it completely.

The SmartList peer lists do loop messages back to the original peer, but, as long as the X-Loop headers remain intact, the original peer knows not to redistribute the messages. This system is less efficient than Listproc; the messages pass between the lists twice, instead of once.*

---

* Because SmartList relies on the X-Loop header, you must be careful when setting up more than two list peers. Peers must be arranged in a *tree* topology without loops, or some subscribers will receive multiple copies of messages. For example, you can connect list *a* to list *b* and list *b* to list *c* as peers, but don't also make lists *a* and *c* peers.

12

Administering LISTSERV Lite

LISTSERV Lite is among the most complex and powerful of the free MLMs available for Unix. Like Listproc, it's ideal for busy lists. It's actively developed, includes a web interface, and offers remote list management capabilities on a par with Majordomo.

This chapter examines the installation, configuration, and operation of LISTSERV Lite in detail. LISTSERV Lite is a simplified version of LISTSERV Classic, L-Soft's well-known commercial MLM. LISTSERV Lite is free for noncommercial use, but is limited to serving 10 mailing lists of up to 500 subscribers. At the time of this writing, the current version of LISTSERV Lite was 1.8c; 1.8d was available as a beta release. Some of the important new features 1.8d will include are:

- A fully functional web interface, including administrative functions and access to private, password-protected archives. The web interface is only partially functional in 1.8c; if this feature is important to you, consider waiting for 1.8d or trying the beta version.

- A "change of address" request.

- HTML indexes and digests.

- The ability to review subscribers by subscription date.

What's Different in LISTSERV Classic?

Some of the features available in LISTSERV Classic but not in LISTSERV Lite include:

*   Support for multiple moderators.

*   Peered lists and the ability to distribute messages efficiently by passing them to remote LISTSERV sites for delivery.

*   Lists can have "topics", signified by special keywords in the Subject header, and subscribers can choose which topics they wish to receive.

*   Junk mail, or spam, can be identified and weeded out.

*   Enhanced handling of bouncing messages.

*   The ability to add your own programs to LISTSERV's flow of operations.

*   Additional subscription options, hierarchical archives, and access to databases.

Overview of Operations

The server administrator uses the *go* program to start the LISTSERV Lite server daemon, *lsv. lsv*, and child processes that it forks, handle requests formatted in Command Job Language (CJL). When a request directs *lsv* to distribute mail to list subscribers, it calls *sendmail* to handle the actual delivery.

Users communicate with the LISTSERV Lite server by sending email to the *listserv@host* address. The server administrator creates mail aliases for each mailing list and for *listserv*. Mail sent to these aliases is piped to the *lsv_amin* program, which converts it to CJL, saves it in a spool area, and sends a signal to *lsv* to alert it that mail is waiting to be processed.

LISTSERV Lite can also be accessed by the server administrator with the *lcmd* utility and by users over the Web.

Figure 12-1 shows the relationships between the LISTSERV Lite programs.

Preparing to Install LISTSERV Lite

LISTSERV Lite is extremely powerful and configurable, but at the cost of a fairly complex installation and configuration. Root access is required to set up the *listserv* user and to add mailing list aliases to *sendmail*'s *aliases* file.

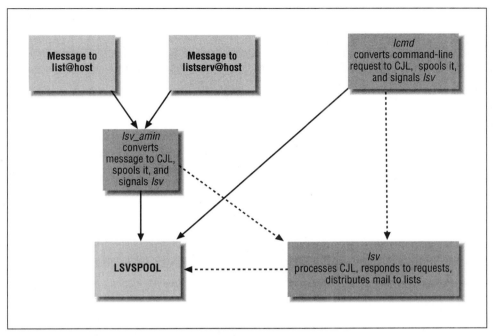

Figure 12-1: Calling relationship among the LISTSERV Lite programs

The LISTSERV installation guide strongly suggests using *sendmail* 8.7 or later with LISTSERV. Earlier versions of *sendmail* aren't capable of the efficient and rapid delivery of the later versions.

Setting Up the Server User

LISTSERV Lite requires a separate account, *listserv*, which runs its processes. The server account can be created the way you'd create any new account on your system. LISTSERV Lite is installed into the server's home directory. This chapter assumes that you're going to install LISTSERV Lite into the */home/listserv* directory, which is the default. The entry in */etc/passwd* for the server user should look like:*

```
listserv:A1AHACIb1MdTq:150:150:LISTSERV Lite:/home/listserv:/bin/csh
```

It's also helpful (although not necessary) to establish a LISTSERV Lite group. The */etc/group* entry should look something like:

```
listserv:*:150:listserv
```

---

* If your system uses shadow passwords, the encrypted password won't appear in */etc/passwd*. The other fields should be similar.

The *listserv* account can be set up to use any shell; choose your favorite.

Getting LISTSERV Lite

Once the *listserv* account is established, log in as *listserv* and create a temporary directory to hold the preinstalled files. Then download the LISTSERV Lite source code from *ftp.lsoft.com* by anonymous FTP. The files are in */LISTSERV-Lite/UNIX/*; you have to select the distribution that matches your operating system. Versions are available for AIX, BSDi, HP/UX, Irix, Linux, Digital Unix, SCO Unix, Solaris86, Solaris 2.x, SunOS 4.1.x, and Ultrix.

LISTSERV Lite is distributed as a compressed *tar* archive. To unpack it, use the *uncompress* and *tar* programs. Unpack it in a temporary directory:

```
% mkdir tmp
% cd tmp
% ftp ftp.lsoft.com
  Once the file is downloaded...
% uncompress SunOS-Lite.tar.Z
% mkdir home
% tar xf SunOS-Lite.tar
% rm SunOS-Lite.tar
```

The mkdir home step is necessary because the *tar* files for some of the distributions are built incorrectly and do not create the *home* directory the distribution needs for some of its files.

Compiling and Installing

The source code for the core of LISTSERV Lite is not distributed. Instead, source code stubs for programs are linked with a precompiled *lsv.o* object file. This limits your ability to modify the operation of LISTSERV Lite, but makes compilation simple.* All steps but one are performed as the *listserv* user:

1. Edit *Makefile* to define compilation options.

2. Optionally edit *lsv_amin.c*.

3. Compile the various system components.

4. Install the system with *make install*.

5. As *root*, set up the *listserv* mail aliases.

Each of these steps is described in greater detail in the following sections. More information can be found in the Unix installation document, *u-install.memo*, also

---

* In fact, if you're willing to accept the default directory and file locations, you can use the precompiled executables and skip compiling at all. Because the defaults may not be suitable for everyone, however, I suggest recompiling the executables anyway.

available on the Web at *http://www.lsoft.com/unixinst.html*. Other LISTSERV manuals are available at *http://www.lsoft.com/manuals/index.html*.

Editing the Makefile

Because the LISTSERV Lite distributions are already tailored to particular flavors of Unix, little needs to be changed in the *Makefile*. Here are the few variables that are worth a look:

BINDIR

> BINDIR should be set to the directory in which to install LISTSERV Lite's command-line interface program, *lcmd*. *lcmd* lets you send commands to LISTSERV Lite without having to send email to the *listserv* address. By default, BINDIR is set to */usr/local/bin*. If other users on your host don't need to access *lcmd*, it may be better to create a new directory (e.g., */home/listserv/bin*) and set BINDIR to point there.

LSVROOT

> Set LSVROOT to the directory in which LISTSERV Lite should be installed. By default, this is */home/listserv*. You might prefer to store these files in a subdirectory, however. I'll assume that you've created */home/listserv/root* and set LSVROOT to that directory.

LSVSPOOL

> LISTSERV Lite spools incoming messages in the LSVSPOOL directory. By default, this is a subdirectory under LSVROOT called *spool*.

LSVNAME

> Set LSVNAME to the *listserv* user name, usually *listserv*.

ALIASES

> ALIASES should be set to the full path to the *sendmail aliases* file.

LSVAMIN_TYPE

> LSVAMIN_TYPE determines how the *lsv_amin* program should be called from list aliases. It can be set to either flags or links. If LSVAMIN_TYPE is flags, *aliases* looks like this:

```
mylist: "/home/listserv/root/lsv_amin -t mylist"
```

> If LSVAMIN_TYPE is links, *aliases* looks like this:

```
mylist: "/home/listserv/root/mylist"
```

In this case, */home/listserv/root/mylist* is a symbolic link to *lsv_amin*. Unless you're using *Zmailer* as your MTA, stick with the default flags option.

Optionally Edit lsv_amin.c

lsv_amin.c is the source code for the *lsv_amin* program, through which incoming mail is piped. As distributed, it's suitable for systems running *sendmail* or *Zmailer*. You may have to modify it if you use a different MTA.

lsv_amin uses the *syslog* system logging facility to log status and error messages. By default, it uses the `LOG_MAIL` logging facility. You can change it to use another logging facility by changing the line that reads:

```
#define LOG_FACILITY LOG_MAIL
```

Compiling the System Components

To compile LISTSERV Lite, you perform a series of **make** commands:

% **make mailer**	*Builds lsv_amin*
% **make lcmd**	*Builds lcmd*
% **make server**	*Builds lsv*

Installing the System

To install the system, simply use **make install**.

Setting Up the listserv Aliases

Before you proceed to customize your installation, you can take advantage of a simple way to set up the *listserv* and *owner-listserv* aliases. As *root*, use *make aliases*. The following aliases are added to the end of your *aliases* file:

```
# -- Aliases for LISTSERV server
listserv: "|/home/listserv/bin/lsv_amin -t listserv"
owner-listserv: "|/home/listserv/bin/lsv_amin -t owner-listserv"
```

The *make aliases* script also tries to send a HUP signal to *sendmail*, to induce *sendmail* to reread its configuration files. It does so using the command:

```
kill -HUP `cat /etc/sendmail.pid`
```

On some shells, signals can't be specified by name (HUP) but must be given by number (in this case, 1). If *kill* fails for you, you can determine the *sendmail* process ID number from */etc/sendmail.pid* and issue this command by hand:

```
% kill -1 process-id
```

Most modern versions of *sendmail* don't require a HUP signal when updating *aliases*. Accordingly, you can probably ignore it if *kill* fails.

Guide to the Files

A LISTSERV Lite system, installed as described above, has a directory structure like that shown in Figure 12-2.

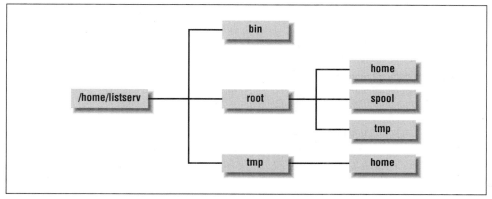

Figure 12-2: The LISTSERV Lite directory structure

Here's a quick look at what each subdirectory contains:

/home/listserv/bin

> Contains the *lcmd* and *lsv_amin* programs.

/home/listserv/root

> Holds the *lsv* program, a copy of *Makefile*, and the scripts *go*, *go.user*, and *go.sys* that are used to start LISTSERV Lite.

/home/listserv/root/home

> Holds the data files that LISTSERV Lite uses and serves as an archive for files it can send to users. The *listmast.memo* file is a guide for server administrators; *listownr.memo* is a guide for list administrators.

/home/listserv/root/spool

> A spool directory that holds incoming messages to *listserv* or mailing lists.

/home/listserv/root/tmp

> LISTSERV Lite's temporary work directory.

Once you've finished the installation, you can delete the preinstalled files and the */home/listserv/tmp* directory. Don't do this until you're sure you don't need any of the files that remain there, however, such as *wa* (the web interface).

Configuring the Server

Little initial configuration needs to be performed for a LISTSERV Lite server. Configuration options are set in the file *go.user* in the *root* directory. *go.user* is a Bourne shell script, so variables are set with a simple *VARIABLE=value* syntax. Lines beginning with a pound sign (#) are comments.

Tell LISTSERV Lite About Its Site

The NODE variable should be set to the fully qualified domain name of your site. If your site is known by more than one fully qualified name (mine is known by at least nine), MYDOMAIN can be set to a space-separated list of all the names.

LISTSERV Lite needs to know which mailing addresses are local to your site. The LOCAL variable should be set to a pattern that matches all local addresses. An asterisk (*) is a wildcard.

You can set MYORG to the name of your organization; it's included in the header of messages from LISTSERV Lite.

LISTSERV was developed in the days of BITNET, and LISTSERV Lite reflects that history. By default, it handles BITNET addresses by passing them to a mail server at L-Soft. If a mail server at your organization knows how to route BITNET addresses, you can uncomment the BITNET_ROUTE variable and set it to the name of that host. This improves the efficiency of sending mail to subscribers with BITNET addresses. You may need to check that the postmaster at your BIT-NET_ROUTE host allows mail from your site to be relayed through hers.

Tell LISTSERV Lite Who's Boss

POSTMASTER is a space-separated list of email addresses of people who are responsible for maintaining the LISTSERV Lite system. Don't include *listserv* as a maintainer!

Tell LISTSERV Lite Its Own Name

The USERID variable should be set to the name of the *listserv* user, usually *listserv*.

Establish a List-Creation Password

The list-creation password is used when you want to set up a new LISTSERV Lite mailing list. Unlike the other MLMs described in this book, list creation is performed entirely by email. Set CREATEPW to your desired list-creation password.

Set Up the Web Interface

LISTSERV Lite comes with a CGI script to allow users to access list archives and other files through the Web. If you have a web server running at your site, you can set `WWW_ARCHIVE_CGI` to the path to the *wa* CGI script (which you'll install later) and set `WWW_ARCHIVE_DIR` to a subdirectory in your web document tree where you'd like to store the list archive files. Installation of the web interface is discussed later in this chapter.

Here's what the *go.user* variables might look like for the *northpole.org* LISTSERV Lite installation:

```
NODE=northpole.org
MYDOMAIN=northpole.org santa-workshop.org
LOCAL=*@northpole.org
MYORG=Santa's Workshop
POSTMASTER=rudolph@northpole.org
USERID=listserv
CREATEPW=xmas
```

The list is at *northpole.org* (also know as *santa-workshop.org*), and all email addresses ending in *northpole.org* are local. The Organization header of LISTSERV Lite messages contains "Santa's Workshop." The server administrator is *rudolph@northpole.org.** The LISTSERV Lite user is *listserv*, and the list-creation password is *xmas*.

Starting and Stopping the Server

Once you've configured the *go.user* script, you can start the LISTSERV Lite server (*lsv*) by running the *go* script as the *listserv* user from the *listserv/root* directory. To start the server operating in the background, use *./go bg*. When LISTSERV Lite is started in the background, its output is sent to the file *listserv.log*. Here's what the log file from the first startup looks like:

```
9 Oct 1997 21:10:22 LISTSERV(R) for unix version 1.8c starting...
9 Oct 1997 21:10:22 Copyright L-Soft international 1986-1997
9 Oct 1997 21:10:22 SIGNUP data is being re-hashed...
9 Oct 1997 21:10:22 SIGNUP files are being compressed...
9 Oct 1997 21:10:22 -> No entry removed.
9 Oct 1997 21:10:22 Host name changed - network tables must be rebuilt.
9 Oct 1997 21:10:22 The peers tables are being rebuilt...
9 Oct 1997 21:10:22 File peers.namesum has been rebuilt.
9 Oct 1997 21:10:22 Nearest backbone host is LISTSERV@SWGATE.LSOFT.COM
9 Oct 1997 21:10:22 Initialization complete.
9 Oct 1997 21:10:22 License merged successfully:
```

---

* "Then one foggy Christmas Eve, Santa came to say ... 'Rudolph, with your nose so bright, won't you set up LISTSERV Lite?'"

```
> LISTSERV-LITEFE-UNIX
>           UNITS=10
>           EXP=NEVER
>           REL=1.8d
>           OPT=NONE
>           SCOPE=MAXSUB(500),PERLIST
>           SERIAL=FREE-EDITION-UNIX;728996
 A long banner describing the license agreement
 9 Oct 1997 21:10:24 Generating daily nondelivery monitoring reports...
 9 Oct 1997 21:10:24 Rebuilding WWW archive files...
 9 Oct 1997 21:10:25 WWW archive files updated.
 9 Oct 1997 21:10:25 Press Ctrl-C at any time to enter a command
```

Once the server is started, you can issue commands by using the *lcmd* program in
the *bin* subdirectory. To stop the server, log in to the *listserv* account and from the
home directory, use *bin/lcmd stop*. An email message in response to the stop command is sent to the addresses defined as **POSTMASTER** in *root/go.user*.

To start the LISTSERV Lite server whenever your system reboots, add a line like
this to your startup files (*/etc/rc.local* on BSD Unix systems, or one of the files in
/etc/rc2.d on System V Unix systems):

```
/bin/su - listserv -c "/home/listserv/root/go bg"
```

Adding Lists

Now you're ready to start adding lists to the server. The list owner may let you
know how she wants the list to operate, or you may have to make some of the
decisions yourself. Here's a step-by-step look at how to add a list, using the *nice-
children* list from Chapter 6, *Maintaining Lists with LISTSERV Lite*, as an example.
Note that unlike the other MLMs discussed in this book, list creation, like all other
list operations, is performed remotely by email. Only adding MTA aliases requires
access to the host machine.

Creating a List Header

To create a LISTSERV Lite list, you submit a "list header" to *listserv*. The list header
describes how the list functions. The syntax of the header is straightforward. Every
line must begin with an asterisk (*). The first line is a description of the list. Lines
thereafter can contain one or more header keywords, followed by an equal sign,
optional white space, and the value of the keyword (*keyword= value*). There
are keywords to control all aspects of the list's operation, and for the most part,
these functions can be configured by the list owner and are covered in Chapter 6.
Here's a rundown on the most common things you need to do with keywords.

Defining the list owners

The `Owner` keyword should be set to the email address of the list owner. The keyword can be used repeatedly to define multiple list owners. The special value `Quiet:` signifies that subsequent owners should not receive error messages generated by the list. A typical header might include lines like this:

```
* Owner= listowner@remotehost
* Owner= Quiet:
* Owner= serveradministrator@listservhost
```

Determining how errors are handled

LISTSERV Lite can be configured to receive and process bounced email, optionally removing users whose email addresses no longer work.

The `Auto-Delete` keyword turns automatic removal on (`Auto-Delete= Yes`) or off (`Auto-Delete= No`). When automatic removal is on, LISTSERV Lite automatically unsubscribes users whose email addresses bounce with hard errors and passes soft bounces on to the list owner.

The `Errors-To` keyword determines who receives copies of error messages sent to list users. It defaults to `Postmaster`—the server administrator—and probably should be changed to `Owners`, the list owners.

Setting a few security options

The `Confidential` option controls whether the list is hidden from the `LIST` request (`Confidential= Yes`) or not (`Confidential= No`). No is the default.

The `Validate` keyword protects users and list owners from other people modifying their list settings or issuing list requests on their behalf. Here are the values it can take:

`No` No protection. This is the default and is suitable for most casual mailing lists.

`Yes`

> Specifies that requests other than `SUBSCRIBE` and `SET` use a password (given as `PW=password` at the end of the request) or obtain the approval of the list owner. Users can set personal passwords with the `PW ADD password` request. Note that the `UNSUBSCRIBE` request is one of those that requires a password or approval, so leaving the list becomes less convenient. This method also relies on the secrecy of passwords.

`Yes,Confirm`

> Most requests result in LISTSERV Lite sending a confirmation message to the user's email address. When the user replies to the confirmation message, the

request is run. However, passwords are also accepted in requests, and pass-worded requests circumvent the confirmation process.

`Yes,Confirm,NoPW`

Most requests result in confirmation messages. Passwords are no longer accepted. This is a highly secure operation mode, and I recommend it for lists where security is a concern.

`All,Confirm`

Like `Yes,Confirm`, but all requests except `PUT` and purely informational requests require validation by password or confirmation message.

`All,Confirm,NoPW`

Like `Yes,Confirm,NoPW`, but all requests except `PUT` and purely informational requests require validation by confirmation message.

`PUT` is an exception to the `Validate` rules; it must always be accompanied by a password.

Putting it all together

The header file for *nice-children@northpole.org* might look like this:

```
* A list for conversation between nice children
*
* Owner= santa@northpole.org
* Owner= Quiet:
* Owner= rudolph@northpole.org
* Owner= mrsclaus@northpole.org
* Subscription= Open,Confirm
* Filter= Also,*@*naughty.com
* Auto-Delete= Yes
* Errors-To= Owners
* Reply-To= Sender,Respect
* Validate= Yes,Confirm,NoPW
*
```

The list is owned by *santa*, *rudolph*, and *mrsclaus*, but only *santa* receives list error messages. The list password is *hohoho*. The list is open, but requires confirmation of subscriptions. Users from *naughty.com* may not subscribe. The SMTP From header points back to the list, and bouncing email addresses are automatically removed from the subscriber list. Copies of error messages are sent to the list owner. The Reply-To header contains the sender's address, but an existing Reply-To header is respected and passed on without modification. Requests that affect users must be confirmed.

Sending the List Header to listserv

Once you've got the list header in a file, you need to send it to *listserv*, prefaced by a PUT request. PUT is used to store files in the *listserv/root/home* directory. List definitions (including subscriber addresses and settings) are stored in files called `listname.LIST`. To create the list, you use PUT to store your list header as this file. For *nice-children*, the list-creation message looks like this:

```
From: rudolph@northpole.org
To: listserv@northpole.org
Subject: Making a list

put nice-children.list pw=xmas
* A list for conversation between nice children
*
* Owner= santa@northpole.org
etc.
```

The password used in the PUT command must be the list-creation password (CREATEPW) you set in *go.user*, and the command must be sent from an address that LISTSERV Lite recognizes as a POSTMASTER.

If the list header is all correct, LISTSERV Lite responds with an acknowledgment that the list has been created. If not, the response indicates where the error in the list header is.

Adding Aliases for the List to the MTA

LISTSERV Lite requires each list to have a number of aliases set up in your MTA's *aliases* file. Fortunately, the process is very easy. As *root*, use `make list name=listname` from the *listserv/root* directory:

```
% cd root
% su
# make list name=nice-children
```

The *Makefile* runs a series of commands to add aliases for the list and rebuild the *aliases* database. The resulting aliases look like this:

```
# -- Aliases for 'nice-children' mailing list
nice-children: "|/home/listserv/bin/lsv_amin -t nice-children"
owner-nice-children: \
  "|/home/listserv/bin/lsv_amin -t owner-nice-children"
nice-children-request: \
  "|/home/listserv/bin/lsv_amin -t nice-children-request"
nice-children-server: \
  "|/home/listserv/bin/lsv_amin -t nice-children-server"
```

Each alias pipes mail to *lsv_amin* along with the name of the alias. Mail to *nice-children* is saved to the *spool* directory with CJL instructions to process it as list mail. Mail to *owner-nice-children* is saved with instructions to forward it to the list owner. Mail for *nice-children-request* is treated similarly, but the sender also receives a message explaining that administrative requests are handled by the *listserv* address. Mail to *nice-children-server* is saved with instructions to treat the mail as requests to LISTSERV Lite.

You may also find a *-search-request* alias. This alias is used for LISTSERV database searching. LISTSERV Lite doesn't support the LISTSERV database functions, so you can safely remove this alias from your *aliases* file.

Informing the List Owner

Finally, tell the list owner the list's name and address. Remind the owner to subscribe to the list, and to use the **PUT** request to submit a *listname.welcome* and possibly a *listname.farewell* file.

Any list owner can modify the list's configuration by requesting a copy of the list's header file, editing it, and sending it back to *listserv*. To request a copy of the header file, the list owner sends the following request:

```
GET listname (header PW=password
```

LISTSERV Lite sends back a file containing:

*   The **PUT** command required to send the header back (password missing)

*   The list header itself*

Here's what the response to **GET nice-children (header** looks like:

```
From: "L-Soft list server at NORTHPOLE (1.8c)" <LISTSERV@NORTHPOLE.ORG>
Subject:       File: "NICE-CHILDREN LIST"
To: Santa Claus <santa@NORTHPOLE.ORG>

PUT NICE-CHILDREN LIST PW=XXXXXXXX
* A list for conversation between nice children
*
* Owner= santa@northpole.org
* Owner= Quiet:
* Owner= rudolph@northpole.org
* Owner= mrsclaus@northpole.org
* PW= hohoho
* Subscription= Open,Confirm
* Filter= Also,*@*naughty.com
* Auto-Delete= Yes
* Errors-To= Owners
```

---

* If you leave out the "**(header**" in the **GET** request, the list header is followed by a list of subscribers and their settings, in a strange encoded format. Don't attempt to modify or send back the subscriber list! It's easy to make a mistake and thoroughly disrupt your list. Use "**(header**"; it's safer.

```
* Reply-To= Sender,Respect
* Validate= Yes,Confirm,NoPW
*
```

To update the list header, edit the message. Replace the **XXXXXXX** with your personal password.* Send the resulting PUT request back to *listserv*.

After you GET the header, the header file is locked to prevent another list owner from modifying it at the same time. If you choose not to update the list header, send an UNLOCK *listname* request to *listserv*. The UNLOCK request is important; new subscriptions aren't allowed while a list is locked.

LISTSERV Lite backs up the current header when you PUT a new one. If you make a mistake and need to retrieve the old header, use GET *listname*.LIST (old to have the old header emailed to you. You can then PUT it back to restore it.

Archives

LISTSERV Lite is not only a list server but also a file server. LISTSERV Lite archives can contain mail messages or any other text files. Archive access can be permitted to anyone, list members, list owners, particular users, or any combination.

LISTSERV Lite associates a file alias with each file in the archive. Files are retrieved by their file aliases, not their true filenames. Aliases aren't case-sensitive and must contain a period. For example, the Frequently Asked Questions document for the *nice-children* list might be associated with the alias *nice-children.faq*.

The archived files themselves can be stored in any directory to which the *listserv* user has read and write access. Filenames, like aliases, must contain a period; moreover, they must be lowercase. LISTSERV Lite works best if directory names do *not* contain periods.†

The examples below assume that you've set up an *archives* directory beneath */home/listserv*, with a subdirectory for each list beneath. That is, files for the *nice-children* list are kept in the directory */home/listserv/archives/nice-children*.

LISTSERV Lite can automatically archive list messages and can also archive other text files. We'll look at each of these in turn.

---

* For some operations, such as turning archiving on, the list-creation password, known only to the server administrator, must be used instead. This ensures that only the server administrator can determine directories in which the list looks for archived files.

† The strange rules about periods are due to LISTSERV's historical development on IBM VM mainframes, where filenames are sometimes referred to as NAME.EXTENSION.DISK, and there are no subdirectories. If you need to access a file in a directory path that contains a period (e.g., */usr.local/myfiles/a.file*), you must refer to it as *a.file./usr.local/myfiles*, or LISTSERV assumes the file's name is */usr*, its extension is *local/myfiles/a*, and it's in the directory *file*.

Archiving List Messages Automatically

The NOTEBOOK keyword in the list header controls whether and how list messages are archived. Its default value is No, which disables archiving. To enable archiving for a list, add the line below to the list header:*

```
* Notebook= Yes,location,frequency,access
```

location can be either the name of the directory in which to store the list archives (preferred), or the special value A, which refers to the *home* directory beneath the *listserv/root* directory. For *nice-children*, the appropriate location is */home/listserv/archives/nice-children*.

frequency determines how the archive is organized. It can be:

single
   Archive all messages in a single file *listname.notebook*.

yearly
   Archive by year in files with names such as *listname.log98*, *listname.log99*, etc.

monthly
   Archive by month in files like *listname.log9801*, *listname.log9802*, etc.

weekly
   Archive by week in files like *listname.log9801a*, *listname.log9801b*, etc.

separate
   Archive each message in its own file, with names like *listname.98-0001*, *listname.98-0002*, etc.

If you plan to allow web access to the archives, you must use yearly, monthly, or weekly archives. Our *nice-children* list is archived yearly.

access determines who can search and retrieve files from the archive. It can be:

public
   Anyone may access.

postmaster
   Only the server administrator may access.

private
   List subscribers may access.

---

* The server administrator's list-creation password is always necessary in order to enable archiving, even on an existing list.

`owner`

    The list owner may access.

`(`*`listname`*`)`

    Subscribers of *listname* may access.

`owner(`*`listname`*`)`

    The owners of *listname* may access.

`private`, `owner`, `(`*`listname`*`)`, and `owner(`*`listname`*`)` can be used together in any combination.

Our *nice-children* list is `private`. Here's what the NOTEBOOK keyword for *nice-children* looks like:

```
* Notebook= Yes,/home/listserv/archives/nice-children,Yearly,Private
```

Archiving Files Manually

You can also manually archive any text file (to archive a binary file, first encode it as text using *uuencode*). Here are the steps to add files to the LISTSERV Lite archive:

1. Log in to the *listserv* account and change to *root/home*.

2. Edit the file *site.catalog*. Each line in the file lists a file alias, its associated filename, who may retrieve the file, and who may update the the file:

    ```
    NICE-CHILDREN.FAQ /home/listserv/archives/nice-children/nc.faq ALL
    OWNER(nice-children)
    ```

    The filename must be a full path to the file. The permissions for getting or updating are each comma-separated lists of the values `ALL` (anyone may access), `PRIVATE(`*`listname`*`)` (subscribers to *listname* may access), `OWNER(`*`listname`*`)` (owners of *listname* may access), `NOTE-BOOK(`*`listname`*`)` (whoever could access *listname*'s archive may access), and specific user email addresses.

3. Put the files in the appropriate archive directories.

4. Test your archive by sending mail to LISTSERV Lite with commands like:

    ```
    index                    List the files in the archive
    get nice-children.faq    Get one
    ```

LISTSERV Classic supports hierarchies of archives, so you can establish an archive for each list and let list owners manage their own archives. LISTSERV Lite, however, supports only a sitewide archive that must be maintained by the server administrator. You can keep things organized by maintaining separate directories for each list's archive files, and by consistently using the list name as the first part of file aliases for files associated with the list (*NICE-CHILDREN.FAQ, NICE-CHILDREN.SANTAS-FAVORITE-COOKIES*, etc.).

The Web Interface

LISTSERV Lite includes its own CGI script, *wa*, which allows subscribers to access LISTSERV Lite over the Web. From their browser, subscribers can request personal passwords, send messages to lists, read list archives, subscribe to or unsubscribe from lists, and change mail options.*

Setting Up the Web Interface

The web interface isn't difficult to set up, but requires some careful attention to permissions. Here's a checklist for setting up the web interface:

1. Install the *wa* program in your web server's *cgi-bin* directory. *wa* can be found with the preinstalled files. Make *wa* setuid to the listserv user. As *root*:

   ```
   # cd /home/listserv/tmp
   # cp wa /webserver/cgi-bin
   # chown listserv /webserver/cgi-bin/wa
   # chmod 4755 /webserver/cgi-bin/wa
   ```

2. Decide where the web pages that LISTSERV Lite creates should reside. LIST-SERV Lite must have read and write access to this directory. Obviously, the web server must have read access to this directory as well. LISTSERV Lite assumes that this directory is called *archives* and is at the URL *http://yourhost/archives*, but for our example, let's use *listserv* as the name of our subdirectory. If your web server's document tree is rooted at */webserver/htdocs*, you might create a subdirectory */webserver/htdocs/listserv* like:

   ```
   # mkdir /webserver/htdocs/listserv
   # chown listserv /webserver/htdocs/listserv
   # chmod 755 /webserver/htdocs/listserv
   ```

3. Decide which lists should be accessible from the Web. For each list that should be accessible, create a subdirectory under the directory you just made:

   ```
   # cd /webserver/htdocs/listserv
   # mkdir nice-children
   # chown listserv nice-children
   # chmod 755 nice-children
   ```

---

* The web interface is distributed with LISTSERV Lite 1.8c, but is only partially functional; for example, posting doesn't work correctly. A working web interface is distributed with LISTSERV Lite 1.8d, now in beta. It also allows list owners to manage their lists through the Web.

4. Create the file */etc/lsv-wa.config*. This file tells LISTSERV Lite where the top of your LISTSERV web tree is and how it's accessed by URL. It looks like this:

```
PATH /webserver/htdocs/listserv
URL /listserv
```

The `PATH` statement is followed by the path to the top of the LISTSERV web tree. `URL` is followed by the URL that brings up this directory, relative to *http://yourhost*.

5. Edit *root/go.user* and set the values of `WWW_ARCHIVE_CGI` and `WWW_ARCHIVE_DIR`. `WWW_ARCHIVE_CGI` is the relative URL to the *wa* CGI script. Usually, it is */cgi-bin/wa*. `WWW_ARCHIVE_DIR` is the same directory you used for `PATH` in */etc/lsv-wa.config*.

6. If you didn't use */archives* as your URL, edit *root/home/default.mailtpl*. *default.mailtpl* contains templates for email messages and web pages generated by LISTSERV Lite. Replace the three references to */archives* with */listserv*.

7. Stop and restart the LISTSERV Lite server. As *listserv*:

```
% cd /home/listserv
% bin/lcmd stop
% cd root
% ./go bg
```

Testing the Web Interface

You should now be able to access your lists through the Web. Point your web browser at *http://yourhost/listserv/*. You should see a page that lists each of the lists that you've made accessible. Following a link to a list should bring up a page that lets you read the list's archives or post to the list (once you've established a personal password).

WARNING | Although the web interface enforces the same privacy rules that the email interface does, it may be possible for people to access archives of closed lists directly through the Web by pointing their browser at *http://yourhost/listserv/closed-list-name/*. Check your web server documentation to see how to prevent access to subdirectories of the */webserver/htdocs/listserv* directory. For the Apache web server, you might add something like this to *access.conf*:

```
<Directory /webserver/htdocs/listserv/*>
Options None
AllowOverride None
Order deny,allow
deny from all
</Directory>
```

Daily Maintenance and Troubleshooting

LISTSERV Lite largely takes care of itself. When something goes wrong, however, there are a few places you can look to try to diagnose the problem.

The Log File

As you continue to run LISTSERV Lite, you should periodically check the log file, *root/listserv.log*. The file can be particularly helpful when you experience problems with LISTSERV Lite. Old log files are archived in *root/listserv.log.OLD*. The LIST-SERV Site Manager's Manual (*root/home/listmast.memo*) includes an entire chapter on how to interpret the LISTSERV logs. Because LISTSERV Lite uses *sendmail* as its delivery agent, the *sendmail* logs may also be helpful.

The Mail Spool

When LISTSERV Lite can't deliver a message, it leaves a copy of the message in a numbered file in its *root/spool* directory. This directory also holds the file *listserv.PID*, which contains the process ID number for the top-level *lsv* process, and the program *jobview. jobview* can be used to examine *.job* files in the *spool* directory; *.job* files are machine-readable files that LISTSERV Lite creates while it's working. Other types of files also appear in the *spool* directory; see *root/home/listmast.memo* for details.

A

Listproc Reference

Subscribers can retrieve extensive help on list requests from Listproc. Listproc also provides complete information for server administrators in the manual pages distributed with it. This appendix summarizes this information. It also provides a guide to the directories and files in a Listproc installation and the Listproc configuration directives.

User Commands

User commands don't require the list owner's password.

General Commands

General commands can be used by anyone, whether or not they are subscribed to a list, though some lists may restrict these commands to subscribers:

help [*command*]
> Request a help message listing commands or for a given command.

lists
> Request the list addresses and descriptions of lists served by the Listproc. Lists may be concealed from this request.

info *listname*
> Request the list's information file.

recipients *listname*
> Request a list of subscribers' email addresses. Subscribers may conceal themselves from this request. On some lists, only subscribers may issue this request. review does the same thing.

`statistics `*`listname email-addresses`*` | -all`

Request a report of the number of postings made by the given email addresses (or all subscribers if `-all` is given). Subscribers may conceal themselves from this request. On some lists, only subscribers may issue this request.

`release`

Request to know the version number of the Listproc software.

Subscriber Commands

Subscriber commands are used to subscribe to the list or are restricted to list subscribers:

`subscribe `*`listname fullname`*

Subscribe to mailing list *`listname`*. *`fullname`* is the subscriber's full name. If the list is private, subscription requests are forwarded to the list owner.

`unsubscribe `*`listname`*

Unsubscribe from a list. `signoff` also works.

`set `*`listname [option value]`*

Sets a list option for a subscriber, or, if no option is given, shows the subscriber's current option settings. Options and their values are:

address

Changes the subscriber's subscription address. The value of this option should be the subscriber's current password followed by their desired address. This option may not be allowed for some lists.

conceal

Controls whether the subscriber is concealed from **recipients** and **statistics** requests. Can be set to **yes** (conceal yourself) or **no** (don't conceal yourself).

mail

Controls how mail is received from the list. Can be set to **ack** (receive messages individually and receive copies of your own messages as well), **noack** (receive messages individually, but don't receive copies of your own messages), **digest** (receive messages as digests), or **postpone** (don't receive any messages until you reset your mail option).

password

Followed by the subscriber's current password and desired password, changes the password to the desired password.

`which`

Request to know to which lists you have subscribed.

```
run listname [password command [arguments]]
```
> Given the correct command password for *command*, execute the command and return the output. If no password and command are given, list all commands that subscribers may execute. Commands are usually external Unix programs.

Archive Commands

Archive commands let users search archives and retrieve files. Archives may be password-protected; if an archive is password-protected, archive requests must include the password, preceded by a slash (/). In addition, archives are hierarchically structured. Commands that accept the argument -all can operate on an archive and all of its subarchives.

```
index archive [/password] [-all]
```
> Request an index of the files in a given *archive*, which may be specified by name or, if many archives have the same name, by its unique path from the master archive.

```
search archive [/password] [-all] 'pattern'
```
> Search files in *archive* for files containing *pattern*. *pattern* is a case-insensitive *egrep* regular expression with these additional operators:

> ~ At the beginning of the pattern, reverses its meaning; shows lines that don't match the pattern.

> & Combines multiple subexpressions as a logical AND; all subexpressions must match for the expression to match.

> | Combines multiple subexpressions as a logical OR; any subexpression must match for the expression to match.

> <> Group regular expressions together.

```
get archive file [/password] [parts]
```
> Request the file *file* from *archive*. The file may be sent in multiple parts; specifying a space-separated list of *parts* sends only those parts requested. Binary files are uuencoded before being sent.

```
fax fax-number archive file [/password] [parts]
```
> Request to have *file* from *archive* faxed to *fax-number*.

List Owner Commands

These commands require the list owner password; they must come from an email address listed in the *owners* file as being an owner of the list.

`system listname password address #request`

> Execute `request` on behalf of `address`, ignoring any restrictions except that the `address` must be in the list's *.subscribers* file for subscriber commands, and the request must specify `listname` as its list.
>
> For example, to unsubscribe a user from a list:
>
> ```
> system mylist mylistpassword olduser@somewhere #unsubscribe mylist
> ```

`approve | discard listname password tag`

> If the list is moderated using *catmail*'s moderation system, *listproc* sends a copy of the message and its unique `tag` to the list owner. The owner uses the `approve` command to approve a posting to the list. The `discard` command rejects a message and removes it from the list's *moderated* file.

`reports listname password`

> Request the list's log reports. Once sent, the list's accumulated report file (*.rep.list.acc*) is cleared. This request has no effect if *syslog* is used instead of report files.

`edit listname password file`

> Request a copy of the `file` for `listname`. Valid values for `file` are: `aliases`, `ignored`, `info`, `subscribers`, `welcome`, `news`, and `peers`.

`put listname password alias alias address`

> Add an `alias` for `address` to `listname`'s *.aliases* file.

`put listname password ignore address`

> Add an `address` to be ignored in `listname`'s *.ignored* file.

`put listname password file`

> Replace `listname`'s `file` with a new version, which should be given imme- diately after the `put` request. Valid values for `file` are: `aliases`, `ignored`, `info`, `subscribers`, `welcome`, `news`, and `peers`. For example, to replace the list's *welcome* file:
>
> ```
> put mylist mylistpassword welcome
> Welcome to mylist!
> File continues here
> ```
>
> When `put` is issued by email, the rest of the email message contains the replacement text. When issued via *ilp*, use a single period on a line by itself to terminate the text.

Server Administrator Commands

Listproc has a single request that's designed for use by the server administrator:

execute *password* #*command [arguments]*

If the server administrator has defined *command* and its *password* in the *config* file, the **execute** request runs *command* and emails the results back.

Listproc Files

Figure A-1 shows the Listproc directory structure.

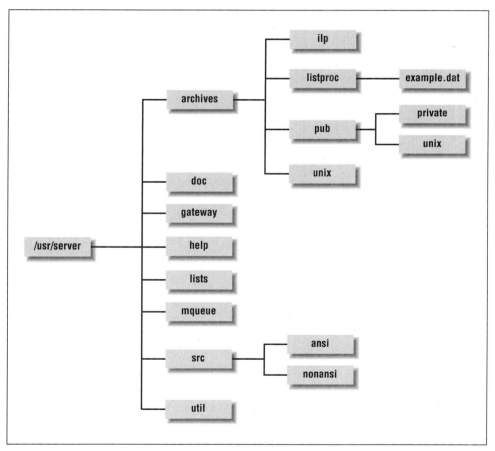

Figure A-1: The Listproc directory structure

Files in /usr/server

Many files reside in */usr/server* (or whatever directory you choose for HOMEDIR) once the system is compiled. Here's a list of the most important (see the manual page for *server* for a complete list):

.aliases

This file contains aliases for users whose incoming and outgoing email addresses may be different. For example, a subscriber who sends mail from a cluster of workstations might have SMTP From headers that include the specific workstation he used when he sent his mail (e.g., *red.cluster.foo.com*, *blue.cluster.foo.com*), but should receive email at a specific address (e.g., *cluster.foo.com*). The *.aliases* file contains a list of regular expressions to check the SMTP From header for and the corresponding subscriber address to assume.

```
^(.*)@.*\.cluster\.foo\.com$   \1@cluster.foo.com
^jsimmons@somesite\.edu$       Jane.Simmons@somesite.edu
```

The aliases in */usr/server/.aliases* are checked when mail is sent to Listproc itself. Each list directory contains its own *.aliases* file that is checked when mail is sent to a list address.

.ignored

This file lists addresses from which email should be ignored. Typically this includes the server user, to help prevent mail loops.

.message.ids

This file stores a list of recent message IDs and senders. This information is used to prevent mail loops; if the system sees a message with a matching message ID and sender, it ignores the message.

*.report.** and *.rep.*.acc*

The *.report.** files (*.report.catmail*, *.report.daemon*, *.report.list*, *.report.server*, and *.report.start*) contain current status reports logged by the Listproc programs if Listproc has not been configured to use *syslog* for logging. The *.rep.*.acc* files (*.rep.server.acc*, *.rep.serverd.acc*, and *.rep.start.acc*) contain the accumulated past status reports from those programs.

catmail

This program deposits incoming mail messages for Listproc or any of its lists into the appropriate mail box (*requests*, *lists/listname/mail*, or *lists/listname/moderated*) for later processing by the system.

config

This file is the heart of Listproc's configuration and controls the operation of Listproc. Configuration directives are explained in detail later in this appendix.

farch

This program creates file archives, and can add and remove files from archives.

ilp Listproc can be configured to allow users to connect interactively over the Internet, and perform subscription and file archive functions. The *ilp* program is the Interactive ListProcessor client.

list This program distributes email to a Listproc mailing list.

listproc

This program responds to user requests sent to the *listproc* address.

mbox

This file contains email sent to the *listproc* address.

news

This shell script creates a Usenet news connection for a list. News connections are discussed in Chapter 9, *Administering Listproc*.

owners

This file contains email addresses of the server administrator and list owners, as well as information about whether primary list owners should be notified when users issue various commands or when the list detects an error.

peer

This shell script creates a peer list. Peer lists are discussed in Chapter 9.

priv.hosts and *unwanted.hosts*

If the file *priv.hosts* exists, hosts that attempt to connect to the Interactive List-Processor must match one of the regular expressions in the file. Otherwise, if *unwanted.hosts* exists, hosts that don't match any of the regular expressions in *unwanted.hosts* are allowed to connect.

queued

This daemon runs *pqueue* at regular intervals to redeliver queued outgoing messages.

requests

This file contains email sent to *listproc* that is waiting to be processed. A similar file, *requests.live*, holds requests received from Interactive ListProcessor connections.

serverd

This program is the Listproc server daemon. It periodically runs *listproc* and *list* to manage requests and distribute list messages. On an operational Listproc system, this program is always running.

setup
>   This shell script compiles and installs Listproc.

welcome.live
>   This file is shown to users who connect to the Interactive ListProcessor using
>   *ilp*.

Files in /usr/server/archives

Each of the subdirectories in */usr/server/archives* contains information about an
archive of files that Listproc can deliver. The files themselves need not be in these
subdirectories, though they often are; Listproc can serve files from */usr/spool/ftp* or
any other directory it can access. Archives can be hierarchically organized into further subdirectories and can be private (password-protected). Archive directories
contain, at minimum, two important files:

DIR
>   This file contains a directory of all the files in the archive and where they are
>   located.

INDEX
>   This file contains a list of subarchives, the paths to their *DIR* and *INDEX* files,
>   and their passwords, if any.

The *listproc* archive is the master archive; *listproc/INDEX* gives information about
all of the archives.

WARNING   As distributed, the master archive directory */usr/server/archives/list-
                 proc/DIR* includes an entry that delivers the file */etc/service*. On most
                 Unix systems, that file doesn't exist (probably */etc/services* was
                 meant), but you don't want to deliver it if it ever does. Remove the
                 appropriate line from the *DIR* file before starting Listproc.

Files in /usr/server/doc

The */usr/server/doc* directory contains manual pages (formatted and unformatted)
for each of the Listproc programs: *catmail, farch, ilp, list, listproc, queue, server,
serverd*, and *start*.

Files in /usr/server/help

The files in */usr/server/help* are help files that Listproc users can request from the
list server. The *TOPICS* file contains a list of help topics and their corresponding
files. Help files can be added and deleted by inserting or removing lines from
TOPICS.

The help files themselves may be either plain-text files or executable scripts beginning with #!. Help scripts should direct their output to *stdout.*

Files in /usr/server/lists/<LISTNAME>

Listproc creates a subdirectory in */usr/server/lists* for each mailing list, identified by the list's name. The most important files in each list directory include:

.aliases

> Aliases for subscribers to the list. See the discussion of */usr/server/.aliases* above.

.ignored

> Mail from senders whose email addresses match one of the regular expressions in the *.ignored* file is ignored. To prevent mail loops, this file usually contains the email address of the list itself.

.info

> Listproc sends the contents of the *.info* file in response to an info request for the list.

.news and *.peers*

> The *.news* file lists newsgroups that are connected to the list. The *.peers* file lists the names of peer lists for the list and the email addresses of their Listproc servers.

.report.list and *.rep.list.acc*

> These files contain the current (*.report.list*) and accumulated (*.rep.list.acc*) status reports for the list, if *syslog* is not being used for logging.

.restricted

> If a list is set up to support restricted users (see the section on *config* file directives later in this appendix), the *.restricted* file contains a list of restricted users and either the alternate recipients file containing the subscribers who should receive mail sent by a restricted user or the word NONE, which prevents mail from that sender from being distributed. Using this feature, mail sent by different senders can be distributed to different groups of subscribers.

.subscribers

> The *.subscribers* file contains the email addresses of the list subscribers, as well as their mail mode (ACK, NOACK, DIGEST, or POSTPONE), password (for Interactive ListProcessor access), conceal setting (YES or NO), and real name.

.welcome

> Listproc sends the list's *.welcome* file to new subscribers, along with standard Listproc information.

archive

> This file contains copies of all the messages distributed to the list. It can be placed in a file archive using the *farch* program. If the list is being archived automatically, and this file isn't needed, it can be replaced by a link to */dev/null.*

mail and *moderated*

> *catmail* stores messages for unmoderated lists that are ready to be distributed in the *mail* file. Once Listproc delivers a message, it's removed from the *mail* file. If the list is moderated, newly arrived mail is held in the *moderated* file until the moderator approves the messages.

mbox

> The *mbox* file contains all the email sent to the list address. Unlike *archive*, it includes messages that weren't distributed to the list (e.g., blank messages, messages containing administrative requests, messages from mailer daemons, etc.)

removed.users and *removed.alias*

> If `ERROR_MAIL_ANALYSIS` is defined in *src/Makefile* (see Chapter 9), Listproc automatically removes subscribers from the *.subscribers* file when mail to their addresses bounce, with "User unknown," "Host unknown," or other irrecoverable errors. Listproc records removed subscribers in the *removed.users* file. Aliases for removed subscribers are also removed from the *.aliases* file and added to *removed.alias.*

Other Subdirectories

Listproc queues messages that it can't deliver in the */usr/server/mqueue* directory. This directory is usually empty. The */usr/server/src* directory contains the Listproc source code. */usr/server/util* contains some utilities and patches distributed with Listproc.

config File Directives

Each line in the *config* file controls an aspect of the server's operation. A sample *config* file is distributed with Listproc, but it needs extensive editing. Each configuration directive must be given on a single line; don't use an editor that wraps long lines when editing the *config* file. Any line beginning with a pound sign (#) is treated as a comment and ignored.

Server-Related Directives

Here are the general directives that affect the server as whole:

manager *email address*

> This directive sets the email address of the person responsible for the Listproc server. Use a full email address, including a fully qualified domain name (i.e., *kiwi@fruit.ora.com* rather that simply *kiwi* or *kiwi@fruit*). The manager receives messages from Listproc when problems occur.

mailmethod *method*

> This directive controls how Listproc delivers email. It's important that Listproc sends messages with the right SMTP From header. The SMTP From header for a message on a list should be:

    From listname@your-host

> Messages from *listproc* itself should have this SMTP From header:

    From listproc@your-host

> Each of the methods achieves this in a slightly different way.

> With the *system* method, Listproc opens a TCP socket to an SMTP server (usually the local *sendmail* daemon) and transfers outgoing mail using SMTP. This is the most reliable and efficient method, and works on almost all systems that have TCP/IP capability.

> If the system method doesn't work for some reason, but your system has a working *telnet* program, the *telnet* method can be used. It uses the *telnet* program to connect to an SMTP server.

> Finally, as a last resort, use the env_var method. It's specified as:

    mailmethod env_var LOGNAME mail-program

> where mail-program is usually either */bin/rmail* (on UUCP systems) or */usr/lib/sendmail -ba*, though other mail-delivery programs may work as well. This method works by resetting the environment variable LOGNAME to the name of the list (or *listproc*), and then using a mail program that gets the user's name from LOGNAME to deliver the mail.

server listproc@*your-host options*

> This directive gives the request address of the MLM and some options to use when the *listproc* program is run.

> The -a *LISTNAME* option makes a list private. Subscriptions to private lists are forwarded to the list owner for review. The *LISTNAME* should be in uppercase. Multiple -a options make more than one list private.

The -c *LISTNAME* option conceals a list. A concealed list doesn't appear when a user sends a `lists` request. As with -a, the *LISTNAME* should be in uppercase, and multiple -c options can be used.

The -d *request* option disables a request. Users can't use disabled requests. Multiple requests can be disabled.

The -r *request* option restricts a request to times when few users are on line. By default, restricted requests can only be used when fewer than 100 users are on line; the restriction directive, discussed below, changes this limit. The -r option is often used with the `statistics` request, which can be computationally expensive. Multiple requests can be restricted.

The -b *request* option causes the specified request to be batched. Batched requests are stored in a file and processed once a day (just after midnight) when, ideally, there are fewer demands on the host. Batched requests are disabled when using Interactive ListProcessor. Multiple requests can be batched.

The -D option turns on debugging for requests. When debugging is on, a copy of the last commands sent to the SMTP server is stored in the file *sent*, and the response of the SMTP server is stored in the file *received*.

Here's an example of a complete server directive. The list *private* is made private, the list *hidden* is concealed from the `lists` request, the `recipients` request is disabled, and the `statistics` request is restricted to times of low usage. While the directive is broken up onto two lines in the example, it should be entered as a single long line:

```
server listproc@mellers1.psych.berkeley.edu -a PRIVATE
      -c HIDDEN -d recipients -r statistics
```

restriction *number-of-users*
  This directive sets the number of users above which restricted commands are disallowed. See also the discussion of the -r option of the `server` directive above.

batch *start-hour stop-hour*
  This directive sets the hours between which batched requests (specified with the -b option in the `server` directive) are added to the batch queue, rather than processed immediately. The hours are given in 24-hour time and `start-hour` must be less than `stop-hour`. By default, batching is done between 8 A.M. and 8 P.M. To batch all requests, use `batch 0 23`.

serverd *options*
  This directive (not to be confused with the `server` directive!) controls how the Listproc server daemon runs.

If the `-i` *seconds* option is given, the Interactive ListProcessor server daemon is started.* Each interactive connection may last for a maximum of *seconds* seconds. When live connections are allowed, the welcome message sent to new subscribers by Listproc includes a list password and instructions for changing it.

The `-l` *load* option prevents *serverd* from running when the system's load average (as reported by *uptime*) is higher than *load*, unless 300 seconds have passed without being able to run *serverd*.†

The `-e` option causes *serverd* to echo its messages to the screen. It has no effect if *syslog* is used for logging.

frequency *seconds*

This directive controls how long the server daemon waits between checking for new mail. Setting frequency to 0 causes the server daemon to check continuously; this may use excessive processing power.

limit message *number-of-bytes*

This directive allows you to set a limit on the size of email messages that Listproc delivers. Messages longer than the limit are rejected, and the sender is notified.

limit files *number-of-bytes*

This directive sets the maximum archive file size that is sent out in a single email message when a user requests a file from the archive. If an archive file exceeds the specified size, it is automatically split into parts, and each part is sent separately.

precedence *precedence-level*

This directive sets the value of the Precedence header on all outgoing mail messages. Valid precedence levels are determined by your system's MTA; typical values are `bulk`, `junk`, and `first-class`.

The default precedence is `bulk`, which instructs the MTA to give lower priority to processing the message and prevents vacation programs from replying to mailing list messages. However, some mail programs preserve Precedence headers in replies, so users replying to list messages may find their replies rejected by Listproc, which rejects incoming `bulk` messages to help avoid mail loops. One solution to this problem is to define a new precedence level

---

* If you use *ps* to see the server user's processes when using this option, two *serverd* processes are listed. One is the master server daemon; the other, its child process, is the Interactive ListProcessor server daemon listening for interactive requests.

† The 300-second rule is based on 30 * `MAX_TRIES`. `MAX_TRIES` is defined in *src/serverd.h*, should you want to adjust it.

in your MTA and use that with Listproc. *sendmail* users, for example, might add this line to their *sendmail.cf* file:

```
Plist=-50
```

Now you can use `precedence list` in your Listproc *config* file.

comment server #*comment message*

Any message given after the pound sign (#) in the `comment server` directive is included as the X-Comment header of all email sent out in response to user requests. This can be used to help users who forget Listproc commands:*

```
comment server #For help, send a message to listproc@your-host with
'help' in the body of the message.
```

organization *name*

This directive sets the name of your organization. Listproc uses the organization name in two ways. First, if a mailing list is being gatewayed to a news group, postings from the list have an Organization header set to *name*. Second, if Interactive ListProcessor is enabled, users who connect interactively will see a welcome message that includes the organization name.

fax *path-to-fax program [fax-program-options]*

If your host has a fax modem, Listproc can accept requests to fax files from its archives. The fax directive tells Listproc the location of the fax program, and any options that should be given to the program on the command line. Listproc calls the fax program with the specified options followed by the phone number to fax to. The file to fax is given on the standard input. If your fax program expects a different syntax, you have to write a script for Listproc that can call your fax program correctly. If you don't include a fax directive in the *config* file, faxing is disabled.

option *keyword*

This directive sets miscellaneous system-dependent options. The *systest* script suggests setting some of these. Others are matters of taste or local policy.

By default, when Listproc receives a request it doesn't understand, it stops processing the rest of the message. If the `ignore_invalid_requests` option is set, Listproc simply ignores invalid requests and continues checking the message for valid requests.

If the `relaxed_syntax` option is set, Listproc accepts user requests with more than the expected number of arguments. By default, Listproc rejects such requests.

---

* As with all *config* file directives, the `comment server` directive can be only a single long line.

The `sysv_ps` option should be set if the *ps* program uses System V Unix syntax; the `bsd_ps` option should be set if *ps* uses BSD Unix syntax. *systest* suggests this option if necessary.

The `bsd_mail` option should be set if the UCB mail program is available. The path to the UCB mail program is given in *src/Makefile*'s `UCB_MAIL` definition. If `bsd_mail` is set, the server manager is emailed when errors occur. *systest* suggests this option when UCB mail is available.

When a mailing list is connected to a Usenet newsgroup, messages can be sent to the newsgroup in two ways. If the `post_mail` option is set, messages are sent to the newsgroup by using *inews*. The path to *inews* is given in *src/Makefile*'s `INEWS` definition. If the `gate_mail` option is set, messages are emailed to a news gateway rather than posted with *inews*.

The `bad_telnet` option is used if the system sends out only a single message when the `telnet` mail-method is in use. A better idea is to avoid the `telnet` mail method entirely.

List-Related Directives

The directives below apply to individual lists served by Listproc. Many of these directives appear in the *config* file once for each list you create, though all but the `list` directive (which defines a list) are optional:

list *listname list-address owner-address password options*
> This directive defines a list to Listproc and must be used before any other directives related to the list. *listname* should be the name used to define the list's alias for the local MTA. *list-address* is the list's full email address, *owner-address* is the full email address of the primary list owner, and *password* is the list's password.* Finally, a number of *options* control how mail to the list is handled.

> Normally, Listproc rejects messages from people who aren't subscribed to the list and returns a copy to the sender. The `-f` option causes the rejection message to be forwarded to the list owner instead of the sender.†

---

* Because the list owner must include the list password in email messages sent to Listproc to maintain the list remotely, the password is easily compromised, and should not be the same as the list owner's account password, the server account password, or any other important password.

† While notes in *src/list.c* suggest that you could use this feature to allow a list to have the same email address as its owner (because messages from nonsubscribers continue to reach the owner), the formatting of the rejection message makes that inconvenient.

The -s option allows nonsubscribers to send email to the list. Lists of product announcements, for example, might benefit from vendors sending announcements without subscribing to the list.

The -m *number* option controls the number of recipients per message. By default, Listproc sends out messages with one recipient per message. The recipient's address is listed in the To header. It is more efficient and often more useful to send out messages to multiple recipients at once, and to have the To header contain the list address. The -m option causes messages to be sent out to *number* recipients at a time and changes the To header to read:

```
To: Multiple Recipients of List <listname@your-host>
```

The -P option sets the Reply-To header of outgoing list messages to the address of the message sender. By default, Listproc sets the Reply-To header to point back to the list address, which causes most MUAs to always send replies to the whole list. By using both the -m and -P options, you can create headers that allow subscribers to choose to reply to either the list or the message sender.

The -M option is one way to create a moderated mailing list.* Mail sent to lists defined with -M is forwarded to the primary list owner, who can then forward it back to the list (possibly after editing.) Mail from any list owner is sent directly to the list.

When the -r option is set, Listproc consults the *.restricted* file in the list directory for subscribers whose mail shouldn't be sent out to the entire list. The *.restricted* file allows you to specify a file containing the list of addresses that should, and should not, receive mail from that sender. In earlier versions of Listproc, this flag could simulate peer lists by subscribing two lists to one another and using the *.restricted* file to insure that mail from the other list would not be distributed back to it. The current version of Listproc supports true peer lists, but the -r option may still be useful if you need to connect a Listproc list and a non-Listproc list as peers.

The -D option turns on debugging for list messages, just as the -D option in the **server** directive turns on debugging for *listproc* requests. When debugging is on, a copy of the last commands sent to the SMTP server is stored in the file *sent* in the server user's home directory, and the response of the SMTP server is stored in the file *received.*

---

* The other way is to give the -m flag to *catmail* in the alias for the list in your MTA's aliases file. Using *catmail* for moderation sends the list owner a copy of the message and instructions on how to approve or discard the message by sending commands to Listproc. This can reduce bandwidth, as the owner doesn't have to forward the entire message back to Listproc. However, the owner can't post an edited version of the message as easily.

header *listname* { *Header:* ... }

This directive specifies headers that should be preserved from the original sender's message. Headers defined here are case-sensitive. Headers can be listed on multiple lines. Here's how you'd use the header directive to preserve MIME headers on incoming mail:

```
header mylist {
    MIME-Version:
    Mime-Version:
    Mime-version:
    Content-Type:
    Content-type:
    Content-ID:
    Content-id:
    Content-Description:
    Content-description:
    Content-Transfer-Encoding:
    Content-transfer-encoding:
    References:
    references:
    In-reply-to:
    In-Reply-To:
}
```

default *listname* { *option* = *value* ... }

This directive sets defaults for list subscribers. Default option/value pairs may be listed on multiple lines, and there must be a space both before and after the equal sign.

The **address** option may be set to **fixed** or **variable**. When the address option is set to **fixed**, users may not change the address they subscribe with. They must unsubscribe from their old address and resubscribe at their new address. When the address option is set to **variable**, users may use the following command to change their addresses:

> set *listname* address *subscriber-password new-address*

This setting also causes Listproc to notify a new subscriber of her list password and how to change it. The default is **fixed**.

The **conceal** option may be set to **yes** or no. By default, subscriber email addresses can be seen by issuing a **recipients** or **statistics** request. Subscribers who prefer not to reveal this information can ask Listproc to conceal their email addresses. The conceal option determines whether subscribers are concealed by default or not. Its value can be **yes** (conceal new subscribers) or **no** (don't conceal new subscribers, the default).

The **mail** option controls how new subscribers receive list messages. Values include **ack** (subscribers receive copies of their own messages), **noack** (subscribers don't receive copies of their own messages), `digest` (subscribers receive list digests instead of individual messages), and `postpone` (subscribers receive no messages). The default is `noack`, which can be confusing for some users; if you use it, be sure to explain in your list's welcome message that subscribers shouldn't expect to see their own messages to the list.

The `password` option sets a single list password that is assigned to all new subscribers if Interactive ListProcessor or variable addresses are enabled. Without this option, Listproc assigns a different random nine-digit number to each subscriber.

ceiling *listname number-of-messages*

This directive sets a maximum number of messages that Listproc processes for the list each day, including messages that are rejected. Messages sent after the ceiling has been reached aren't processed until the next day.

disable *listname request*

Disables the use of the request *request* on *listname* by anyone but a list owner. Subscribers who attempt to use a disabled request are sent a rejection message.

comment *listname #comment*

This directive defines a comment to be included in the X-Comment header in each outgoing list message. The pound sign (#) is required in the directive, but doesn't appear in the X-Comment header. List comments are also shown in response to a `lists` request; accordingly, the comment should reflect the list's purpose or function.

digest *listname number-of-lines number-of-hours*

This directive determines how often a list digest is sent to subscribers who choose to receive digests. Listproc sends digests when the length of the digest exceeds *number-of-lines* or when *number-of-hours* have passed since the last digest.

unix_cmd *listname cmd-password cmd-alias 'unix-cmd [args]'* #comment

This directive allows list subscribers who know the command password *cmd-password* to execute the specified Unix command by using the following request:

```
run listname cmd-password cmd-alias [args]
```

The arguments, *args*, to the command may include the variables $1 to $9, which are set to the first through ninth arguments given in the run request, and $*, which is set to all the arguments passed to the `run` request. Users can list all defined Unix commands for a list by issuing a `run list` request;

Listproc includes the comment following the pound sign in response to that request.

WARNING   The `unix_cmd` directive is a good way to make your Unix sys-
           tem vulnerable to malicious subscribers. The only security List-
           proc provides is to prevent the arguments from containing
           dangerous shell metacharacters. If you must use this directive,
           be absolutely certain that your command can handle any argu-
           ments and can't do any harm. The list owner should have the
           CCRUN owner preference set in the *owners* file (see Chapter 9)
           to keep track of the use of the `run` request.

`remote` *rmt-listname rmt-list-addr rmt-listproc-addr*
[host [port]] #*comment*

This directive informs your local Listproc server about a list served by a
remote Listproc server. Lists defined by a `remote` directive are included in the
response to a `lists` request, along with the *comment* describing them.
Requests or messages meant for the remote list are forwarded to the remote
Listproc address *rmt-listproc-addr* or remote list address *rmt-list-*
addr respectively. If your server and the remote server allow interactive connections, giving the remote server's *host* (either its hostname or IP address)
and *ilp* port (372 if not given) allows your Interactive ListProcessor to transfer
users to the remote Interactive ListProcessor.

Archive-Related Directives

`archive` *listname archive-dir format [index-dir]*
[archive-password] [digest]

This directive causes messages to *listname* to be automatically archived in
archive-dir, a full path to a directory writable by the server user. The files
DIR and *INDEX* are kept in the *index-dir*, which is a relative path under
/usr/server/archives. If you include an *archive-password*, requests for files
from the archive must be accompanied by the password. A password of – is
the same as no password. If you use the `digest` keyword, only digests of the
mailing list are archived.

The *server* manual page suggests that you can leave out the *index-dir* or
use a default directory by using –. This doesn't really work well; it overwrites
the *archives/listproc/DIR* file with the new list's directory. The manual page
also suggests that *index-dir* should be a relative path under *listproc*, for
example *listproc/mylist*. While that works fine, it's often simpler to simply use
the list's name as the index directory, rather than making it a subdirectory of
listproc. If the archive directory is */usr/server/archives/mylist*, and the index

directory is *mylist*, all the archived files and the *DIR* and *INDEX* files are stored together, which is convenient. Another variation is to make the archive directory a directory accessible by FTP or gopher and keep the *DIR* and *INDEX* files in a similarly named directory under */usr/server/archives*.

The `format` specifies how the files in the archive are named. Format can include lowercase letters, numbers, and some special sequences:

%m Month of the year, a number from 01–12.

%h Month name, Jan–Dec.

%d Day of the month, a number from 01–31.

%y The last two digits of the year.

%j Day of the year, a number from 001–366.

%a The value of the Archive-Name header, if any, that may appear in either the mail headers or the body of the message. Because digests might have multiple Archive-Name headers, %a can't be used when archiving digests.

%# The digest number, if digests are being archived.

%1 The first word of the body of the message.

%v and %n
    Volume and issue numbers. To use %v and/or %n, the message should begin with a "Volume <#> Number <#>" line.

When using the sequences %a, %v, or %n, Listproc only archives messages that fit the required format (an Archive-Name header, or a Volume-Number line.) You can use these to archive only files that are sent to the list, while leaving ordinary messages out of the archive.

The Subject header of an archived message is stored along with the archive filename, size, and location in the archive's directory file, *DIR*. (If a message would be archived with the same filename as an earlier message, it's appended to the file, but only the first message's Subject header is listed in the archive file's description. There is code commented out in *src/list.c* (line 2956) that might change this behavior to give each archived message a unique filename by appending a period and a number.)

B

Majordomo Reference

This appendix summarizes the Majordomo user commands and list owner commands. It also provides a guide to the directories and files in a Majordomo installation and the Majordomo configuration directives.

User Commands

User commands do not require the list owner's password.

General Commands

General commands can be used by anyone, whether or not they are subscribed to a list, though some lists may restrict these commands to subscribers:

`help`
> Request a help message listing commands and the version of Majordomo that's in use.

`lists`
> Request the list addresses and descriptions of lists served by Majordomo. Lists may be concealed from this request.

`info` *listname*
> Request the list's information file.

`who` *listname*
> Request a list of subscribers' email addresses. On some lists, only subscribers may issue this request.

`end`
> Causes Majordomo to ignore the rest of the message. A line that starts with a dash (–) also stops Majordomo from reading the rest of the message.

Subscriber Commands

Subscriber commands are either used to subscribe to the list or are restricted to list subscribers:

subscribe *listname [address]*
> Subscribe to mailing list *listname*. If *address* is given, subscribe that email address instead of the sender's address (which may require list owner approval).

unsubscribe *listname [address]*
> Unsubscribe from a list. If *address* is given, remove that email address from the list (which may require list owner approval).

which *[address]*
> Request to know to which lists you have subscribed. If *address* is given, request to know to which lists *address* is subscribed.

Archive Commands

Archive commands let users search list archives and retrieve files. These commands may be restricted to list subscribers:

index *listname*
> Request an index of the files in *listname*'s archive.

get *listname file*
> Request the file *file* from *listname*'s archive.

List Owner Commands

List owner commands let the list owner control the configuration of the list. They require the list password:

config *listname list-password*
> Request a copy of the list's configuration file.

newconfig *listname list-password*
> Replace the list's configuration file with a new file. The new file must appear below the newconfig command and be followed by a line containing EOF.

newintro *listname list-password*
> Replace the list's intro file with a new one. The new file must appear below the command and be followed by a line containing EOF.

newinfo *listname list-password*
> Replace the list's info file with a new one. The new file must appear below the command and be followed by a line containing EOF.

`writeconfig` *listname list-password*
> Rewrite the list's configuration file to include all the comments and variables in the distributed configuration file. Useful when upgrading from earlier versions of Majordomo.

`password` *listname current-backup-password new-backup-password*
> Change the backup list password.

`mkdigest` *listname list-password*
> Issue a digest immediately for a digested list.

`approve` *list-password* `subscribe` *listname email-address*
> Subscribe an email address to the list.

`approve` *list-password* `unsubscribe` *listname email-address*
> Unsubscribe an email address from the list.

`approve` *list-password* `who` *listname*
> Get a list of subscribers to a list, even if the `who` request is disabled for that list.

Majordomo Files

Figure B-1 shows the files and subdirectories in */home/majordomo* that you should have at the end of an installation, if you follow the instructions in Chapter 10, *Administering Majordomo*.

Files in /home/majordomo/archives

The *archives* directory contains subdirectories for each list with archived messages. Only files in these subdirectories (or others specified in the configuration file) can be requested by users.

Files in /home/majordomo/digests

The *digests* directory is used as a work area for building list digests. Each digested mailing list requires a subdirectory under the *digests* directory.

Files in /home/majordomo/lists

The *lists* directory contains the configuration files for lists. A list named `listname` may have these files:

listname
> The list's subscribers are kept in a file named for the list, with one subscriber per line. This file is required.

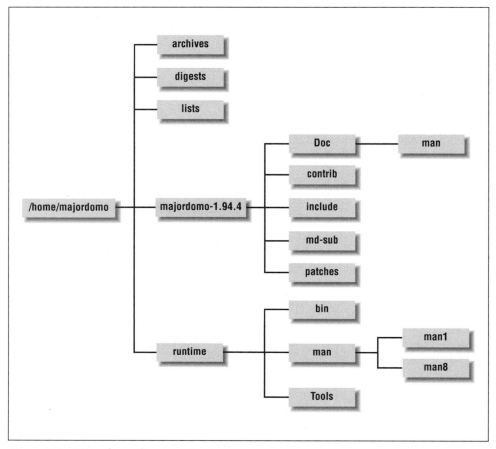

Figure B-1: Majordomo directory structure

listname.config

> The list's configuration file, which controls most aspects of the list's operation. This is a required file.

listname.info

> This file is sent in response to an **info** request. It typically contains a description of the list's purpose or perhaps the entire list charter.

listname.passwd

> This file contains the default administrative password for the list. *listname.config* also contains the administrative password, but even if the list owner changes the password in the configuration file, the default password still works, which makes it possible to recover when a configuration file is cor-

rupt. The password is unencrypted, so don't use a login password! This file is required.

Files in /home/majordomo/majordomo-1.94.4

The *majordomo-1.94.4* directory, of course, contains the Majordomo source code that you installed. You can remove it if you're short on disk space, but it's often helpful to have it available, as it contains contributed programs that you may not have installed. In addition, when it comes time to upgrade to a later version of Majordomo, you'll have the *Makefile* around as a guide.

Files in /home/majordomo/runtime

The *runtime* directory (or, more generally, the W_HOME directory), contains the Majordomo programs themselves, the server configuration file, and supporting scripts (which end in *.pl*):

Log

> When Majordomo responds to requests, it records them in the *Log* file. A piece of a *Log* file might look like this:

```
Apr 14 20:53:17 gshp.com majordomo[472] {Rex <rex@obedience.edu>} help
Apr 14 20:55:13 gshp.com majordomo[478] {Rex <rex@obedience.edu>} lists
Apr 16 15:43:54 gshp.com majordomo[1027] {Fido <fido@spaniel.com>} help
```

> Each line records the date, time, Majordomo host, program (and process ID number), email sender, and request processed.

bounce-remind

> Majordomo can help manage subscribers to whom email bounces. You can set up a special list called *bounces*, and list owners can use the *bin/bounce* program to unsubscribe addresses from their list and subscribe them to the bounces list. The *bounce-remind* script sends a reminder to users who have been placed on the *bounces* list, telling them how to remove themselves from bounces and resubscribe to the list they were subscribed to. It's meant to be run nightly from the Majordomo user's *cron* file. Chapter 10 has more information about setting up and using a *bounces* list.

config-test

> This script (called with *./wrapper config-test*) provides information about your configuration that can be extremely useful in tracking down problems.

digest

> This script adds mail messages to a list digest. It's called from the *sendmail* alias for the digested list.

majordomo

> This is Majordomo's administrative request server; it answers mail sent to the *majordomo* address and processes commands in the message.

new-list

> This script simply returns a message saying that a mailing list is new and not yet ready for messages. It's used in the *sendmail aliases* file to respond to the list address when a list is new and still acquiring subscribers.

request-answer

> Returns a message explaining that administrative commands should be sent to *majordomo@host*, not `listname-request@host`.

resend

> This program is responsible for actually processing and distributing list mail, optionally adding or removing special headers, filtering out administrative requests, and enforcing a maximum message length. There's also a *resend.README* file that you should delete; the arguments it describes are now set in the list's config file rather than on the *resend* command line.

wrapper

> A setuid and setgid wrapper program that is used to invoke the Majordomo programs.

majordomo.cf

> The master configuration file for the Majordomo suite. Configuration directives are explained in detail later in this appendix.

config_parse.pl, majordomo.pl, majordomo_version.pl, and *shlock.pl*

> The files ending in *.pl* are Perl packages that are used by the Majordomo programs to parse mailing list configuration files, manipulate mail headers, report the version number, and lock files.

Files in /home/majordomo/runtime/bin

The *bin* directory contains two Perl scripts that are useful for list owners (*approve* and *bounce*) and one for the server administrator (*medit*). Owners of moderated lists can pipe messages to *approve* in order to approve them for posting to the list. The *bounce* script makes it easy for list owners to unsubscribe users whose email is bouncing. *medit* is used to edit Majordomo files; it locks the files to prevent them from being used by Majordomo while they are in an inconsistent state, runs your editor, and then unlocks the files.

Files in /home/majordomo/runtime/man

The *man* directory contains two manual pages (formatted with *nroff*) that you might want to install in your system's manual page directories or distribute to list owners. The file *man/man1/approve.1* is the manual page for the *approve* script; *man/man8/majordomo.1* is an old manual page for Majordomo itself.

Files in /home/majordomo/runtime/Tools

The *Tools* directory contains tools that Majordomo uses for archiving, indexing, and digesting lists.

config File Directives

List owners configure their lists by requesting a copy of the list's configuration file, `listname`.*config*, editich10 ng the file, and mailing it back to Majordomo.

The configuration file is nearly all valid Perl. Lines in the configuration file that begin with a pound sign (#) are comments. Other lines define the value of list options. Most list options take string values, numbers, or filenames, and are in the format `option = value`. Others take lists of strings or regular expressions and are defined like this:

```
option    << END
Values are listed here, one per line or this might be a paragraph value
To include a blank line, use a line with a single hyphen:
-
Normally, multiple spaces    like this are treated as a single space
If it's important to preserve them, start the line with a hyphen:
-1     2     3     4     5
To get a single hyphen at the beginning of a line, double it:
-- is a hyphen
the definition ends with the line END
END
```

Here are the directives in the configuration file:

`admin_passwd`

> The administrative password must accompany administrative commands from the list owner. Each list has two administrative passwords. One is stored in the file `listname`.*passwd*. The other is given in the configuration file by defining `admin_passwd`. `admin_passwd` defaults to `listname.admin` and should definitely be changed.

`administrivia`

> If `administrivia` is set to **yes**, suspected administrative requests sent to the list address are forwarded to the list owner; setting it to **no** disables request filtering. The default value is **yes**. The variables `$admin_headers`

and $admin_body in *majordomo.cf* control which patterns are considered to
be administrative requests.

advertise and noadvertise

The `advertise` and `noadvertise` options control the visibility of the list in
response to a `lists` request. These options take arrays of regular expressions
as values, like this:

```
advertise        << END
/@.*.myhost.com/
/sarah@friendly.org/
END
noadvertise      << END
END
```

Each line in the list is a regular expression, enclosed by slashes. Lists are
always visible to their subscribers. For nonsubscribers, if the email address of
the sender of a `lists` request matches a regular expression in `noadver-`
`tise`, the list doesn't appear in Majordomo's response. If not, the list appears
if the sender's address *does* match a regular expression in `advertise`. Either
or both of these options may be left undefined by including no regular
expressions between the `<< END` and `END`. Undefined options are effectively
disabled.

In the example above, the list is only visible to requests which come from
.myhost.com addresses or from *sarah@friendly.org*. To make a list totally invisible, define `noadvertise` like this:

```
noadvertise      << END
/./
END
```

announcements

If `announcements` is set to `yes`, the list maintainer receives notification
whenever someone subscribes or unsubscribes from the list. If `announce-`
`ments` is set to `no`, no notifications are sent.

approve_passwd

If a list is moderated, its moderator approves messages by resending them to
the list with an `Approved:` *password* header. `approve_passwd` sets the
password for message approval. It defaults to *listname*`.pass` and should
be changed.

comments

The `comments` option is a place to put comments into the configuration file
that are preserved even when the file is rewritten. Its value is a paragraph:

```
comments << END
This configuration file is maintained by jerry
END
```

date_info and date_intro

If `date_info` is set to `yes`, the date that the list's info file was last updated with the `newinfo` command is placed at the top of the info file. If set to `no`, the date isn't placed in the file (though it's still included in the response to an `info` request). Placing the date in the file is handy if the file might be looked at in some other way than an `info` request. `date_info` defaults to `yes`. `date_intro` performs the same function for the list's intro file.

debug

Setting `debug` to `yes` prevents the *resend* program from actually distributing list messages; instead it sends the list owner a message containing the commands that it would have executed. The default is `no`.

description

`description` is a single string that describes the mailing list in Majordomo's response to the `lists` request.

digest_volume and digest_issue

If the mailing list is digested, `digest_volume` gives the next volume number; `digest_issue` is the next issue number. `digest_issue` is automatically updated as each digest is produced. `digest_volume` must be updated manually when a new volume should be issued.

digest_maxdays and digest_maxlines

These options control how many days can pass between digests and how long (in lines) a digest can grow before being distributed. See also `maxlength`, which controls digest size in characters.

digest_name

If the mailing list is digested, the digest's subject line contains the value of `digest_name`, followed by the volume and issue numbers. It defaults to the name of the mailing list.

digest_work_dir

You can define `digest_work_dir` to direct Majordomo to build digests in a particular directory; if undefined, Majordomo uses the *listname* subdirectory in the *digests* directory. Generally, you shouldn't define this.

get_access

This option controls who can use the `get` command to retrieve a file from the list's archive. Three values are possible: `open` allows anyone to issue a `get` command, `list` only allows list members, and `closed` prevents anyone from using the command. Actually, the list's owners can override closed access by using the `approve` command. For example:

```
approve listname password get filename
```

A *command_access* option is available for the commands `get`, `index`, `info`, `intro`, `which`, and `who`.

maxlength

Sets the maximum number of characters a message may contain in order to be distributed without approval. It's also the size at which digests are automatically distributed if the list is digested. The default value is 40000.

message_fronter, message_footer, and message_headers

These options allow you to define a paragraph of text that is inserted in the headers (`message_headers`), at the beginning of the body (`message_fronter`), or at the end of the body (`message_footer`) of each message or digest distributed to the list. In addition to static text, certain special strings are automatically expanded by Majordomo in useful ways:

$LIST

Expands into the name of the mailing list. Only undigested lists may use `$LIST`.

$SENDER

Expands into the sender's address from the message's From header. Only undigested lists may use `$SENDER`.

$VERSION

Expands into the Majordomo version number. Only undigested lists may use `$VERSION`.

SUBJECTS

Expands into a table of contents for a digest. It may only be used in the `message_fronter` of a digested list.

Majordomo discards anything after two blank lines in these options, so be sure to leave only single blank lines between paragraphs.

moderate

When `moderate` is set to `yes`, the list is moderated. All messages sent to moderated lists are forwarded to the moderator(s) for approval. Default is `no`.

moderator

If `moderator` is set to an email address, messages requiring approval are bounced to that address, rather than the list owner.

mungedomain

Majordomo allows users to subscribe themselves at addresses that differ from their From address, but requires list-owner approval in the most common configuration (see the description of `subscribe_policy` below). If `mungedomain` is set to `yes`, users whose mail comes from *user@host.domain.xxx* may subscribe the address *user@domain.xxx* without approval. Because such situations are increasingly common, this can be a valuable time saver. Its value defaults to `no`.

precedence

The `precedence` option, if defined, sets the value for the Precedence header for outgoing messages. It defaults to `bulk`, which prevents vacation programs from responding to the list, but also instructs *sendmail* to discard messages that bounce rather than send them back to Majordomo for processing.

purge_received

If `purge_received` is set to `yes`, *resend* removes all Received headers before distributing messages to the list. This can produce headers that are shorter and more uniform, and makes it easier to conceal the identity of message senders, which may or may not be desirable. It also defeats *sendmail*'s built-in loop detection feature that rejects messages with too many Received headers.

reply_to

The `reply_to` option, if defined, sets the value for the Reply-To header of outgoing messages. To set the Reply-To header to match the From header, set this option to `$SENDER`. Digested lists with undigested counterparts use this option to direct replies to the digested list back to the undigested list. This option is undefined by default, which results in no Reply-To header on outgoing messages.

resend_host

`resend_host` sets a hostname that is appended to addresses used by *resend*. Alternatively, *resend* can be called with a `-h` *host* argument. This option is undefined by default.

restrict_post

The `restrict_post` option may be defined as a list of files (separated by spaces or colons) that are checked for addresses of approved message senders. Only senders whose addresses match a line in one of the listed files may send messages to the list. Because remote list owners generally can't access these files, however, this option has limited utility, and its comment in the *config* file says that it will be replaced in the future.

`sender`

> The `sender` option sets the SMTP From address and Sender header for outgoing messages. `@hostname` is appended, so only a local alias name is used. `sender` defaults to `owner-listname`.

`strip`

> Most people's From headers include more than just their email address. Often, their full name or other comments appear in the From: header. If the `strip` option is set to `yes`, these comments are stripped off when new subscriber addresses are added to the list's subscriber file. The option was originally added because the *smail* MTA objected to comments in subscriber files. `strip` defaults to `yes`.

`subject_prefix`

> If defined, the `subject_prefix` is prepended to the subject line of outgoing list messages unless it already appears in the message subject. The `subject_prefix` can be only a single word. The expansion strings used in `message_footer`, `$LIST`, `$SENDER`, and `$VERSION`, are also available; setting `subject_prefix` to `$LIST` is often valuable.

`subscribe_policy`

> A particularly important configuration option, `subscribe_policy` controls who may subscribe to the list without the approval of the list owner. It can take one of these values:

`auto`

> Means that anyone can subscribe to the list without approval. Further, third-party subscriptions are allowed; anyone can ask to subscribe an address different than that in their From header.*

`auto+confirm`

> Works like `auto`, but Majordomo sends an authentication number to the subscriber, which he must send back to Majordomo to complete the subscription. This prevents people from subscribing others unwittingly and protects the list from addresses with typos in them.

`open`

> Allows anyone to subscribe themselves to the list without approval. Attempts to subscribe other addresses require approval.

`open+confirm`

> Works like `open`, but also requires confirmation.

---

* This is a dangerous option; it's all too easy for someone to subscribe the list to itself, creating a mail loop, or to subscribe an unwitting and unwilling victim to an unwanted list. Consider using `auto+confirm` instead.

`closed`

> Requires list owner approval for every subscription request.

`closed+confirm`

> Works like `closed`, but also requires confirmation.

`taboo_body` and `taboo_headers`

> These options help protect lists against unwanted mailings. If a message's headers match any regular expression listed in `taboo_headers`, or its body matches any regular expression listed in `taboo_body`, the message is sent to the list owner or moderator for approval. This provides great flexibility in keeping junk mail, abusive posters, or users at rogue sites from disrupting your list.

`unsubscribe_policy`

> `unsubscribe_policy` controls who may unsubscribe from the list without the approval of the list owner. Its values are similar to those of `subscribe_policy`:
>
> `auto`
>
> > Means that anyone can unsubscribe from the list without approval. Further, third-party unsubscriptions are allowed; anyone can ask to unsubscribe an address different than that in their From header. This is probably too liberal for most mailing lists.
>
> `open`
>
> > Allows anyone to unsubscribe themselves from the list without approval. Attempts to unsubscribe other addresses require approval. This is the default.
>
> `closed`
>
> > Requires list-owner approval for every unsubscription request. This is rarely useful.

`welcome`

> If the `welcome` option is set to `no`, welcome messages aren't sent to new subscribers. The default is `yes`.

Unused options

> The options `archive_dir`, `digest_archive`, `digest_rm_footer`, and `digest_rm_fronter` are included in the configuration file but are not operational and shouldn't be defined.

C

SmartList Reference

All SmartList requests are sent to the individual list's request address in the Subject of the message. In keeping with its small and simple philosophy, SmartList has few requests. It does, however, understand that there are many ways to say "subscribe." Some of the many subscribe requests that SmartList recognizes include:

- Subscribe
- Join
- Please add me to the list
- Sign on the list
- Could you please put me on the list?

User Commands

User commands don't require the list owner's password.

General Commands

General commands can be used by anyone, whether or not they are subscribed to a list, though some lists may restrict these commands to subscribers:

`help`
> Request a help message, and, if available, the list's *info* file. `info` does the same thing.

Subscriber Commands

Subscriber commands are used to subscribe to the list or are restricted to list subscribers:

`subscribe`
> Subscribe to the list.

`unsubscribe`
> Unsubscribe from the list.

Archive Commands

Archive commands let users search a list's archives and retrieve files. To use the archive, users send email to the list's request address with `Subject: archive` and the archive commands in the body of the message. If the Subject is `archive help`, a help file is sent. These commands may be restricted to list subscribers:

`archive help`
> Send a help file listing archive commands.

`version`
> Request the version number of the archive server.

`maxfiles` *number*
> Set the maximum number of files that are returned per request to *number* to protect yourself against mistakenly requesting the entire archive. Setting `maxfiles` to 0 removes the limit.

`ls` *[directories]*
> Request a listing of files in the archive or in a particular directory in the archive. `dir`, `directory`, `list`, and `show` are synonyms for `ls`.

`egrep` *[egrep-flags] pattern files*
> Search *files* (which may include wildcards) for *pattern*. *pattern* is a case-insensitive *egrep* regular expression.

`get` *files*
> Request the files *files* from the archive. Files are sent back MIME-encoded.

List Owner Commands

List owner commands are executed by sending email to the list's request address with an X-Command header.* The format of the header is:

---

* Many SmartList server administrators change the name of this header to something other than X-Command.

X-Command: *owner-address list-password command*

owner-address is the email address of the list owner. The results of any command are emailed back to the list owner's address, with X-Command renamed to X-Processed. The available ***command***s are:

`help | info`
Show a list of available commands.

`subscribe | unsubscribe` ***address***
Subscribe or unsubscribe an email address to the list.

`checkdist` ***address***
Return a list of the eight email addresses most similar to ***address*** that are subscribed to the list.

`showdist`
Return the list of subscribers.

`showlog`
Return the list's log file.

`wipelog`
Clear the list's log file.

SmartList Files

Figure C-1 shows the directory structure after SmartList is installed.

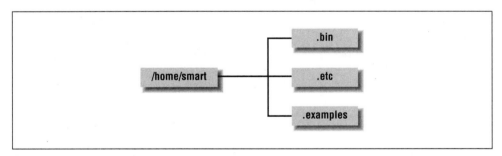

Figure C-1: SmartList directory structure

Files in /home/smart

The SmartList user's home directory need contain only two files: *.forward* and *.procmailrc.**

---

* In fact, if *procmail* is used as the local mail delivery agent on your system, even *.forward* is unnecessary. But it doesn't hurt to have it anyway.

SmartList uses *procmail* to scan incoming mail messages for administrative requests and act on them. The *.forward* file created during the installation forwards incoming mail to *procmail*. The *.procmailrc* file controls the operation of *procmail*.

Files in /home/smart/.bin

The *.bin* subdirectory contains the SmartList programs themselves. Five of these files, *choplist, flist, idhash, multigram,* and *senddigest,* are links to the same setuid *root* program, which behaves differently depending on its name when run.* The other files are Bourne shell scripts.

arch_retrieve

This script is SmartList's archive server. It's run in response to a request to get a file from the archive or search the archive.

arch_trunc

In order to limit the number of archived messages for each list, *arch_trunc* is occasionally run. It removes older messages from the archive.

choplist

When SmartList is ready to distribute a message to a mailing list, the *choplist* program splits up the list of subscribers into reasonably-sized chunks and passes them to multiple *sendmail* processes to deliver the mail.

createlist and *removelist*

The *createlist* script is used to create a new mailing list or archive server (if the −a command-line option is given). Its syntax is:

```
createlist [-a] listname [list-owner]
```

Unrecognized administrative requests for the list are forwarded to the list owner. If no *list-owner* is given, these requests are stored in the list's *request* file.

The command **removelist** *listname* removes a mailing list.

cronlist

This script is meant to be called daily by *cron*. By default, it runs *flush_digests* to send out any digests that are due for delivery.

delink and *showlink*

When a list is initially created, many of its configuration files are linked to the master configuration files in *.etc/*. In order to customize an *rc* file, you must

---

* The source code for this program is *multigram.c* in the *procmail sr* directory.

create a separate, unlinked copy of the file. The *delink* script automates this process. The *showlink* script lists all links between *rc* files.

digest

rc.submit calls the *digest* script to build digests from incoming list messages.

donatelist

The *donatelist* script gives a local user complete control over a list's directory and files without putting the user in the SmartList group. Its syntax is:

```
donatelist list-owner listname
```

On many systems, this script must be run by *root*, as it uses *chown* to change file ownership. Local list owners should set their umask to 007 in order to insure that user and group permissions are maintained when list files are edited.

flist

This program is run from */etc/aliases* when mail for any list or list-request addresses is received. Its primary function is to execute the appropriate *procmail* script for processing incoming mail.

flush_digests

Mails out any digests that are due to be delivered. Digests are checked for readiness whenever incoming mail is received and periodically via *cronlist*.

idhash

The *idhash* program computes a hash value for an email message. These hash values are used to prevent mail loops when messages bounce.

led It's dangerous to edit SmartList's scripts and configuration files while SmartList is active; your editor might save a file in an unfinished state while you're working on it and cause errors when list mail is received. The *led* script allows you to use your editor safely. It creates lock files that prevent SmartList from processing mail until your editing is complete, and insures that your editor hasn't modified the file permissions on the files. *led* uses the editor specified by your VISUAL environment variable, or *vi* if VISUAL isn't set.

mimencap, mimencap.local, and *mimesend*

SmartList uses the *mimesend* script to send out a MIME-encapsulated message. The script calls the *mimencap procmail* script to encapsulate archive files using MIME headers prior to sending them out. The *mimencap.local* script contains the rules that decide which Content-Type a file should be assigned. The rules are primarily based on file extensions (e.g., a file with a name in *.ps* is PostScript) or file contents (e.g., a file that begins with the characters %! is PostScript).

multigram

This program tries to match email addresses in mail messages to email addresses on a subscriber list, even if the addresses in the messages aren't quite the same. SmartList uses this program in its scripts to find subscribers.

procbounce

When a bounce message from a mailer daemon is received, the *procbounce* script is called to keep track of the bounced addresses and possibly remove them from the subscriber list.

senddigest

This program determines if a digest is ready to be sent. It is used by *flush_digests*.

sendmails

This script emulates the behavior of *sendmail*'s -t (use the To header to determine where to send the message) option when *sendmail* isn't available.

subscribe and *unsubscribe*

These scripts are called by *rc.request* in response to a request to subscribe to or unsubscribe from a list.

x_command

This script is called by *rc.request* when SmartList receives an X-Command request from a list owner.

Files in /home/smart/.etc

Most of the files in the *.etc* subdirectory are master copies of the *procmail* scripts that control the operation of lists. When a new list is created, its directory initially includes links to these master files. By modifying these files you can change the default behavior for newly created lists. The *.etc* subdirectory also contains the help files for list subscribers.

Manual

A copy of the SmartList manual can be found in the *.etc* subdirectory. It's a little different than the manual in the source distribution; this copy has been customized to use the SmartList user's home directory in place of */home/list* in a couple of places.

help.txt and *archive.txt*

The *help.txt* file is sent in response to a help request. It explains how to subscribe and unsubscribe from a list. The *archive.txt* file is sent in response to an archive help request and explains the archive commands.

subscribe.txt and *unsubscribe.txt*

The *subscribe.txt* and *unsubscribe.txt* files are sent as part of the message users receive when they subscribe or unsubscribe from a SmartList mailing list.

The *rc.** scripts

The files beginning with *rc.* are the *procmail* scripts that constitute SmartList itself:

rc.init

Initializes all the variables used in the other scripts. It also calls *rc.custom*, which initializes per-list variables.

rc.post

Saves a copy of a message to the file *.etc/request* and sends a copy to the SmartList listmaster, if one has been defined.

rc.request

Processes mail sent to a list-request address. It recognizes administrative requests and calls the programs to handle them. Unrecognized requests are stored in the list's *request* file, forwarded to the list owner, and passed to *rc.post*.

rc.submit

Processes mail sent to a SmartList mailing list address. It identifies administrative requests sent to the list address and redirects them to *rc.request*, and distributes legitimate messages to the mailing list, digest, and archive.

rc.archive

Processes mail sent to an archive server. It calls *arch_retrieve* to handle archive requests. Unrecognized requests are stored in the archive's *request* file, forwarded to the archive owner, and passed to *rc.post*.

rc.main

A link to */home/smart/.procmailrc*, the script that handles mail sent to the SmartList user itself. It uses *rc.init* to initialize its variables and then runs *rc.post*.

rc.lock

This file doesn't appear in the *.etc* directory by default, but if you create it, SmartList postpones processing of incoming mail for up to 17 minutes from its last-access date. You can use this if you need to modify important files, such as *rc.init* on an active SmartList account. If you need more than 17 minutes, *touch* the *rc.lock* file every 15 minutes or so. Remove the file to resume normal operation.

Files in /home/smart/.examples

The *.examples* directory contains examples of files and scripts that may be useful in working with SmartList. Many of the files are duplicates of files in other directories. Unique files include:

doxcommand

> This script can be used by list owners to send remote list commands conveniently. See the discussion of X-Command in Chapter 5, *Maintaining Lists with SmartList.*

gatherinfo

> Each SmartList mailing list can have an *info.txt* file that is included in responses to help requests. The *gatherinfo* script is an example of how all such files could be concatenated into a single *info.txt* file that can be made available by FTP or archive server.

putfile

> This script is an example of how an archive server might allow file submissions by email.

rc.local.s20

> Many of the *rc* scripts offer the ability to customize the script's behavior by having it run local *procmail* recipes. This file gives examples of what might go into the RC_LOCAL_SUBMIT_20 recipe, which is called before distributing list messages. See Chapter 11, *Administering SmartList*, for complete details.

retrieve.local

> The *retrieve.local* file gives an example of how the archive server can be extended to support new commands. It includes instructions and an example of a `find` command much like SmartList's `search` command.

subscreen

> If a *subscreen* script exists in a list directory, it is called to see if a user is allowed to subscribe to the list. The sample *subscreen* shows how to write such a script to accept or reject users based on their email addresses.

uuencode.dif

> This file contains two patches (in unified diff format) for *.bin/mimencap*, which causes it to send its files in uuencoded format instead of using other MIME encodings. This might be useful if most of your subscribers have non-MIME-compliant mail agents and access to a uudecoder.

Configuration Directives

The basic configuration file is *rc.custom*. By setting directives in *.etc/rc.custom*, you set the defaults for all new lists. An individual list is customized by editing its copy of *rc.custom*.

Like the other *rc* files, *rc.custom* is a *procmail* script. Its format, however, is extremely simple. It sets a number of variables using a shell-like syntax, where `variable=value` sets a variable, and `variable` alone clears a variable. Lines beginning with pound signs (#) are comments, and variables that aren't set receive default values from *rc.init*. Here is a list of all the variables in *rc.custom*:

maintainer

> Set to the email address of the list owner. If you leave `maintainer` blank, list requests are stored in the list's *request* file, rather than being sent to the list owner.

LOGABSTRACT and VERBOSE

> The **LOGABSTRACT** and **VERBOSE** variables control the amount of detail that is logged during SmartList operation. They are special *procmail* variables.

size_limit

> The size in bytes of the largest allowable message. Defaults to 512 KB.

idcache_size

> To prevent mail loops, SmartList caches message IDs. This variable sets the size (in bytes) that the cache may grow to. Defaults to 8 KB.

archive_hist

> The number of recent messages the list should archive. By default, the list archives the last two messages sent.

archive_log and subscribe_log

> These log files should be used to note archive requests and administrivia requests. By default, they point to $LOGFILE, the default *procmail* log file, which is the file *log* in the list directory.

maxhist

> The number of bounces to keep track of. Defaults to 32.

minbounce

> The number of bounces at which a subscriber is automatically unsubscribed. Defaults to 4.

`cutoff_bounce`

> The number of lines that are examined in a bounced message in order to determine why the message bounced and to whom it was intended. Defaults to 256.

`match_threshold`, `medium_threshold`, and `loose_threshold`

> The threshold variables control how closely an email address must match a list of addresses. These values are used by *multigram*. They default to 30730, 28672, and 24476, respectively.

`auto_off_threshold`

> This variable controls how closely an email address must match in order to automatically remove it from the subscriber list due to repeated bounced mail. Defaults to the value of `medium_threshold`.

`off_threshold`

> This variable controls how closely an email address must match when a subscriber tries to unsubscribe themselves from the list. Defaults to the value of `loose_threshold`.

`reject_threshold`

> This variable controls how closely an email address must match an address in the *reject* file when rejecting subscription requests. Defaults to the value of `match_threshold`.

`submit_threshold`

> This variable controls how closely an email address must match an address in the *accept* file when accepting submissions to the list.

`unsub_assist`

> When set to a number, subscribers who attempt to unsubscribe, but fail, are sent a list of the specified number of closest matches to their address, to help them pin down the exact address they wish to unsubscribe. When undefined, unsubscribers aren't assisted. Assisting unsubscribers is helpful, but permits them to learn the email addresses of other subscribers to the list, which may be undesirable. It is undefined by default.

`foreign_submit`

> If set to **yes** (the default), nonsubscribers may send mail to the list. If undefined, only those in the *accept* file may mail the list. By default, the *accept* file is linked to the *dist* file, so all subscribers can mail the list.

`restrict_archive`

> If set to **yes**, only users in the *accept* file may retrieve files from this list's archive. If undefined (the default), anyone may retrieve files.

force_subscribe

If set to **yes**, people who send mail to the list are automatically subscribed if they aren't already subscribers. It is undefined by default.*

auto_unsubscribe

If set to **yes** (the default), subscribers may unsubscribe themselves without the aid of the list owner. If undefined, the list owner must process all unsubscriptions.

auto_subscribe

If set to **yes** (the default), subscribers may subscribe themselves without the aid of the list owner. If undefined, the list owner processes all subscriptions.

auto_help

If set to **yes**, users who send requests SmartList doesn't recognize are sent a copy of the help file for the list. The list owner is sent a copy of the request whether **auto_help** is defined or not. Defining **auto_help** makes sense if list administration is to be primarily mechanized; undefining it makes sense if users are expected to be able to reach the list owner personally at the list-request address.

moderated_flag

If set to **yes**, the list is moderated. List messages are sent to the list moderators, who can approve them by adding an Approved header containing their email address. It is undefined by default.

cc_requests

If set to **yes**, copies of requests to subscribe to the list and requests for help are sent to the list owner. It is undefined by default.

cc_unsubrequests

If set to **yes**, copies of requests to unsubscribe from the list are sent to the list owner. It is undefined by default.

pass_diverts

SmartList tries to filter out administrative requests that are sent to the list address. By default, such requests are handled as if they were sent to the list-request address. If **pass_diverts** is set to **yes**, however, the requests are sent to the list owner unprocessed instead.†

---

* In SmartList 3.10, forced subscriptions don't work correctly for moderated lists. Also, the *reject* file isn't checked when **force_subscribe** is enabled, so people whom you don't want to subscribe may be able to. These bugs have been fixed in SmartList 3.11.

† SmartList 3.11 adds another *rc.custom* variable, **divertcheck** that controls whether SmartList filters out administrative requests at all.

`reply_to`

> By default, SmartList doesn't include a Reply-To header in outgoing list mail. If you'd like one, set `reply_to` to the header you'd like added. The variable `$listaddr` contains the address of the list, so to force replies to be sent to the list, you could use:
>
> ```
> reply_to = "Reply-To: $listaddr"
> ```

`digest_flag`, `igest_age`, `digest_size`, and `undigested_list`

> By default, `digest_flag` is undefined, and the list isn't digested. If `digest_flag` is set to **yes**, the list sends out digests rather than individual messages. When the list is digested, `digest_age` controls how long to wait (in seconds) between digests; it defaults to 262144 (a little more than 3 days). `digest_size` sets how large (in bytes) a digest can grow before it must be sent out; it defaults to 32 KB.
>
> The `undigested_list` variable sets the Reply-To address for digested lists. By default, replies are directed back to the digested list. If, however, you want to offer a list in both digested and undigested versions, you can simply create two lists, add the digested list address to the undigested list's *dist* file, and set `undigested_list` to the list address of the undigested list.

`X_COMMAND` and `X_COMMAND_PASSWORD`

> Remote list owners can subscribe and unsubscribe users, and perform other administrative functions by sending email to their list's request address with a special header field. By default, the header field is X-Command followed by the owner's email address, the list password, and the command to execute. The `X_COMMAND` variable is used to change the name of the header from X-Command to something else. The `X_COMMAND_PASSWORD` header sets the list password; it defaults to **password**. It's a good idea to change both to prevent other users from executing list-owner commands.

`daemon_bias`

> This variable allows mail from addresses that SmartList would usually treat as mailer daemons (and hence ignore) to be considered acceptable. An example of the format is given in the *rc.custom* file, and using it requires a strong understanding of *procmail*'s weighted scoring recipes (described in *procmailsc*). This variable is rarely necessary.

`RC_LOCAL_*`

> SmartList's behavior can be customized at predefined points by writing local procmail recipes and uncommenting these lines to tell SmartList when to run the local recipe. Here are some examples:

RC_LOCAL_SUBMIT_00

> If defined, *rc.local.s00* is called in *rc.submit* immediately after loading *rc.init* and *rc.custom*, but before any other action.

RC_LOCAL_SUBMIT_10

> If defined, *rc.local.s10* is called in *rc.submit* after the incoming message has been accepted as not containing an administrative request and coming from a valid sender. This is a good place to filter the message for other criteria that might make it unsuitable for the list.

RC_LOCAL_SUBMIT_20

> If defined, *rc.local.s20* is called in *rc.submit* just before the message is distributed to the list subscribers. This is a good place to add or remove headers.

RC_LOCAL_REQUEST_00

> If defined, *rc.local.r00* is called in *rc.request* immediately after loading *rc.init* and *rc.custom*, but before any other action.

RC_LOCAL_REQUEST_10

> If defined, *rc.local.r10* is called in *rc.request* before checking for requests in the message. This is a good place to add request recipes that override the standard requests.

RC_LOCAL_REQUEST_20

> If defined, *rc.local.r20* is called in *rc.request* just after checking for standard requests in the message. This is a good place to add new request recipes.

RC_LOCAL_REQUEST_30

> If defined, *rc.local.r30* is called in *rc.request* when no requests have matched, after the X-Diagnostic header has been set, but before the failed message is sent on to the list maintainer. This could be used to automate responses to invalid requests.

D

LISTSERV Lite
Reference

This appendix summarizes the LISTSERV Lite user commands, list owner commands, and server administrator commands. It also provides a guide to the directories and files in a LISTSERV Lite installation.

User Commands

LISTSERV Lite commands may require the user to have a personal password, depending on the list's security settings. When a password is required, it should be included in the command by adding PW=*password* to the end of the command. Three LISTSERV Lite requests are used to manage your personal password:

PW ADD *password*
> Defines a personal password that can be used to authenticate password-protected list commands.

PW CHANGE *newpassword* PW=*oldpassword*
> Changes the personal password.

PW RESET
> Deletes the personal password.

User commands may also require confirmation. If confirmation is required, LISTSERV Lite sends a message to the user asking him to confirm the command by replying to the message.

General Commands

General commands can be used by anyone, whether or not they are subscribed to a list, though some lists may restrict these commands to subscribers:

HELP

>   Requests a file listing commands.

INFO *topic*

>   Requests information on a given topic. If no topic is given, requests a list of topics.

INFO *listname*

>   Requests information about a list.

LISTS

>   Requests the list addresses and descriptions of lists served by the MLM. Lists may be concealed from this request.

REVIEW *listname*

>   Requests the list header and a list of subscribers' email addresses. Subscribers may conceal themselves from this request, and list owners may restrict who may use this request for their list.

RELEASE

>   Requests to know the version of the LISTSERV Lite software and the address of the server administrator.

Subscriber Commands

Subscriber commands are used to subscribe to the list or are restricted to list subscribers:

SUBSCRIBE *listname fullname*

>   Subscribes to mailing list *listname*. *fullname* is the subscriber's full name or the word **ANONYMOUS**. If the list is private, subscription requests are forwarded to the list owner.

SIGNOFF *listname*

>   Unsubscribes from a list. **UNSUBSCRIBE** also works. If *listname* is *, unsubscribes from all lists at that server.

SET *listname options*

>   Sets a list option for the subscriber. Options are:

>   ack | noack

>>   Determines whether or not LISTSERV Lite sends a message acknowledging receipt of postings to the list.

>   conceal | noconceal

>>   Controls whether or not the subscriber is concealed from **REVIEW** requests.

`mail | nomail`

Controls whether or not the subscriber receives mail from the list.

`mime | nomime`

Controls whether or not the subscriber receives digests in MIME format.

`digests | nodigests | index | noindex`

Controls whether or not the subscriber receives digests or indexes. Digests contain the complete text of messages sent to the list. Indexes contain only a list of subjects; subscribers must retrieve the messages from the list archives with GETPOST.

`repro | norepro`

Controls whether or not the subscriber receives copies of his own list postings.

QUERY *listname*

Shows which options the subscriber has set for *listname*. Using a *listname* of * shows options set for all lists to which the subscriber belongs.

Archive Commands

Archive commands let users search archives and retrieve files or messages:

INDEX *listname*

Requests an index of *listname*'s file archive, showing all the files in the archive. If *listname* isn't specified, requests an index of all archived files other than message archives.

GET *filename*

Requests the file *filename*.

GETPOST *listname message-number-list*

Requests a message sent to *listname* from the *listname* archives. This command is used by subscribers who receive lists as indexes. The list index includes the message numbers.

PUT *filename*

Replaces *filename* with a new version, given below the PUT command. *filename* must already have been set up by the server administrator, and you must have permission to update it.

List Owner Commands

These commands require the list owner's password, and must come from an email address listed as an owner in the list's header file:

GET `listname` [options]

> With no *options*, locks the list (preventing new subscriptions) and retrieves the list's header file and subscriber list. *options*, which are given as a space-separated list after a left parenthesis ((), include `header` (send only list header, not subscribers: recommended), `nolock` (don't lock the list), and `old` (retrieve the backup list header from before the last PUT command).

PUT `listname`.LIST

> Updates the header file for `listname` and unlocks the list. The header file should follow the PUT request. Never modify the subscriber list with GET and PUT; use the ADD and DELETE commands discussed below instead.

UNLOCK `listname`

> Unlocks `listname` without updating the header file after a GET.

HOLD | FREE `listname`

> HOLD locks a list, preventing mail from being processed until a FREE request is sent.

[QUIET] ADD `listname email fullname`

> Adds a subscriber to `listname`. *email* is the subscriber's email address and *fullname* is the subscriber's full name or a * (in which case LISTSERV Lite tries to determine the full name from other lists, or replaces it with (No Name Available).) If preceded by QUIET, the subscriber doesn't receive notification of the subscription or welcome messages.

[QUIET] DELETE `listname email` [TEST]

> Removes a subscriber from `listname`. *email* is the subscriber's email address, and may be a wildcard pattern. If preceded by QUIET, the subscriber isn't notified and doesn't receive the farewell message. If followed by TEST, the deletion isn't actually performed; this allows you to test wildcard patterns before really using them.

QUERY `listname` FOR `email`

> Checks the subscription options of the address *email* on `listname`. *email* may be a wildcard pattern.

[QUIET] SET `listname options` FOR `email`

> Sets subscription options for address *email* on `listname`. If preceded by QUIET, the subscriber isn't notified. Options include those discussed for the SET subscriber command above as well as three others:

`post | nopost`

Controls whether or not the subscriber can post to the list.

`editor | noeditor`

Controls whether or not the subscriber has "editor" privileges and can post to a moderated list without going through the moderator.

`review | noreview`

Controls whether or not all postings by the subscriber must be reviewed by the list owner or moderator before appearing on the list.

Server Administrator Commands

The server administrator uses the same commands as the list owner. However, by using the server's list-creation password in place of a personal password, the server administrator can create a new list by writing a header file and issuing a `PUT` command.

LISTSERV Lite Files

Figure D-1 shows the LISTSERV Lite directory structure.

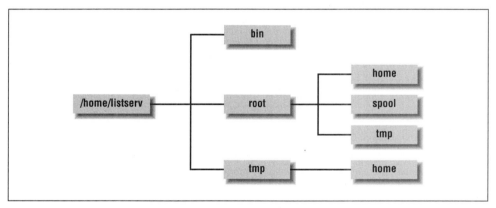

Figure D-1: The LISTSERV Lite directory structure

Files in /home/listserv/bin

/home/listserv/bin contains the *lcmd* and *lsv_amin* programs. *lcmd* is a command-line interface to LISTSERV Lite; it allows the server administrator to issue commands to LISTSERV from the *listserv* account. *lsv_amin* processes incoming mail to LISTSERV Lite-managed lists and to *listserv* itself.

Files in /home/listserv/root

/home/listserv/root contains the heart of the LISTSERV Lite system. Here's a list of the most important files:

Makefile

The *Makefile* is useful even after LISTSERV Lite is installed, because it includes a target that adds list aliases to */etc/aliases*. To use *Makefile* to add aliases for a list called *newlist*, do the following as *root*:

```
# make list name=newlist
```

go, go.sys, and *go.user*

These shell scripts start up LISTSERV Lite. *go.user* contains user-configurable variables. *go.sys* contains variables configured at compile-time. *go* does the actual work. See Chapter 12, *Administering LISTSERV Lite*, for a discussion of compilation, configuration, and startup.

listserv.log

listserv.log contains a record of LISTSERV Lite's actions since its last startup. *listserv.log.OLD* is an archive of old *listserv.log* files.

lsv *lsv* is the LISTSERV Lite daemon itself.

Files in /home/listserv/root/home

The *root/home* directory contains the data and help files for LISTSERV Lite. Files ending in *.memo* and *.refcard* are help files. Those ending in *.file* are LISTSERV Lite data files.

Each LISTSERV Lite list has a file in this directory called `listname.LIST`, containing the list header and subscribers, and possibly a file `listname.oldlist`, containing a backup copy of the list header and subscribers. Lists may also have `listname.welcome` and `listname.farewell` files for their welcome and farewell messages. Moderated lists store messages waiting to be approved in this directory as well.

Other important files include:

default.mailtpl

default.mailtpl contains the templates LISTSERV Lite uses to construct its standard messages to users, as well as some of its web pages. You can modify this file to modify these messages.

default.wwwtpl

default.wwwtpl contains the templates LISTSERV Lite uses to construct most of its web pages for the web interface.

site.catalog

> If present, *site.catalog* lists all files available from the server's archive other than message archives. Chapter 12 explains how to add new files to archives by creating *site.catalog*.

Files in /home/listserv/root/spool

The *root/spool* directory is a storage area for email waiting to be processed or distributed by LISTSERV Lite. Under normal operations, this directory always contains the *jobview* program, and the file *listserv.PID*. *jobview* can be used to decode *.job* files that LISTSERV Lite temporarily stores in this directory. *listserv.PID* contains the process ID of the *lsv* process.

List Header Keywords

For an excellent and comprehensive list of keywords that can be used in list headers, see the LISTSERV Site Manager's Manual (*listmast.memo*) available in */home/listserv/root/home* or from any LISTSERV site by sending the request GET listmast.memo.

Index

About the Author

Alan Schwartz is an assistant professor of clinical decision making in the Department of Medical Education at the University of Illinois at Chicago. In his spare time, he develops and maintains the PennMUSH MUD server and brews beer and mead with his wife. Alan runs multiple mailing lists for the Society for Judgment and Decision Making and for PennMUSH users and developers; he has been managing mailing lists for at least five years now. Turn-ons for Alan include sailing, programming in Perl, playing duplicate bridge, and drinking Anchor Porter. Turn-offs include subscription requests sent to list addresses and watery American lagers.

Colophon

The animal featured on the cover of *Managing Mailing Lists* is a three-toed woodpecker. There are approximately 380 species of woodpeckers scattered all over the world, with the exception of Madagascar, New Guinea, Australia, and New Zealand. Woodpeckers use their strong, straight bills to drill or chisel tree trunks in order to reach the insects inside. Their quest for dinner is also aided by tongues that are extremely extensible and often covered in barbs and a sticky saliva-like substance. They support themselves upright against tree trunks with their stiff tail feathers. Most woodpeckers also support themselves with the use of four toes, two facing forward and two facing back.

The three-toed woodpecker, however, lacks the first, backward-facing toe. These birds get at their food by chiseling at the tree trunk, requiring that they throw their heads far back before each blow. Having an additional backward-facing toe would impede these efforts. Three-toed woodpeckers prefer swampy woods and the remnants of burned forests, as insects are abundant in these habitats. They are harder workers than many of their fellow woodpeckers, and they search each tree thoroughly to get every last larva. A final distinction between the three-toed woodpecker and many other woodpeckers is that their heads are yellow, not the red commonly associated with woodpeckers.

Edie Freedman designed the cover of this book using a 19th-century engraving from the Dover Pictorial Archive. The cover layout was produced with Quark XPress 3.3 using the ITC Garamond font.

The inside layout was designed by Nancy Priest and implemented in gtroff by Lenny Muellner. The text and heading fonts are ITC Garamond Light and Garamond Book. The illustrations that appear in the book were created in Macromedia Freehand 7.0 by Robert Romano. This colophon was written by Clairemarie Fisher O'Leary.

Whenever possible, our books use RepKover™, a durable and flexible lay-flat binding. If the page count exceeds RepKover's limit, perfect binding is used.

More Titles from O'Reilly

Network Administration

Managing IP Networks with Cisco Routers

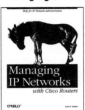

By Scott M. Ballew
1st Edition October 1997
352 pages, ISBN 1-56592-320-0

Managing IP Networks with Cisco Routers is a practical guide to setting up and maintaining a production network. It discusses how to select routing protocols and how to configure protcols to handle most common situations. It also discusses less esoteric but equally important issues like how to evaluate network equipment and vendors and how to set up a help desk. Although the book focuses on Cisco routers, and gives examples using Cisco's IOS, the principles discussed are common to all IP networks, regardless of the vendor you choose.

Topics covered include:

- Designing an IP network
- Evaluating equipment and vendors
- Selecting routing protocols
- Configuring common interior protocols (RIP, OSPF, EIGRP)
- Connecting to external networks, and configuring exterior protocols (BGP)
- Ongoing network management: troubleshooting and maintenance
- Security and privacy issues

Virtual Private Networks

Charlie Scott, Paul Wolfe & Mike Erwin
1st Edition February 1998 (est.)
184 pages (est.), ISBN 1-56592-319-7

Historically, only large companies could afford secure networks, which they created from expensive leased lines. Smaller folks had to make do with the relatively untrusted Internet. Nowadays, even large companies have to go outside their private nets, because so many people telecommute or log in while they're on the road. How do you provide a low-cost, secure electronic network for your organization?

The solution is a virtual private network: a collection of technologies that creates secure connections or "tunnels" over regular Internet lines—connections that can be easily used by anybody logging in from anywhere. This book tells you how to plan and build a VPN. It starts with general concerns like costs, configuration, and how a VPN fits in with other networking technologies like firewalls. It continues with detailed descriptions of how to install and use VPN technologies that are available for Windows NT and UNIX, such as PPTP and L2TP, the Altavista Tunnel, and the Cisco PIX Firewall.

sendmail, 2nd Edition

By Bryan Costales & Eric Allman
2nd Edition January 1997
1050 pages, ISBN 1-56592-222-0

This new edition of *sendmail* covers sendmail Version 8.8 from Berkeley and the standard versions available on most systems. It is far and away the most comprehensive book ever written on sendmail, the program that acts like a traffic cop in routing and delivering mail on UNIX-based networks. Although sendmail is used on almost every UNIX system, it's one of the last great uncharted territories—and most difficult utilities to learn—in UNIX system administration.

This book provides a complete sendmail tutorial, plus extensive reference material on every aspect of the program. Part One is a tutorial on understanding sendmail; Part Two covers the building, installation, and m4 configuration of sendmail; Part Three covers practical issues in sendmail administration; Part Four is a comprehensive reference section; and Part Five consists of appendices and a bibliography.

In this second edition an expanded tutorial demonstrates hub's *cf* file and *nullclient.mc*. Other new topics include the #error delivery agent, sendmail's exit values, MIME headers, and how to set up and use the user database, *mailertable*, and *smrsh*. Solution-oriented examples throughout the book help you solve your own sendmail problems. This new edition is cross-referenced with section numbers.

sendmail Desktop Reference

By Bryan Costales & Eric Allman
1st Edition March 1997
74 pages, ISBN 1-56592-278-6

This quick-reference guide provides a complete overview of the latest version of sendmail (V8.8), from command-line switches to configuration commands, from options declarations to macro definitions, and from m4 features to debugging switches—all packed into a convenient, carry-around booklet co-authored by the creator of sendmail. Includes extensive cross-references to *sendmail*, second edition.

O'REILLY™

TO ORDER: **800-998-9938** • *order@oreilly.com* • *http://www.oreilly.com/*
OUR PRODUCTS ARE AVAILABLE AT A BOOKSTORE OR SOFTWARE STORE NEAR YOU.
FOR INFORMATION: **800-998-9938** • **707-829-0515** • *info@oreilly.com*

Network Administration *(continued)*

DNS and BIND, 2nd Edition

By Paul Albitz & Cricket Liu
2nd Edition December 1996
438 pages, ISBN 1-56592-236-0

This book is a complete guide to the Internet's Domain Name System (DNS) and the Berkeley Internet Name Domain (BIND) software, the UNIX implementation of DNS. In this second edition, the authors continue to describe BIND version 4.8.3, which is included in most vendor implementations today. In addition, you'll find complete coverage of BIND 4.9.4, which in all probability will be adopted as the new standard in the near future.

In addition to covering the basic motivation behind DNS and how to set up the BIND software, this book covers many more advanced topics, including using DNS and BIND on Windows NT systems; how to become a "parent" (i.e., "delegate" the ability to assign names to someone else); how to use DNS to set up mail forwarding correctly; debugging and troubleshooting; and programming. Assumes a basic knowledge of system administration and network management.

Getting Connected: The Internet at 56K and Up

By Kevin Dowd
1st Edition June 1996
424 pages, ISBN 1-56592-154-2

A complete guide for businesses, schools, and other organizations who want to connect their computers to the Internet. This book covers everything you need to know to make informed decisions, from helping you figure out which services you really need to providing down-to-earth explanations and configuration instructions for telecommunication options at higher than modem speeds, such as frame relay, ISDN, and leased lines. Once you're online, it shows you how to set up basic Internet services, such as a World Wide Web server. Tackles issues for PC, Macintosh, and UNIX platforms.

Using & Managing PPP

By Andrew Sun
1st Edition March 1998 (est.)
400 pages (est.), ISBN 1-56592-321-9

Covers all aspects of PPP, including setting up dial-in servers, debugging, and PPP options. Also contains overviews of related areas, like serial communications, DNS setup, and routing.

Networking Personal Computers with TCP/IP

By Craig Hunt
1st Edition July 1995
408 pages, ISBN 1-56592-123-2

This book offers practical information as well as detailed instructions for attaching PCs to a TCP/IP network and its UNIX servers. It discusses the challenges you'll face and offers general advice on how to deal with them, provides basic TCP/IP configuration information for some of the popular PC operating systems, covers advanced configuration topics and configuration of specific applications such as email, and includes a chapter on on integrating Netware with TCP/IP.

TCP/IP Network Administration, 2nd Edition

By Craig Hunt
2nd Edition December 1997
630 pages, ISBN 1-56592-322-7

TCP/IP Network Administration, 2nd Edition, is a complete guide to setting up and running a TCP/IP network for administrators of networks of systems or lone home systems that access the Internet. It starts with the fundamentals: what the protocols do and how they work, how addresses and routing are used to move data through the network, and how to set up your network connection.

Beyond basic setup, this new second edition discusses advanced routine protocols (RIPv2, OSPF, and BGP) and the *gated* software package that implements them. It contains a tutorial on configuring important network services, including PPP, SLIP, sendmail, Domain Name Service (DNS), BOOTP and DHCP configuration servers, some simple setups for NIS and NFS, and chapters on troubleshooting and security. In addition, this book is a command and syntax reference for several important packages including *pppd, dip, gated, named, dhcpd,* and *sendmail*.

Covers Linux, BSD, and System V TCP/IP implementations.

Web Server Administration

Managing Usenet

By Henry Spencer & David Lawrence
1st Edition January 1998
508 pages, ISBN 1-56592-198-4

Usenet, also called Netnews, is the world's largest discussion forum, and it is doubling in size every year. This book, written by two of the foremost authorities on Usenet administration, contains everything you need to know to administer a Netnews system. It covers C News and INN, explains the basics of starting a Netnews system, and offers guidelines to help ensure that your system is capable of handling news volume today—and in the future.

Web Security & Commerce

By Simson Garfinkel with Gene Spafford
1st Edition June 1997
506 pages, ISBN 1-56592-269-7

Learn how to minimize the risks of the Web with this comprehensive guide. It covers browser vulnerabilities, privacy concerns, issues with Java, JavaScript, ActiveX, and plug-ins, digital certificates, cryptography, web server security, blocking software, censorship technology, and relevant civil and criminal issues.

Building Your Own WebSite™

By Susan B. Peck & Stephen Arrants
1st Edition July 1996
514 pages, Includes CD-ROM
ISBN 1-56592-232-8

This is a hands-on reference for Windows® 95 and Windows NT™ users who want to host a site on the Web or on a corporate intranet. This step-by-step guide will have you creating live web pages in minutes. You'll also learn how to connect your web to information in other Windows applications, such as word processing documents and databases. The book is packed with examples and tutorials on every aspect of web management, and it includes the highly acclaimed WebSite™ 1.1 server software on CD-ROM.

Apache: The Definitive Guide

By Ben Laurie & Peter Laurie
1st Edition March 1997
274 pages, includes CD-ROM
ISBN 1-56592-250-6

Despite all the media attention to Netscape, Apache is far and away the most widely used web server platform in the world. This book, written and reviewed by key members of the Apache Group, is the only complete guide on the market today that describes how to obtain, set up, and secure the Apache software. Includes CD-ROM with Apache sources and demo sites discussed in the book.

Managing Internet Information Services

By Cricket Liu, Jerry Peek, Russ Jones, Bryan Buus & Adrian Nye
1st Edition December 1994
668 pages, ISBN 1-56592-062-7

This comprehensive guide describes how to set up information services and make them available over the Internet. It discusses why a company would want to offer Internet services, provides complete coverage of all popular services, and tells how to select which ones to provide. Most of the book describes how to set up Gopher, World Wide Web, FTP, and WAIS servers and email services.

Managing Mailing Lists

By Alan Schwartz
1st Edition March 1998
302 pages, ISBN 1-56592-259-X

Mailing lists are an ideal vehicle for creating email-based electronic communities. This book covers four mailing list packages (Majordomo, LISTSERV, ListProcessor, and SmartList) and tells you everything you need to know to set up and run a mailing list, from writing the charter to dealing with bounced messages. It discusses creating moderated lists, controlling who can subscribe to a list, offering digest subscriptions, and archiving list postings.

System Administration

How to stay in touch with O'Reilly

1. Visit Our Award-Winning Web Site

http://www.oreilly.com/

★ "Top 100 Sites on the Web" —*PC Magazine*
★ "Top 5% Web sites" —*Point Communications*
★ "3-Star site" —*The McKinley Group*

Our web site contains a library of comprehensiveproduct information (including book excerpts and tables of contents), downloadable software, background articles, interviews with technology leaders, links to relevant sites, book cover art, and more. File us in your Bookmarks or Hotlist!

2. Join Our Email Mailing Lists

New Product Releases

To receive automatic email with brief descriptions of all new O'Reilly products as they are released, send email to:
listproc@online.oreilly.com
Put the following information in the first line of your message (*not* in the Subject field):
subscribe oreilly-news

O'Reilly Events

If you'd also like us to send information about trade show events, special promotions, and other O'Reilly events, send email to:
listproc@online.oreilly.com
Put the following information in the first line of your message (*not* in the Subject field):
subscribe oreilly-events

3. Get Examples from Our Books via FTP

There are two ways to access an archive of example files from our books:

Regular FTP

- ftp to:
  ftp.oreilly.com
  (login: anonymous
  password: your email address)
- Point your web browser to:
  ftp://ftp.oreilly.com/

FTPMAIL

- Send an email message to:
  ftpmail@online.oreilly.com
  (Write "help" in the message body)

4. Contact Us via Email

order@oreilly.com
To place a book or software order online. Good for North American and international customers.

subscriptions@oreilly.com
To place an order for any of our newsletters or periodicals.

books@oreilly.com
General questions about any of our books.

software@oreilly.com
For general questions and product information about our software. Check out O'Reilly Software Online at **http://software.oreilly.com/** for software and technical support information. Registered O'Reilly software users send your questions to: **website-support@oreilly.com**

cs@oreilly.com
For answers to problems regarding your order or our products.

booktech@oreilly.com
For book content technical questions or corrections.

proposals@oreilly.com
To submit new book or software proposals to our editors and product managers.

international@oreilly.com
For information about our international distributors or translation queries. For a list of our distributors outside of North America check out:
http://www.oreilly.com/www/order/country.html

O'Reilly & Associates, Inc.
101 Morris Street, Sebastopol, CA 95472 USA
TEL   707-829-0515 or 800-998-9938
       (6am to 5pm PST)
FAX   707-829-0104

International Distributors

UK, Europe, Middle East and Northern Africa (except France, Germany, Switzerland, & Austria)

INQUIRIES
International Thomson Publishing Europe
Berkshire House
168-173 High Holborn
London WC1V 7AA
United Kingdom
Telephone: 44-171-497-1422
Fax: 44-171-497-1426
Email: itpint@itps.co.uk

ORDERS
International Thomson Publishing Services, Ltd.
Cheriton House, North Way
Andover, Hampshire SP10 5BE
United Kingdom
Telephone: 44-264-342-832 (UK)
Telephone: 44-264-342-806 (outside UK)
Fax: 44-264-364418 (UK)
Fax: 44-264-342761 (outside UK)
UK & Eire orders: itpuk@itps.co.uk
International orders: itpint@itps.co.uk

France

Editions Eyrolles
61 bd Saint-Germain
75240 Paris Cedex 05
France
Fax: 33-01-44-41-11-44

FRENCH LANGUAGE BOOKS
All countries except Canada
Telephone: 33-01-44-41-46-16
Email: geodif@eyrolles.com
English language books
Telephone: 33-01-44-41-11-87
Email: distribution@eyrolles.com

Germany, Switzerland, and Austria

INQUIRIES
O'Reilly Verlag
Balthasarstr. 81
D-50670 Köln
Germany
Telephone: 49-221-97-31-60-0
Fax: 49-221-97-31-60-8
Email: anfragen@oreilly.de

ORDERS
International Thomson Publishing
Königswinterer Straße 418
53227 Bonn, Germany
Telephone: 49-228-97024 0
Fax: 49-228-441342
Email: order@oreilly.de

Japan

O'Reilly Japan, Inc.
Kiyoshige Building 2F
12-Banchi, Sanei-cho
Shinjuku-ku
Tokyo 160-0008 Japan
Telephone: 81-3-3356-5227
Fax: 81-3-3356-5261
Email: kenji@oreilly.com

India

Computer Bookshop (India) PVT. Ltd.
190 Dr. D.N. Road, Fort
Bombay 400 001 India
Telephone: 91-22-207-0989
Fax: 91-22-262-3551
Email: cbsbom@giasbm01.vsnl.net.in

Hong Kong

City Discount Subscription Service Ltd.
Unit D, 3rd Floor, Yan's Tower
27 Wong Chuk Hang Road
Aberdeen, Hong Kong
Telephone: 852-2580-3539
Fax: 852-2580-6463
Email: citydis@ppn.com.hk

Korea

Hanbit Media, Inc.
Sonyoung Bldg. 202
Yeksam-dong 736-36
Kangnam-ku
Seoul, Korea
Telephone: 822-554-9610
Fax: 822-556-0363
Email: hant93@chollian.dacom.co.kr

Singapore, Malaysia, and Thailand

Addison Wesley Longman Singapore PTE Ltd.
25 First Lok Yang Road
Singapore 629734
Telephone: 65-268-2666
Fax: 65-268-7023
Email: daniel@longman.com.sg

Philippines

Mutual Books, Inc.
429-D Shaw Boulevard
Mandaluyong City, Metro
Manila, Philippines
Telephone: 632-725-7538
Fax: 632-721-3056
Email: mbikikog@mnl.sequel.net

China

Ron's DataCom Co., Ltd.
79 Dongwu Avenue
Dongxihu District
Wuhan 430040
China
Telephone: 86-27-3892568
Fax: 86-27-3222108
Email: hongfeng@public.wh.hb.cn

All Other Asian Countries

O'Reilly & Associates, Inc.
101 Morris Street
Sebastopol, CA 95472 USA
Telephone: 707-829-0515
Fax: 707-829-0104
Email: order@oreilly.com

Australia

WoodsLane Pty. Ltd.
7/5 Vuko Place, Warriewood NSW 2102
P.O. Box 935
Mona Vale NSW 2103
Australia
Telephone: 61-2-9970-5111
Fax: 61-2-9970-5002
Email: info@woodslane.com.au

New Zealand

Woodslane New Zealand Ltd.
21 Cooks Street (P.O. Box 575)
Waganui, New Zealand
Telephone: 64-6-347-6543
Fax: 64-6-345-4840
Email: info@woodslane.com.au

The Americas

McGraw-Hill Interamericana Editores, S.A. de C.V.
Cedro No. 512
Col. Atlampa 06450
Mexico, D.F.
Telephone: 52-5-541-3155
Fax: 52-5-541-4913
Email: mcgraw-hill@infosel.net.mx

South Africa

International Thomson Publishing
South Africa
Building 18, Constantia Park
138 Sixteenth Road
P.O. Box 2459
Halfway House, 1685 South Africa
Telephone: 27-11-805-4819
Fax: 27-11-805-3648

O'REILLY™

O'REILLY™

O'Reilly & Associates, Inc.
101 Morris Street
Sebastopol, CA 95472-9902
1-800-998-9938

Visit us online at:
http://www.ora.com/

O'REILLY WOULD LIKE TO HEAR FROM YOU

Which book did this card come from?

_____

Where did you buy this book?
- ❏ Bookstore   ❏ Computer Store
- ❏ Direct from O'Reilly   ❏ Class/seminar
- ❏ Bundled with hardware/software
- ❏ Other _____

What operating system do you use?
- ❏ UNIX   ❏ Macintosh
- ❏ Windows NT   ❏ PC(Windows/DOS)
- ❏ Other _____

What is your job description?
- ❏ System Administrator   ❏ Programmer
- ❏ Network Administrator   ❏ Educator/Teacher
- ❏ Web Developer
- ❏ Other _____

❏ Please send me O'Reilly's catalog, containing a complete listing of O'Reilly books and software.

Name _____ Company/Organization _____

Address _____

City _____ State _____ Zip/Postal Code _____ Country _____

Telephone _____ Internet or other email address (specify network) _____

neteenth century wood engraving
a bear from the O'Reilly &
sociates Nutshell Handbook®
sing & Managing UUCP.

POST CARD

BUSINESS REPLY MAIL
FIRST CLASS MAIL   PERMIT NO. 80   SEBASTOPOL, CA

Postage will be paid by addressee

O'Reilly & Associates, Inc.
101 Morris Street
Sebastopol, CA 95472-9902